FUGITIVE LIFE

FUGITIVE LIFE THE QUEER POLITICS

OF THE PRISON STATE **STEPHEN DILLON**

Duke University Press Durham and London 2018

Text designed by Courtney Leigh Baker
Cover designed by Matt Tauch
Typeset in Whitman by Westchester Publishing Services

Library of Congress Cataloging-in-Publication Data
Names: Dillon, Stephen, [date–] author.
Title: Fugitive life : the queer politics of the prison state / Stephen
    Dillon.
Description: Durham : Duke University Press, 2018. | Includes
    bibliographical references and index.
Identifiers: LCCN 2017051974 (print) | LCCN 2017060640 (ebook)
ISBN 9780822371892 (ebook)
ISBN 9780822370673 (hardcover : alk. paper)
ISBN 9780822370826 (pbk. : alk. paper)
Subjects: LCSH: Gays—Political activity—United States—
    History—20th century. | Prisoners—Civil rights—United States. |
    Social movements—United States—History—20th century. |
    Protest movements—United States—History—20th century. |
    Gay activists—United States. | Anti-racism—United States—
    History—20th century. | Neoliberalism—Social aspects—United
    States—History.
Classification: LCC HQ76.8.U6 (ebook) | LCC HQ76.8.U6 D55 2018
    (print) | DDC 306.76/60973—dc23
LC record available at https://lccn.loc.gov/2017051974

Cover art: Coco Fusco, still from *a/k/a Mrs. George Gilbert*, 2004.
Black-and-white single-channel video. Courtesy of the artist.

ACKNOWLEDGMENTS

In an interview about his relationship with Michel Foucault, Gilles Deleuze describes Foucault, not as an individual subject, but as a diffuse force he called "passion." The intensity of passion was contrasted to the feeling of "love." Love was a name for becoming through other people—a relation between discrete individuals. In contrast to love, passion named an attempt to comprehend how one can become "dissolved into something undifferentiated." Passion is a state wherein "being oneself no longer made any sense." It is a state wherein it is no longer possible to say "That's you" and "This is me." Being "me" is simply incomprehensible. Passion is an affective intensity where love is no longer the right word. For Deleuze, Foucault wasn't "like a person." He was a laugh, a gesture, "a changed atmosphere," an "event," a "magnetic field," or simply and indescribably, "something." Foucault was a piece of Deleuze—but not quite a piece—because one can remove a piece, identify it, name it, mark it. Being a part of someone is still under the analytic of love. Passion can't be undone.

I begin with this anecdote because it describes the problem with thanking the "you" that helped "me" with completing what has become a book under the name I was given. The people named here, and many more who are not, did not simply help me write, read, and think; they are entangled with what is here. The fiction of me wouldn't be possible without everyone that made me, me. With that in mind, what is here would simply not exist without the physical, emotional, and epistemological support and encouragement of my advisors in graduate school, Regina Kunzel and Roderick Ferguson. Rod's patience, kindness, humor, generosity, and genius will always be a model for me as I navigate a world that so often leaves people unable to laugh in the face of so much stress, frustration, violence, and despair. He always helped me find my way when I got lost, and I think of him in moments large and small when what looks like the right way is never simply that. He continues to provide a path for me to follow—a comfort when so much seems incomprehensible and impossible. Five years ago I wrote that I didn't know how to describe Reg's dedication, compassion, generosity, humility, brilliance, and insight. I said that one day I would figure out how to describe her impact on me. Now that the time is here, the task still eludes me. But this failure now feels appropriate—I'd rather leave it with the words *gesture, event, atmosphere*, and *something*.

The Department of American Studies at the University of Minnesota offered me a place to do what I wanted and needed to do in a world where that is often not possible. I'm grateful to have learned so much from Kevin Murphy, Jennifer Pierce, Laurie Ouellette, and Zenzele Isoke. I'm also grateful to have had a community of so many wonderful people engaged in similar epistemological struggles: Jasmine Mitchell, Kate Beane, Patricia Marroquin Norby, Benjamin Wiggins, Matthew Schneider-Mayerson, Raechel Tiffe, Elizabeth Ault, Juliana Hu Pegues, Tom Sarmiento, Rudy Aguilar, Ryan Cartwright, Karisa Butler-Wall, Ryan Murphy, Michael David Franklin, Daniel LaChance, Aniruddha Dutta, Tammy Owens, Michelle Garvey, Jessica M. Petocz, and Karla M. Padrón. Remembering Jesús Estrada Pérez always makes me smile in the darkest of times.

Myrl Beam, A. J. Lewis, and Eli Vitulli helped me through many aspects of the early stages of this project. Their friendship, support, humor, and insight during and after graduate school have been invaluable. I'm so grateful for their thinking and presence. As a transplant to New England, I am always excited to be near people from the Midwest. It was such a joy to spend two years with Eli as colleagues in the Five Colleges. I was also lucky enough that my Minnesota friend Elizabeth Sharrow got a job at the University of Massachusetts at the same time I accepted a position at Hampshire College. She's been such a support through moments large and small, hilarious (bears!), bizarre, and horrifying. I'm also grateful for new friends I've made in a new part of the country: Jules Rosskam, Alex Samets, Mara Toone, Deborah Schwartz, and Aeryca Steinbauer. Pooja Rangan and Josh Guilford have always been unflinchingly supportive, hilarious, and excited. Pooja helped demystify much of the process of writing a book. Bernadine Mellis, Andrea Lawlor, Hart, and Jordy Rosenberg are the most amazing friends I could ask for. Their encouragement, curiosity, questions, excitement, knowledge, and support have meant everything to me. Creating work in the same small world as them has been a true joy. I'm thankful to Jordy for helping with the fourth chapter and talking through my many questions and concerns on our impromptu walks. Bernadine gave me a title in our many title workshops on snowy nights that I did not use. I'm grateful for it because it helped as I edited and revised. I'm holding on to it for another time.

I'm so appreciative of my colleagues at Hampshire College for their support and encouragement: Angie Willey, Jennifer Hamilton, Amy Jordan, Chris Tinson, Jutta Sperling, Uditi Sen, Hiba Bou Akar, Rachel Ama Asaa Engmann, Djola Branner, Wilson Valentín-Escobar, Marlene Fried, Lili Kim, Susana Loza, Kristen Luschen, Flavio Risech-Ozeguera, George Fourlas, Michele Hardesty, and many more. My students helped me think through many of the book's central questions. Their openness, curiosity, and excitement is inspiring and their brilliance is often breathtaking.

A dispersed group of people have supported my work by inviting me to give a talk, publish an article, or participate on a panel, or have offered me encouragement in ways minor but significant. I first read Dean Spade's work as an eighteen-year-old a decade and a half ago; to have had him engage my work over the past decade has been thrilling. Eric Stanley, Craig Willse, Jason Stahl, and Michelle Potts were wonderful interlocutors and editors of some of my earlier thinking. Sarah Haley gave me a boost at an early morning panel that meant so much to me. Abbie Boggs has been supportive and excited even after moving all the way to Connecticut. I always look forward to a chance to see Perry Zurn and Andrew Dilts; they have been supportive and excited about my work from the moment I met them and learning from them has been a true pleasure.

Ken Wissoker believed in this project from the beginning and guided me through the editing process so that my memories of finishing are full of grace and ease. Elizabeth Ault was there for all my questions and concerns; I'm thankful for her kindness and encouragement. I'm also deeply grateful and indebted to two anonymous reviewers for their care, insight, concerns, questions, and enthusiasm. Susan Albury guided the book through copy editing and production and the copy editing of Judith Hoover was a joy to work with. The artist Henry Schneiderman created the index.

My twin sister, Michelle, cheered and clapped and chanted me on every step of the way. We have been together since before our first breath—I hope some of that breath comes through here. My parents, Michael and Marcia, were always there with questions, support, and encouragement even when I could only leave them confused. I hope the book lives up to the core values I learned from them. My brother, Jeff, will always be my intellectual sparring partner; he has made me a sharper thinker. Kevin and Marcie are always lighthearted, even when things feel so heavy. My nieces and nephews, Jacob, Steve, Ben, Katherine, and Megan, have brought me so much joy over the past decade. They've given me perspective and scope when I needed it most. I hope the world is slightly better for them. Finally, Allison Page has read, edited, and commented on every single thing I have written for more than the past decade. What is here would not be here without her. I hope her brilliance and energy shine through. As Fred Moten and Stefano Harney write, "We owe each other everything."

"ESCAPE-BOUND CAPTIVES" RACE, NEOLIBERALISM,

AND THE FORCE OF QUEERNESS

On July 4, 1977, the George Jackson Brigade issued a communiqué that began with the following statement: "Today we bombed the main substation for the state capital complex in Olympia [Washington]. The purpose of this action is to support the struggle of prisoners in the hole at Walla Walla state prison. These men are still on strike as a focus of their militant fight against illegal confinement, barbarism, and torture."[1] From the spring of 1975 until the fall of 1977 the George Jackson Brigade bombed state and corporate institutions throughout the Pacific Northwest. In order to fund their fugitive organization they robbed half a dozen banks to make the state and capital "pay for their own destruction."[2] The George Jackson Brigade was an underground group of working-class former prisoners who were "of different races and sexes" and "different sexual orientations within those races and sexes."[3] The group saw themselves as a form of "armed self-defense" in support of Native sovereignty, domestic national liberation movements, workers' rights, feminism, gay liberation, and, most centrally, prison abolition. Throughout their writings their analysis of power navigated the complicity among race, gender, class, sexuality, capitalism, and incarceration. The Brigade emphasized repeatedly that their choice to go underground was motivated by their involvement with the struggles of "women, prisoners, Third World people, gays and young people."[4] Prisons were the analytical center of the Brigade's theoretical and political work, informing their analysis of white supremacy, sexual violence, colonialism, and heterosexism. When prisoners at Walla Walla took hostages and seized the prison's hospital wing as part of a decade-long struggle for more humane conditions, the Brigade bombed the office of the director of the Department of Corrections in Olympia, causing more than $100,000 in damage.[5] In addition to calling for the end of the random transferring of rebellious prisoners and the use of "psychofascist" forms of control, such as electroshock therapy, sensory deprivation, and drugs, the Brigade situated the prison rebellion in a larger network of racialized and gendered state power by declaring, "If people want a better society, they can start by becoming active feminists, anti-racists, and anti-imperialists."[6]

Rita Bo Brown, the group's bank robber, was known throughout the Seattle area as the "Gentleman Bank Robber" because she dressed "as a man" during robberies, was acknowledged for her "polite gun-pointing prattle," and was praised by bank tellers for her congeniality.[7] Brown's performance was so effective that the FBI spent two years looking for a man. Narrating her transition from aboveground activist to underground "freedom fighter," Brown wrote, "I was part of the politico lesbian community. I worked on lots of different projects with children, womyn, men and 3rd World peoples but prison work was always the most important in my life. In a couple of years, I heard a lot of folks in a lot of places talk about the revolution, but nobody did anything except talk. The BLA and Assata [Shakur] were working their asses off but nobody in Seattle did a thing."[8] When she was captured and stood in court facing twenty years in federal prison, Brown took the opportunity to describe how her lesbian "white life" was made possible by the fabrication of racialized death and dying. Following Bertolt Brecht, she asked the courtroom, "What is the biggest crime, to rob a bank or found one?" She went on to question the legitimacy of the trial, arguing that the Brigade's theft and bombings meant nothing in the face of chattel slavery, genocide, the "terrorism" of prisons, misogyny and sexual violence, and homophobia. For Brown the prison was at the nexus of these multiple forces: "Prisons are big business too. Nationally, the annual profits reach $2 billion. Prisons promote 'terrorism' by making the denial of human and democratic rights a respectable and common thing. Look at who is in prison and why—75 percent of all adults in amerikkan prisons are 3rd world people."[9] Brown's claim that the prison makes the denial of human rights a "common and respectable thing" theorizes white supremacy and the prison as structures of invisibility. As Brown argued, even as many people may imagine the prison sitting on the edges of social and cultural life in the United States, even as some lives may seemingly never be touched by the terrifying logic of capture, the prison is central to who and where we are, what we know, and what we can become.

Throughout their writings the Brigade placed their bombings in the context of the ongoing rebellion in Walla Walla but also the ways that capitalism and prisons were changing during the 1970s. One communiqué, "Capitalism Is Organized Crime," declared, "Capitalism causes crime. Overwhelmingly, the victims of crime are poor and third world people. Street crime is caused and perpetuated by joblessness and underemployment; by a ruling class that uses people for its own profit and discards them when it has no more profitable use for them. . . . [The prison's] sole purpose is to administer the warehousing and repression of human beings for whom capitalism has no use or no solution."[10] This passage is remarkable for a number of reasons. First, it contests a discourse about the naturalness of criminality that took hold under the mid-twentieth-century politics of law and order as articulated by Barry Goldwater and Richard Nixon. Unlike statist discourses that defined criminality as individual nonnormative behaviors created by racialized, cultural, and biological pathology, the Brigade argued that what was labeled "crime" was created by the profoundly unnatural formation of capitalism. Second, placed in the context of the Brigade's larger body of work, the passage is a feminist and queer theorization of how racial capitalism was changing under an encroaching dominance of neoliberal economics and a new state form in which the prison was foundational. For the Brigade, the expansion of regimes of incarceration and capital accumulation was central to the violent reorganization of gender, sexual, and racialized life in the post–civil rights era. Third, the Brigade described the function of the prison as "warehousing" those discarded by a new form of capitalism that was built on "joblessness and underemployment." A new formation of capitalism was abandoning the employment protocols of Keynesian economics in favor of a regime of accumulation that relied on the racialized mass production of workless and working poor people. These abandoned populations were then *stored* in state and federal prisons. The Brigade averred that the prison warehoused potentially rebellious, disposable people—its logic was not rehabilitation, but immobilization.[11]

As the Brigade argued, the state and capitalism were producing surplus populations no longer necessary to racial capitalism. Brigade members theorized the emergence of this new form of racialized economic power founded on disposable, low-wage labor, the dismantling of welfare, and the creation of human beings as what Angela Davis calls "detritus" as a form of state violence.[12] In the closing statement to his trial for 14 bank robberies and 11 bombings, another member, John Sherman, asked the jury to find him guilty but also to set him free because "capitalism excretes the violence and terror of unemployment, the violence and terror of war, the violence and terror of crushing poverty."[13] Similarly, in an interview after his arrest, a founding member, Ed Mead, placed the group's actions in the context of cuts to welfare and a growing unemployment. He maintained that the "decay" produced by capitalism was a form of state violence cloaked as the natural outcome of the market's governance. The terror of racialized impoverishment and incarceration urgently required the answer to the question "How are we going to overturn this thing if not by armed force?"[14] The judge and jury sympathized with Sherman's passion. They found him guilty on all charges, and the judge sentenced him to the lightest sentence his "conscience [would] permit": twenty years instead of the two hundred demanded by the prosecution.[15]

I begin with the writings of the George Jackson Brigade because they were part of a much larger world of underground, fugitive activists in the 1970s who theorized and challenged the formation of a new form of state power called the neoliberal-carceral state.[16] This term describes the intimacy between the possession of life itself by the market under neoliberal economics and the exponential expansion of systems of racialized capture and caging under law-and-order politics. In this era countless feminist, queer, and antiracist activists were imprisoned or became fugitives as they fought the changing contours of U.S. state power. Indeed the late 1960s and early 1970s saw the emergence of two new voices in national debates about racism, imperialism, poverty, gender, and sexual politics: the prisoner and the fugitive. Although *Fugitive Life* tells a story about post–civil rights feminist, queer, and antiracist activism, it focuses on these two figures and two corresponding spaces: the prison and the underground. In response to police repression in the form of incarceration, sabotage, and assassination, and in order to deploy illegal tactics, hundreds of activists in the 1970s left behind families, friends, jobs, and their identity in order to disappear into a vast network of safe houses, under-the-table jobs, and transportation networks called the underground. While there has been a resurgence of interest in many of these groups (in part prompted by and reflected in the anxiety about Barack Obama's connections to the Weather

Underground member Bill Ayers during the 2008 presidential election), their significance to the post–civil rights landscape—as structured by the prison and neoliberalism—has only begun to be explored.

As increasing numbers of activists were imprisoned or went underground to escape a repressive racial state and engage different tactics, a new body of knowledge arose from the prisoner and the fugitive that negated national narratives of progress, equality, and justice. I use the communiqués, literature, films, memoirs, prison writing, and poetry of underground and imprisoned women activists in the 1970s United States to provide an analysis of the centrality of gender and sexuality to this new mode of racialized state power. I pause on the neoliberal-carceral state's moment of inception in the 1970s to consider how feminist and queer prisoners and fugitive activists reorganized their efforts to respond to a rising wave of incarceration animated by a new mode of governance structured by the market. In this way I offer a reinterpretation and renarration of feminist, queer, and antiracist post–civil rights activism by exploring how it responded to the rise of the prison and the rule of the market. It is my contention that we have much to learn from the writings, art, and films of these activists, who saw what was coming before it took form. As the prison and market continue to engulf life itself, I argue that the fugitive is a queer figure who is the site of a dramatic reimagining of freedom that points the way out even as life is increasingly surrounded.

The Cultures of the Neoliberal-Carceral State

Of course the Brigade was not alone in theorizing the dramatic changes occurring to capitalism, incarceration, and the state in the 1970s. Six years earlier Angela Davis edited a collection of essays from a cell in the Marin County Jail, *If They Come in the Morning: Voices of Resistance*. Davis was imprisoned after spending months underground as a fugitive from the FBI. The text gathered the writings of political prisoners like Davis, Huey Newton, Bobby Seale, Ericka Huggins, George Jackson, John Clutchette, and Ruchell Magee. It also included court statements and letters of support surrounding Davis's imprisonment. The collection documents the various trials of black power activists in the late 1960s and early 1970s, and it marks a moment when activists tried to make sense of the profound racial violence they were subjected to under a rising wave of incarceration. Davis and her coeditor, Bettina Aptheker, described this moment: "Political repression in the United States has reached monstrous proportions. Black and Brown peoples especially, victims of the most vicious and calculated forms of class, national and racial oppression, bear the brunt of this repression. Literally tens of thousands of innocent men and women, the overwhelming majority of them poor, fill jails and prisons; hundreds of thousands more . . . are subject to police, FBI, and military intelligence surveillance."[17] For Davis the imprisonment of tens of thousands of poor people of color meant "fascism" had taken hold in the United States. Aptheker declared, "This is a fascist program. It is a genocidal program."[18] James Baldwin argued that Davis's isolation and loneliness in prison reminded him of a "Jewish housewife in the boxcar headed to Dachau," describing prisons as "concentration camps" under which white Americans could measure their safety in "chains and corpses."[19] These sentiments concerning racism and the prison formed a common sense among the radical and revolutionary left in the 1970s United States and around the world. Prisons, as Michel Foucault noted in an essay from the same year, were "a war having other fronts in the black ghettos, the army and the courts." Incarceration was "an experience of [a] hostage, of a concentration camp, of class warfare, an experience of the colonized."[20] The title of Davis and Aptheker's collection itself emphasized the profound violence the black power movement felt it was confronted with; as Baldwin exclaimed to Davis, "If they take you in the morning, they will be coming for us that night."[21]

What is most astonishing about *If They Come in the Morning* is what it tells us about the changes that occurred to the U.S. prison system just years after Davis and her cohort declared that fascism had gripped the nation. Less than a decade later a convergence between the intensely racialized politics of law and order and the poverty and unemployment created by deindustrialization produced the largest prison system in the world. In 1970 there were roughly 200,000 people imprisoned in the United States. By 1995 there were 1 million, an increase of more than 442 percent in a quarter century.[22] By 2008, 2.5 million human beings—1 percent of the population—were immobilized in U.S. prisons and jails. In the same period 7 million adults were subject to state-supervised surveillance.[23] In a typical year roughly 14 million people pass through the gates of a prison or the bars of a jail.[24] Throughout this massive reorganization of the state and civil society, roughly 70 percent of the people behind bars were, and continue to be, people of color. Race, gender, sexuality, and class are central processes that determine what bodies are captured and immobilized. LGBTQ people (especially poor queer and transgender people of color) are drastically overrepresented in regimes of immobilization.[25] Within just four decades the prison emerged as a technology for the capture and management of racialized and gendered populations considered waste under the logics of late twentieth-century racial capitalism. As Ruth Wilson Gilmore has observed, it is a central regime for producing racism as the "state-sanctioned or extralegal production and exploitation of group-differentiated vulnerability to premature death."[26] In other words, the prison has become a central institution for the state regulation and management of the contours, possibilities, and impossibilities of life itself.

These changes would have been considered practically impossible and epistemologically unthinkable to the people contesting the post–civil rights expansion of the prison system. In fact, 1970s radicals and revolutionaries on the left thought that the worst had arrived and that a new world was dawning. Many of the collection's authors considered the intensity of the era's police and penal violence indicative of the "serious infirmities of the social order." For Davis and her coauthors, the "bourgeois democratic state," especially its judicial system, was "disintegrating," and the "revolutionary transformation of society" was close at hand. The increasing brutality of the police, courts, prisons, and an emerging economic crisis were reflective of a "profound social crisis, of systemic disintegration."[27] If we could speak to the past and issue a warning of what was coming, of the unprecedented regimes of racialized capture and immobilization that we live with today, our warnings would be inconceivable.

Davis and the Brigade theorized and contested these new epistemologies and institutional transformations in their writing. Underground organizations like the Weather Underground, Black Liberation Army, and George Jackson Brigade not only physically attacked symbols of state violence; the members also wrote poetry, stories, memoirs, communiqués, and magazine and newspaper articles and made films and art. They deployed culture to theorize the changes to global capitalism and incarceration happening around them. At the same time they used culture to imagine other ways of organizing life. Culture was a way to understand and see beyond the epistemological and affective dead ends of the forms of thought central to the neoliberal-carceral state. The fugitive activists I analyze understood culture as foundational to the production and survival of alternatives to the violence of the everyday. Thus the neoliberal-carceral state was not only made possible by cultural politics; for fugitive activists, culture was also one of the sites of racial capitalism's ruin. The forms of culture created by fugitive activists are an index that makes visible connections, complicities, and ruptures that the discourses produced by the neoliberal-carceral state attempt to disappear.

For instance, the goal of *If They Come in the Morning* was to archive and distribute voices, feelings, and forms of knowledge that the state was actively trying to eradicate. In their preface Davis and Aptheker write that the collection aims to "decisively counter, theoretically, ideologically, and practically, the increasing fascistic and genocidal posture of the present ruling clique." They remark that the state worked to disappear political insurgents through incarceration, but the state also renders unknowable its violence against workers, students, the black liberation movement, and the antiwar movement in the United States and in Vietnam through discourses of freedom, democracy, and equality.[28] They thus position theory and culture as epistemological tactics in a broader mass-based political movement against capitalism and the racial state. Later in the collection Davis ends her essay "Political Prisoners, Prisons, and Black Liberation" by declaring, "No potential victim of the fascist terror should be without the knowledge that the greatest menace to racism and fascism is unity!" She argues that state violence attempts to "physically decapitate and obliterate the movement" while also working to ideologically isolate and eradicate it. Thus, state power looks like assassination, incarceration, and police violence, but also the ways the state shapes memory, emotion, and knowledge. Davis argues that knowledge, theory, and culture are requirements in a successful multiracial struggle against the terror of prisons and attacks on organized labor, welfare, and the black liberation movement. "Unity" is a name for an epistemology, for a way of knowing grounded in a theory of relational difference whereby white workers can see their relationship to black workers and political prisoners because "their acquiescence" has "only rendered themselves more vulnerable to attack."[29] Yet this conception of unity would remain impossible without a politics of knowledge that could make it visible. A new way of knowing would lead to a new form of political struggle. Like Davis's emphasis on knowledge and culture, the Brigade did not think their bombings were an actual threat to the most powerful military in the history of the world. Bombings were a way to bring attention to forms of state violence that remained in the shadows of dominant ways of knowing. They called this "armed propaganda."[30] Writing and art were sites for the creation of alternative epistemologies that the neoliberal-carceral state continually worked to erase and expunge from the knowable.

This turn to cultural politics allows me to document how neoliberal political philosophy relies on an intimate and constitutive relationship to the carceral. Indeed, the earliest writing of neoliberal economists in the 1940s, 1950s, and 1960s advocated the containment of racialized and gendered populations considered surplus or potentially rebellious to the rule of the free market. At the same time, law-and-order politicians like Goldwater and Nixon argued in speeches and campaign ads that police and prisons were necessary to the freedom of the liberal individual and the deregulated labor market. While neoliberal economists argued that the free market needed the prison, law-and-order politicians argued that the prison would protect the free market and an emergent neoliberal social order. In other words, in the earliest articulations of what law and order and neoliberalism would be—before a wave of new laws and policy changes took hold in the 1980s— neoliberalism was imagined as a carceral project, and law and order as a neoliberal project.

Like the Brigade, Davis situated her imprisonment within the mutually constitutive relationship among racism, incarceration, and a changing economic landscape. According to Davis, prisons were filled with poor people of color and were thus a technology used to contain resistant and surplus populations. This containment occurred within a new formation of global capitalism that scholars and activists have come to call neoliberalism. Many of the contributors to *If They Come in the Morning* argued that the dismantling of the Keynesian welfare state and a wave of deindustrialization produced a massive surge of poverty and unemployment. Law-and-order policies then criminalized the ways of living amid the neoliberal economic production of poverty. In effect, poor people of color were trapped between the abandonment of a crumbling welfare state and the power of an encroaching penal state. Within this context many prisoners and activists argued that the free world started to feel like a prison. Zayd Shakur wrote in 1970, "Prisons are really an extension of our communities. We have people who are forced at gunpoint to live behind concrete and steel. Others of us, in what we ordinarily think of as the community, live at gunpoint again in almost the same conditions. . . . It's the same system—America is the prison."[31] Mark Cook, a "black, ex-convict prison organizer" convicted of working with the Brigade, writes that the separation between the free world and the prison was not distinct for the group: "We get out [of prison] and we don't distinguish between cops and prison guards. It took me *years* to understand that cops and prison guards weren't the same. When you first get out you just see them as guards and it's easy for ex-prisoners to get together and deal with them like we're still in prison." Brown saw the free world as "minimum-security," while Mead argued that in the free world "our leash is a little longer."[32] This theorization of prison undoes normative conceptions of space by exceeding the walls of the prison proper. A changing economic system became coextensive with an emerging carceral apparatus. An assemblage of race, gender, capital, policing, and penal technologies produced a symbiosis between the deindustrialized landscape of the late twentieth-century urban United States and the gendered racisms of an emerging prison-industrial complex. As feminist of color activists argued in this period, dispersed but structural regimes of racism and sexism paralleled and colluded with the cold cement of a cage. Many 1970s activists argued that the intimacy between the market and the prison was much deeper than had been articulated by scholars in the past two decades.

Throughout *Fugitive Life* I examine the economic, epistemological, and affective registers of neoliberalism. As an economic project, neoliberalism is a school of thought and a set of policy recommendations created by a transatlantic association of economists starting in the 1930s, including Friedrich Hayek, Karl Popper, Henry Simons, Ludwig von Mises, and Milton Friedman.[33] This economic project claims to expand the individual liberty of a rational, self-interested actor through the governance of a free market.[34] Neoliberalism attempts to free the individual, the market, and private enterprise from the constraints implemented by the state. This is accomplished by dismantling unions; cutting or eliminating public funding of social services (welfare, education, health care, social security, infrastructure); privatizing public resources, institutions, and goods; undoing environmental, labor, health, and safety regulations; deregulating the financial and banking industries; eliminating wage and price controls; and expanding "free trade."[35] Neoliberalism is a transnational political and economic project that aims to remake the nexus of state, market, and citizenship.[36] It does this by subjecting life to a logic that prioritizes the mobility and proliferation of capital at all costs.[37]

In order to justify and naturalize the capture of life by the economic, neoliberalism creates and requires a complex epistemological regime. I examine the intricacies of this system of knowledge in greater detail in chapters 1 and 2 by analyzing the politics of law and order and the writings of the neoliberal economist Milton Friedman, respectively. Neoliberal economics and the racialized and gendered violence that it produced were narrated into naturalness by discourses of freedom, democracy, equality, opportunity, and justice. These terms became methodologies for making incarceration, imperialism, poverty, racism, heteropatriarchy, and capital accumulation synonymous with the collective good. Put another way, neoliberalism incessantly disavows the centrality of the processes of valuation and devaluation called race, gender, and sexuality to its operation.[38] Race, gender, and sexuality have been folded into the very architecture of neoliberalism, which then constructs itself as neutral to the question of difference.[39] As Ruth Wilson Gilmore argues, one must now document how state racism functions even when it is officially over.[40] Racism and heteropatriarchy are consigned to the shadow of neoliberalism, constitutively haunting neoliberal conceptions of freedom in their present absence. The neoliberal-carceral state thus occludes what it requires and produces. Challenging neoliberal epistemologies requires producing new ways of seeing what seems to not be present and knowing what is impossible within statist epistemologies.

Discourses of personal responsibility, choice, and individuality are also central to neoliberal forms of capture. Under neoliberal regimes of freedom, one's subjection to "the state-sanctioned or extralegal production" of premature death through homelessness, poverty, illness, overwork, addiction, or incarceration is the result of an isolated, individual choice.[41] This logic is used against those subjected to environmental devastation, imperialism, forced famine, privatization, deregulation, the restructuring of paid and unpaid labor regimes, the dismantling of welfare apparatuses, increased policing and surveillance, and the hyperimmobilization of black and brown bodies in an ever-expanding regime of incarceration and detention.[42] Simply, those most susceptible to the production of premature death are blamed for their vulnerability to regimes of power far beyond their control: the drowned, the starved, the imprisoned, the impoverished, the murdered, the bombed, the occupied. Within the systems of knowledge manufactured by neoliberal economists, the world disappears and only the individual remains.

Activists who were aboveground, underground, and locked down all worked furiously to contest these emerging forms of knowledge. In the original introduction to *Soledad Brother*, the best-selling book by the imprisoned black revolutionary George Jackson, Jean Genet wrote that Jackson's prison writing exposed "the miracle of truth itself, the naked truth revealed."[43] For Genet and many readers of this literature, the prisoner had access to a unique formation of knowledge that led to alternative ways of seeing and knowing the world. The books of imprisoned authors like Eldridge Cleaver, George Jackson, and Malcolm X (which sold hundreds of thousands of copies) exposed something about the United States that only they could know. Scholars like Dylan Rodríguez, Michael Hames-García, and Joy James have argued that the knowledge produced by the prisoner exposes a truth about the United States that cannot be accessed from elsewhere.[44] The prisoner could name what others could not even see. Rodríguez writes, "As they are (sometimes literally) buried beneath the complex web of discourses, institutions, and power relations that compose social formation, prisoners encounter a cognitive territory outside common sense, beyond the symbolic and rational universe of civil society."[45] For Rodríguez space and violence are constitutive of epistemology. We can extend his argument to include other spaces outside the prison proper that are structured by penal and policing technologies.

Like imprisoned people in the early 1970s, hundreds of political fugitives wrote devastating critiques of the United States as they bombed and robbed their way to what they hoped would be a better world.[46] These groups understood culture as foundational to the production and survival of alternatives to things as they were. I understand the underground to entail a spatial and temporal shift as well as an epistemological one. Fugitive knowledges emerged to see and name that which normative ways of knowing could not. Going underground meant other analytics arose to narrate the emergence of the neoliberal-carceral state. I explore the forms of knowledge produced from multiple spaces literally and metaphorically beneath the neoliberal-carceral state. It is from the underground that new ways of knowing power and theorizing subjection emerge. By going underground I hope to make visible connections that are not always evident in the light of day. The space of the underground produces an estrangement from normative epistemologies so that the fugitive conceptualizes as profoundly unnatural what may pass as normal and routine.

The cultural products of imprisoned and underground activists are a record of what has been forgotten by hegemonic epistemologies. Roderick Ferguson writes that "epistemology is an economy of information privileged and information excluded," under which "national formations rarely disclose what they have rejected."[47] The prisoner and the fugitive index the histories and forms of knowledge that were erased and excluded by the politics of law and order and neoliberal economics. I explore the ways imprisoned and underground activists responded to the changing operations of (and technologies central to) racialized and gendered power under neoliberalism. In addition I contrast the forms of knowledge arising from the underground to the epistemologies central to the buildup of the neoliberal-carceral state. In this way, the prisoner and the fugitive produced epistemologies that undermined the political and historical fictions underpinning this process. For example, while law-and-order politicians argued that policing and penal technologies were instruments of safety and liberty, and neoliberal economists argued that poverty was the outcome of individual pathology, Davis and countless others labored to name the racialized and gendered violence cloaked by these new discourses. Central to contesting dominant ways of knowing and feeling was a theorization of difference as it related to the state and capital. In addition to describing the neoliberal-carceral state at the moment of its inception, the writings of the Brigade and Davis can help us reimagine queerness not as an individual gender or sexual identity but as a force productive of relational forms of difference.

The Force of Queerness

The Brigade placed incarceration at the center of a vast network of biopolitical power where capitalism and the prison operated symbiotically to manufacture populations vulnerable to devaluation in ways that mirrored but also exceeded older forms of racialized power. They argued that capitalism in the 1970s was changing to produce new forms of racialized and gendered value and disposability. This process was brought into being by the emergence of a new state form, one in which the governance of incarceration was central. Comprehending this new form of state power required an intersectional theorization of the processes that produced "women, the gays, the Blacks," and prisoners as devalued populations.[48] The group was thus part of a broader effort ignited by feminists of color in the late 1960s to open up new epistemological pathways to a different ordering of the world.[49] The Brigade explicitly pushed against a Marxist, feminist, and nationalist politics that attempted to relegate difference to the margins of revolutionary politics or erase it all together. Mead summarized the voice of this politics: "he's a prisoner and therefore he's kind of different"; "he's queer and that makes him different"; "she's a lesbian or a black" and thus different.[50] Instead of assimilating or abandoning difference, the Brigade made it the starting point for their critique of capitalism and incarceration. They worked to imagine modes of coalition, not based on homogeneity or similarity, but on relational difference, or what Kara Keeling calls "difference as an animating logic of belonging."[51] By letting difference guide their insurgent politics, the Brigade hoped to build a new "basis for freedom."[52]

In her classic essay, "Punks, Bulldaggers, and Welfare Queens: The Radical Potential of Queer Politics?," Cathy Cohen challenges a divide within queer politics between heterosexuality and queerness, where "queer activists map the power and entitlement of heterosexuality onto the bodies of all heterosexuals." She instead argues for a coalitional conception of queerness, wherein "one's relationship to power, and not some homogenized identity," shapes political imaginaries. Throughout the essay the punk, bulldagger, welfare queen, prisoner, and slave are differentially connected through their estrangement and expulsion from normative racialized regimes of gender, sexuality, and conceptions of the human. The radical potential of queerness lies not in its ability to name the fact of embodying individually resistive gender or sexual identities but in its capacity to act as a force that could bring together "all those deemed marginal and all those committed to liberatory politics."[53] Significantly, queerness in this formulation is not a static identity; it is an affective and epistemological methodology for making visible the connections across always changing relational differences.

Cohen explains that heteronormativity arises out of the racialized regulation of gender and sexuality central to chattel slavery and its afterlives. Black people under antiblack state, economic, and interpersonal forms of terror (slavery, lynching, Jim Crow, and the prison regime) have been continuously legally and extralegally positioned outside heteronormativity even as they might be engaged in acts called heterosexual. Sarah Haley refers to this process as "forced queering" to describe the ways that "state regimes of violence and exploitative capitalist labor" produced black women as gender-nonconforming in the early twentieth-century convict-lease system.[54] Black women's bodies were considered gender-nonconforming because black women were forced to endure brutal forms of labor typically reserved for men. The forced construction of black women's gender and sexual otherness arose from being treated as though they were men. State and corporate practices of gendered racialized terror solidified black women as outside the normative category of woman.[55] In addition, the category "black" contradicted the whiteness foundational to the category of universal "woman," meaning "black woman" had no meaning in the white imagination.[56] Christina Sharpe names this process "anagrammatical" because words like *mother* and *child* fail to hold meaning in relation to black people—signification slips so that *girl* does not mean *girl* and *mother* fails to reproduce the meanings of motherhood.[57] Black women's subject position existed outside the binary categories "man" and "woman."[58] The expulsion of black women from gender and sexual normativity acted as the condition of possibility for the subject position of "white woman."[59] Black women in the convict-lease system were not women, and *white woman* was defined against the brutality black women survived and resisted.

In a similar vein, Hortense Spillers argues that the captured and caged "human-as-cargo" on the slave ship was neither male nor female because all enslaved people were "taken in 'account' as *quantities*."[60] A quantity does not have a gender because living as a gendered subject requires existing in the realm of the human.[61] Enslaved life on the ship was not human and enslaved women were not women but embodied calculations of space, time, calories, and illness. On the slave ship and plantation, one loses "gender difference in the outcome" so that the black female body is ungendered and produced as inhuman.[62] Spillers and Haley suggest that heteronormativity and gender normativity arose out of the racialized regulation, terror, and extraction foundational to chattel slavery and its institutionalized afterlives in the convict-lease system and the prison. In other words, the whiteness of heterosexuality came into being through its parasitic relationship to the fabrication of racialized inhumanity.[63] "Forced queering" is a name for the way the state and capital produce nonnormative genders and sexualities through racial violence. Queerness, in this formulation, is not a name for freedom but a method for comprehending how power produces racialized, gendered, and sexual difference as a proximity to suffering, subjection, and death. As Omise'eke Natasha Tinsley writes of the gender-queer bodies that survived the terror of the Middle Passage or remain under the shimmering surface of the Atlantic, "their brown bodies are gender fluid not because they choose parodic proliferations but because they have been 'washed of all this lading, bag, and baggage' by a social liquidation that is *not* the willful or playful fluidity of [Judith] Butler's drag queens"; it is a "gender queerness that calls into question the facile linkages between gender trouble and liberation."[64] Thinking of queerness as a form of relational difference produced by racial violence helps us to reconceptualize how the state and capital operate, and also opens up new possibilities for thinking about life, survival, and freedom.

The Brigade describes the queering of similarly different populations when they write that "prisoners, ex-prisoners, old people, young people, people trapped into the lowest paid, most temporary shit jobs, people forced on welfare and forced to remain there. All these people are discarded by capitalism."[65] The populations named here have been abandoned, captured, overworked, targeted for regulation, underpaid, isolated, and left behind by regimes of racialized capital accumulation. In different ways, with unequal consequences, they have been expelled from the racialized regimes of gender and sexual normativity central to an emerging neoliberalism. It is this expulsion that makes abandonment, disposal, exploitation, and death possible. In an open letter supporting the Brigade, the anonymous group Stagecoach Mary Collective describes the processes that produce differently queered populations in the 1970s United States:

> In actuality, the government of this country and the ruling class behind it ranks as the most powerfully destructive force in the world. In the interest of maintaining the huge profits of multi-national corporations it has taken control of the economies and sought to destroy the cultures of Third World countries through genocidal warfare (as in Viet Nam). Forced sterilization, drug experimentation, destruction of the land and natural resources and outright killings of whole populations are just a few of the ways the U.S. government has terrorized the world.
>
> This same system has used these tactics on poor and Third World people here in the U.S. Children, women and men are killed daily on Indian reservations, in prisons and mental hospitals, and on the streets. Violence is institutionalized through racist and sexist court, welfare, education and public health systems. This violence is a fact of life for poor and non-white people. Our children are shot on the streets, workers are killed by unsafe conditions on the job, women die from back alley abortions because they can't support another child and can't afford a safe abortion. Third world and poor women are consistently sterilized without their knowledge or consent—for example: 40% of Native American Women, 33% of Puerto Rican and 25% of Black women of childbearing age have been sterilized.[66]

In this statement work, abortion, sterilization, imperialism, welfare, schooling, incarceration, settler colonialism, environmental destruction, and genocide are differential processes connected across time and space that produce and render multiple populations vulnerable to death and disposability. Race, gender, and sexuality are not biological or essentialist categories static in their naturalness but "processes of valuation and devaluation."[67] For the Stagecoach Mary Collective, the populations and processes named in this statement cannot be grasped in isolation. In order to understand the sterilization of black women, one must also understand the sterilization of Native and Puerto Rican women. And one must understand how sterilization was made possible by and connected to a seemingly disparate network of events: the "slow death" of life on reservations, U.S. imperialism in Vietnam, the deregulation of labor laws, a racist and sexist welfare system, regimes of capture and caging, and the mundane operations of state power in the form of public health and education.[68] Not only do all of these processes harm and kill queer people; they also produce devalued populations outside the racialized regimes foundational to gender and sexual normativity. Forced outside dominant norms, they have been "left queer."[69]

A process like sterilization is a queer issue not only because queer women of color were sterilized but also because sterilization produced women of color, and children of color, as gendered and sexualized threats to white supremacy. The gender and sexuality of women of color were understood to be nonnormative, deviant threats to the life of the racial state. Indeed by preventing women of color from having children and building families, the aftermath of sterilization disallowed the formation of the normative unit of the family. Women of color were thus doubly expelled from normative paradigms of womanhood. Those subjected to forced sterilization were not liberated by the righteous, resistant pleasure of queerness as identity or sexual practice but were made vulnerable to the sexual violence of the state by queerness as a force that produces racialized, gendered, and sexual difference. Here, queerness as a force central to the production of subjects and nonsubjects justifies state violence and simultaneously creates the objects of state violence. As Grace Hong and Roderick Ferguson observe, "Capitalism is centrally structured around the creation of norms and values. These normative categories are racialized, gendered, classed, and sexualized at the same time. Those who do not fit these norms of respectability are dismissed and demonized and are thus subject to all manner of material and social marginalization."[70] We can add the prison to Hong and Ferguson's observation that capitalism produces norms (and thus nonnormativity) and fabricates populations that are subjected to, as Davis argues, the most "calculated forms" of state violence. For example, the racialization of the criminal occurs through discourses of immorality, deviancy, pathology, and abnormality that expunge the criminal from the realm of gender and sexual normativity. The key function of incarceration is to punish people who deviate from racialized, gendered, sexual, and classed social norms.[71] By divesting from low-income communities of color and targeting poor people of color for capture and caging, the neoliberal-carceral state is able to uphold systems of white heteropatriarchal normativity. In short, the prison upholds the normative behavior of individuals and the normative ordering of the world. The prison and neoliberalism queer in the name of safety and accumulation but produce capture, caging, and disposability.

The Fugitivity of Queerness

Conceptualizing queerness as a force that biopolitically produces relational forms of difference that make possible social, civil, and premature death does not mean that queerness is only a process of subjection. The forces that create difference do not determine its future. Something takes flight and escapes even as capture is always immanent. Norms never act once, and since they must be endlessly repeated and have no single origin, their operation is not deterministic. Their future is unknown; flight is possible because the potential of escape is always present.[72] There may be no outside to power because it is already there, but that does not mean power is totalizing in its effects. As Chela Sandoval writes regarding women of color feminism, "U.S. third world feminism rose out of the matrix of the very discourses denying, permitting, and producing difference." Her "methodology of the oppressed" emerges out of the shock, trauma, terror, and forms of resistance experienced under slavery, colonization, and state violence.[73] It is from within populations labeled materially and "existentially surplus" by the neoliberal-carceral state that survival skills, modes of action, and alternative epistemologies emerge to lead toward new worlds and "something else to be."[74] Populations produced as surplus to the neoliberal-carceral state are also sites of fugitivity. Difference is the outcome and the answer.

In a communiqué sent on International Women's Day in 1976, the Brigade declared that they freed John Sherman from police custody, listed tactical errors they made during an earlier bank robbery where Sherman and Mead were captured, and mourned the death of a member, Bruce Siedel.[75] They ended the statement with a poem that described the possibilities of a fugitive politics grounded in a politics of difference. Difference in their writing was a form of fugitivity from the futurity of the imagination of the racial state—a future normalized and restrained by the racialized, heterosexist, and patriarchal regulation of gender and sexuality. The middle stanza is:

Not the vague vanguard
We are a collection
of oppressed people turning
inside out with action
this united few breaks
barriers of
race class sex
workers and lumpen
all going together
combating dull sameness
corporations, government
and the established rule of
straight white cocks.[76]

The group related across a variety of forms of difference without desiring sameness. They did not want the vagueness of a homogeneous vanguard or a movement where the working class abandoned surplus populations expelled from regimes of work. In addition to finding "unity in difference," they also imagined a movement that was "aboveground, underground, and locked down"—where location (prison or free world) and tactics (legal or illegal) did not lead to an isolationist politics of individual action:

I cannot be one
acting alone with my
little toe outside the line
its both feet
whole body
ain't no turning back now.[77]

The Brigade envisioned a coalitional feminist, queer, and antiracist politics whereby knowledge and action were unifying forces that functioned because of difference, not in spite of it.

Members of the Brigade created a queer politics based on epistemology which could take flight from static notions of identity, culture, or biology.[78] In their vision, a multitude of political and epistemological possibilities open up when one disobeyed disciplinary allegiance to a proper political object. The last stanza of the poem makes this clear by connecting the Brigade's coalitional politics to an abolitionist imaginary:

We are cozy cuddly
armed and dangerous
and we will
raze the fucking prisons
to the ground.[79]

This is a fitting finale to the poem because prison abolition was the only political vision that united the group. In other words, the group's politics of difference extended to epistemology because they "were probably all fighting for a different vision."[80]

Unlike many contemporaneous leftist groups, there was no platform, doctrine, or document that members had to obey. Indeed, the group was constantly revising its thinking and apologizing for mistakes. Their political statement, "The Power of the People Is the Source of Life," contains a long note to the reader making clear that the statement is not "static or final. Rather, [we] will continue to change and develop as our experiences of the revolutionary movement lead us to a deeper understanding of revolution."[81] The group then invited criticism, questions, and comments, producing an antidisciplinary queer politics in which the future was always and already unknown. There was no platform or doctrine that would mold the shape of the future. Thought, being, and what was coming were open to being undone, remade, and undone once again. Queerness was a means of traversing and transforming a variety of conceptual boundaries. The Brigade's politics were not based on a proper object or subject.[82] Queerness was unfixed, mobile, and flexible, a fugitive force leading to a place beyond the prison and beyond the knowable.

The modern prison is one of the most powerful, violent, heavily surveilled, and secure institutions ever constructed, yet people still escape, and people contained within it continue to successfully challenge its existence.

In a short essay also written in prison, "Lessons: From Attica to Soledad," Davis writes that the prison is an institution of "unmitigated totalitarianism." This totalitarian logic is aimed at prisoners but also those not yet caged or targeted for capture.[83] Concrete, armed guards, barbed wire, steel, bullet-proof glass, and cameras are of course intended to ensure human beings do not escape social death. But as Davis observes, these technologies also aim to keep the outside world from getting in. The prison is threatened by its captives but also by the world beyond—by books, family and friends, food, drugs, holding hands, mobile phones, a kiss, "usb storage devices," "tattooing equipment," film, a hug from a child, cameras, alcohol, and "portable digital media players."[84] People immobilized in solitary confinement are starved of the ability to see the horizon, sun, or stars. Why deny someone the sensations of fresh air, the greenish tint of trees in the falling daylight, the quiet radiance of a half-moon, the soft touch of another, or the sounds just before first light? Why force death on a still breathing body? What does the prisoner see and feel that is so dangerous to the racial state? What Davis calls the prison's "unmitigated totalitarianism" reveals that it is threatened by the sensations and feelings of its captives.[85] The prison's fragility is evident in the ways it targets the mind, body, and feelings of imprisoned people but also in its paranoia about what might enter its realm of control. In an essay written while in prison after her work with the George Jackson Brigade, Brown states that a black lesbian couple "were just too much in love to be in prison." They were therefore a "threat to the security of the institution" and placed in solitary confinement.[86]

The prison is constantly at war with the possibility of affective, emotional, and physical escape—with the fugitivity of caged human beings. It is for this reason that Davis refers to imprisoned people as "escape-bound captives." Even as the prison attempts to mold human beings "into non-existence," its power is incessantly subverted, resisted, and undone.[87] Prisoners are captives looking for a way out. Escape is not a single act; it is a political ontology that precedes the prison. The prison works to contain "escape-bound" human beings; it captures people looking for an exit. "Escape-bound" describes a force of life within a regime of unimaginable social, civil, and premature death. Brown called this love, and Davis called it being bound to escape. In short, the prisoner is always already a potential fugitive. And the fugitive is a future prisoner on the run.

One of the most significant lessons of the fugitive is that power is fragile even within the prison's dominance, terror, and breadth. Thousands of people evaded capture for years, sometimes decades, and many are still running. The fugitive is a figure of hope, possibility, and futurity. She shows what it means to be "unfit for subjection."[88] She shows that flight is always possible, that escape is always there, even amid the impossibilities of the present. The fugitive runs even when it seems there is nowhere to go. This is because within new modes of control and subordination, new methodologies for escape arise. New operations of power mean new opportunities for its undoing. Power is never static and unmoving; rather it is *becoming*, not being. If it is becoming, changing and mutating in its never-ending production, there is opportunity to run away because power is "always forthcoming and already past."[89] The contradiction of power is that it produces the conditions that will bring about its end: the state of emergency is also the state of emergence.[90] One is in power even as one opposes it, formed by it even as one reworks it.[91] Dan Berger describes this when he writes of the fugitive activist Marilyn Buck, "Fugitive freedom as a political praxis engages a dialectic between repression and liberation: it finds avenues for liberation in regimes of repression."[92] As the neoliberal-carceral state becomes there are slippages, passages, undoings, proliferations, and forms of flight that were impossible yesterday and might be impossible tomorrow. In this context, the fugitive is one figure we can turn to who finds "a way out of no way."[93] The fugitive finds the void, the rupture, the break in power and runs through it. But the fugitive's flight is not only physical; it is also epistemological and affective. The fugitive runs away but leaves in her wake new ways of knowing and feeling. In the trace of her presence—a rumor, a note, half a fingerprint, ashes of a cigarette, coffee grounds in a cup—lay other ways of living, being, feeling, and thinking. This is one of the legacies of Davis's writing from prison, the Brigade's clandestine manifestos, and the fugitive writings I explore throughout the coming chapters. I seek to open up the many affective and epistemological impossible possibilities that are created by running away, hiding, and vanishing into the thick air of the everyday.

The first chapter "'We're Not Hiding but We're Invisible': Law and Order, the Temporality of Violence, and the Queer Fugitive," is divided into two parts. I begin by investigating how the law-and-order politics of Goldwater and Nixon connected the prison to the free market through a normativizing discourse about the future. In their campaign ads and speeches, Goldwater and Nixon argued that the period's leftist social movements threatened the future of American freedom as embodied by the free market and the liberal individual. Containing this threat to the future of freedom necessitated the governance of the prison. For Nixon and Goldwater the very possibility of a future depended on the immobilization of those rendered surplus, resistant, or fugitive to new racialized economic regimes structured around privatization, deindustrialization, deregulation, and finance. In other words, embedded in the emergent discourses of the neoliberal-carceral state was a vision of the future, one where the freedom of individuality and the market required mass incarceration. Within the discourses of law and order lie the foundations of the neoliberal-carceral state—a necessary relationship between the prison and the free market. I argue that the political fugitive haunted the law-and-order state with the threat of queer ways of being and living that were outside the normative systems of sexuality, white supremacy, gender, family, and nation.

In the second part of the chapter I examine how underground lesbian activists of the period theorized the prison, the market, and time in relation to emerging law-and-order discourses. Many 1970s activists did not see the prison and the market as separate systems of power; they understood them as deeply connected and, at times, indistinguishable. I focus on the communiqués and poetry of the women's brigade of the Weather Underground, a group formed in direct response to the repression and violence of the law-and-order state. These writings can be understood as feminist and queer responses to the temporality of progress that supported law and order. I contrast these revolutionary visions with the dreams of Nixon and Goldwater, who understood the prison and the market as foundational to the security and order of the racial state and its future.

Chapter 2, "Life Escapes: Neoliberal Economics, the Underground, and Fugitive Freedom," investigates two paradigmatic notions of freedom in the 1970s that I call "neoliberal freedom" and "fugitive freedom." I continue to explore the ways that penal and policing technologies were imagined as central to the life of the free market, but in this chapter I focus on the writings of early neoliberal thinkers, in particular Friedman's 1962 *Capitalism and Freedom*. As a leader of the Chicago school of economics, Friedman was perhaps the most important opponent to Keynesian economics and is considered central to the development of neoliberal thought and policy. But despite his significance to neoliberal policy across the globe, scholars of neoliberalism and late twentieth-century capitalism have largely ignored his writings. The emergence of neoliberal theories of freedom were, in part, a response to the liberation movements of the 1960s and 1970s. In addition Friedman's theory of freedom relied on the containment of populations he deemed nonnormative and thus not sufficiently responsible for freedom. Therefore neoliberal theories of freedom required the prison.

I compare Friedman's theory of freedom to the underground as a space that escaped—and critiqued—the forms of knowledge central to the constitution of neoliberal freedom. While feminist, antiracist, and queer liberation movements made demands that exceeded the material and epistemological possibilities of the social order, neoliberal freedom confined and restricted what freedom could be within the relations between the individual and the market. Neoliberal thought deployed freedom as a system of regulation and discipline. In other words, the language of neoliberal freedom captured ways of thinking and organizing life that attempted to escape new and emerging modes of subjection. The production of neoliberal freedom thus colluded with the racialized and gendered power of the police and prison. The prison captured bodies while neoliberal thought captured epistemology. In contrast to Friedman's theory, freedom for fugitive activists was not an ontological status produced by the market or the state; rather it was the practice of working toward a different organization of the world. I expand on this conception of fugitive freedom by turning to memoirs written by fugitive activists and Susan Choi's novel *American Woman*, which is the fictional account of the relationship between a queer Asian American fugitive who lived with Patty Hearst for one year after Hearst joined the Symbionese Liberation Army. *American Woman* and the memoirs demonstrate that the space of the underground opened up other ways of seeing and knowing the world and thus gave rise to alternative notions of freedom that negated the regulatory powers of neoliberalism. The underground thus acted as a temporal space that queered normative regimes of living, knowledge, and governance. I argue that the fugitive and the underground are formations that produced a conception of freedom founded on running away.

Chapter 3, "Possessed by Death: Black Feminism, Queer Temporality, and the Afterlife of Slavery," examines the writings of three imprisoned black feminist fugitives—Angela Davis, Safiya Bukhari, and Assata Shakur—in order to investigate the historical foundations of the neoliberal-carceral state. Since the 1960s, scholars, activists, and prisoners have argued that the contemporary prison exists on a historical continuum with nineteenth-century chattel slavery. More recently (as outlined by chapter 2) a growing body of work has made clear the connections between the post-1980s prison and neoliberal economic policies. Although the prison's connection to slavery and neoliberalism has been well explored, the contemporary market's relationship to chattel slavery has largely been overlooked. If slavery's antiblack technologies inhabit and structure the prison, how do they live on in the operations of the market? What is the relationship between an antiblackness inaugurated under the Atlantic slave trade and the methods of population management used under neoliberalism? In analyzing Shakur's "Women in Prison: How We Are," Bukhari's "Coming of Age: A Black Revolutionary," and Davis's "Reflections on the Black Woman's Role in the Community of Slaves," I argue that these prison writings connected an emergent neoliberalism to chattel slavery through a queer conception of temporality I call "possession." Possession names the ways the past haunts the present and also takes hold of it, determining the contours and possibilities of the now. The possessive theory of temporality produced by imprisoned black feminists queered normative conceptions of time central to law and order and neoliberal economics. This chapter's discussion of queer time sets the foundation for the next chapter, which address queer futurity. If slavery possesses the present of the prison and market, how does one get out?

In chapter 4, "'Only the Sun Will Bleach His Bones Quicker': Desire, Police Terror, and the Affect of Queer Feminist Futures," I examine the ways that feminist and queer activists and writers in the 1970s conceptualized the relationships among desire, fugitivity, policing, and police violence. I focus my analysis on the 1970s and early 1980s poetry of June Jordan and Audre Lorde, which theorized the racial politics of police violence and its relationship to desire. Yet this aspect of their work has not been examined as part of a genealogy of queer and feminist antiprison politics. Read together, the writings of Lorde and Jordan comprise a body of queer, feminist, antiprison, and antipolice politics that can help us make sense of the racial, gendered, and sexual politics of the neoliberal-carceral state. Critically, this body of work makes visible the violence of the racial state, but it does so by exploring the terrain of desire. More specifically Lorde and Jordan worked to make sense of an emerging desire for state power and how this desire for subjection authorized and materialized new forms of carceral and economic state power in the late 1970s. Their poetry expands a queer conception of desire beyond sexuality to the racial politics of policing and state power. They warned that the state sought to capture desire to bolster the normative order of things, and policing was one way this was accomplished. At the same time activists and thinkers like Lorde, Jordan, and many others engaged desire as a form of escape from white supremacy, heteropatriarchy, policing, and prisons. While other chapters focus on feminist and queer activists who became political fugitives, this chapter advances a less identitarian conception of fugitivity. Throughout the chapter I explore fugitivity as an epistemological and affective force, as opposed to a social, political, and legal location. I do so by examining the relationship between desire and the neoliberal-carceral state. I argue that a desire for police and prisons is central to the rise of the neoliberal-carceral state but that fugitive desires and affects are foundational to undoing the reign of the carceral and the terror of neoliberalism.

Fugitive Life ends by examining *Top Ranking: A Collection of Articles on Racism and Classism in the Lesbian Community* (1980). This collection includes some of the thinkers central to the development of black feminism—for example, Lorde, Beverly Smith, and Barbara Smith—but it also brings together the writing of the imprisoned butch political prisoner Rita Brown, lesbian antiprison activists, anti-imperialist feminists, and black lesbians who interrogate the policing functions of white lesbian communities. Despite its attention to the racialized politics of gender and sexuality and its unique attention to incarceration, the collection has largely been forgotten in genealogies of feminist, queer, and abolitionist thought. I explore how the modes of thought produced by the collection form a fugitive politics that is necessary for comprehending the systems of marginalization that make the neoliberal-carceral state necessary and possible. Collectively the contributors construct an affective epistemology—a fugitive way of knowing that escapes articulation—that would give rise to a new ontology founded on collective becoming, not the singularity of being. It is this way of inhabiting the world that can navigate the possessive power of the market and the terror of the prison—to survive, thrive, and keep running in the space between escape and capture.

1. "WE'RE NOT HIDING BUT WE'RE INVISIBLE" LAW AND ORDER, THE TEMPORALITY OF VIOLENCE, AND THE QUEER FUGITIVE

Shock waves, light waves through earth
and air moving us all into one time
This time. Our time.

—THE WOMEN'S BRIGADE OF THE
WEATHER UNDERGROUND, *Sing a Battle Song*

In October 1967 Richard Nixon published an article in *Reader's Digest* titled "What Has Happened to America?" In the article, Nixon lamented that just a few years earlier the "nation seemed to be completing its greatest decade of racial progress" and was "entering one of the most hopeful periods in American History." Yet the progress of the early 1960s dissolved into a "blazing inferno" of "urban anarchy" where "snipers," "looters," and "arsonists" led an "armed insurrection" that exceeded the disciplinary capacities of the police. Nixon did not see the urban uprisings of the late 1960s as symptomatic of "the deep racial division between Negro and white." Instead, they were the omen of a culture that no longer respected authority and the rule of law. The warning signs of this disrespect for law and order were embedded in the weakness of lenient judges, "opinion makers" who blamed society for crime and not the criminal, and, most critically, in the actions of those "who defy the law in the pursuit of civil rights." Nixon argued that the right to protest outside the limits of the law should not exist because "in a civilized nation no man can excuse his crime against the person or property of another by claiming that he, too, has been a victim of injustice." For Nixon, antiracist and anti-imperialist activism threatened the most basic and "primary civil right" of all Americans: the right to be free from "domestic violence."[1]

Central to Nixon's campaign of law and order was a discourse about the relationship between time and violence. He argued, "We cannot have patience with urban violence. Immediate and decisive force must be the first response. *For there can be no progress unless there is an end to violence and unless there is respect for the rule of law.*"[2] The violence of the period's liberation movements threatened to unravel the progress of time's passage so that freedom, the social order, and the nation itself would be propelled backward into the barbarity of lawlessness or destroyed altogether. By contrasting the "immediate and decisive force" of the state to "urban violence," Nixon rendered state violence invisible, making it the precondition for the progress of time and the nation. Revolutionary violence stopped time, while state violence allowed progress to unravel a future filled with freedom, security, and peace. This representation of temporality and its connection to police and the prison would be central to remaking the racial state in the post–civil rights era. Most profoundly the progress of time was conceptualized as a form of security in and of itself; if time stopped or changed direction, the nation's order and integrity would disintegrate. In his 1968 speeches and campaign ads Nixon made clear that foundational to the nation's future was the stability of white supremacy and the order of heteropatriarchy. Radical protest and revolutionary violence were thus positioned by Nixon and others as a temporal force that would queer the nation's future, derailing the nation's progress to an unnamed place that haunted the present. Within the vision of law and order, police and prisons would protect time's steady march forward and thus would secure the nation and its future. The future was described as a space of safety and security in order to maintain the violence of the present and to temper the rage of those who refused to wait for the future's warm embrace to arrive. Nixon argued in more than seventy speeches during his 1968 campaign that law and order was the solution to the crises of state and capital brought on by the 1960s social movements: law and order would undo the ruin of Western time.[3] In short, progress and the future needed the security, rule, and order of police and prisons.

This chapter explores different conceptions of the relationships among time, race, queerness, and violence. As outlined in the introduction, I understand queerness to be a nonidentitarian force that can be produced by dominant and subversive formations. In other words, the racial state can produce populations, spaces, and temporalities as queer. Insurgent formations can also produce forms of queerness that disrupt the biopolitical and necropolitical operations of the neoliberal-carceral state. By analyzing multiple and contrasting queer temporalities I examine two contrasting visions of how neoliberalism and the prison were connected to time and the future: I analyze the rhetoric of late 1960s law-and-order politicians and the epistemologies of 1970s underground revolutionaries. Specifically I examine how a discourse about time and the future was used by proponents of law and order to suture the freedom of the market to the incapacitation of the prison. In addition, I explore how underground revolutionary activists named this process through a queer engagement with temporality. Throughout the chapter I analyze what I term the "temporality of violence." As I document, racialized and gendered forms of state violence undo homogeneous conceptions of time. When one centers racialized and gendered violence in a theory of history, time does not flow evenly, progressing into a better or unknown future. Instead, violence can slow time, reverse it, loop it, make it stop or rush by in a moment of terror; it can also make it disappear forever. And if the future is ossified by the stability of the present, one can also see, know, and feel the future before it arrives. The 1970s writings of imprisoned radicals and underground revolutionaries can be understood as feminist and queer responses to the temporality of progress that supported law and order. The political fugitive haunted the law-and-order state with the threat of queer ways of being, thinking, and living that were outside the normative systems of sexuality, white supremacy, gender, family, and nation. She also lived outside the ways the racial state attempted to order temporality. I contrast these revolutionary visions to the dreams of people, like Nixon, who understood the prison and the market as foundational to the security and normative order of the nation and its future. Indeed, for Nixon and others the very possibility of a future depended on the immobilization of those rendered surplus or resistant to new economic regimes structured around privatization, deindustrialization, deregulation, and financialization. In other words, embedded in the emergent discourses of the neoliberal-carceral state was a vision of the future, one wherein the freedom of individuality and the market required the mass immobilization of the prison. By contrasting statist and underground forms of knowledge about the prison and market, I argue that underground activists produced a theory of time and history that understood law and order as a way for the prison and market to colonize the future.

The Future of the Neoliberal-Carceral State

To read the work of early neoliberal thinkers and the speeches of law-and-order politicians is to confront the utopic dreams of the dominant. In the visions of many economic and political leaders of the mid-twentieth century the prison would usher in a post–civil rights utopia aimed at producing the safety and security of white life, while neoliberalism would inaugurate a "utopia of endless exploitation."[4] The power of the market and the prison would accumulate with time's movement to determine and capture the future. As Pierre Bourdieu argues, neoliberalism relies on a "utopic vision" of the world wherein the abstract rationality of the market is pure, perfect, and always "implacably unrolling the logic of predictable consequences."[5] Similarly, David Harvey posits that neoliberalism operates at two levels: the theoretical and the material. Neoliberalism's theoretical vision is a "utopian project" aimed at reorganizing global capitalism in order to liberate the accumulation of capital from any and all constraint. Inherent in this theoretical utopianism is the flourishing of freedom, choice, and individuality. In contrast, neoliberalism's material project is to restore power to the "economic elite."[6] According to Harvey, the utopianism of neoliberalism works to obscure the violence, force, and exploitation of its materialist politics. Neoliberalism's utopic futurity is an epistemological diversion from the violence of its materialist politics. We can place the utopianism of neoliberalism within the utopic politics of the modern state more broadly. The modern state's utopian aim is to reduce the disorderly, chaotic, always changing social order under its purview into a mirror of the administrative knowledge central to its observations and governance. The state works to produce temporal and spatial intelligibility with the goal of manufacturing the orderly administration and regulation of the nation's population, resources, and infrastructure. By disrupting and dismantling spaces, populations, and epistemologies that are illegible to its regimes of knowing and governance, the modern state creates a utopia of visibility and legibility that is open to policing and control.[7]

Law and order was an insurgent mode of state building that attempted to dismantle and eradicate people, spaces, and forms of knowledge that exceeded or challenged the future of the post–civil rights state. I call law and order "state insurgency" to name the way the state deploys legal and extralegal violence in order to remake itself in spectacular moments of crisis like 1968. I also understand the state to be in a constant state of insurgency against forms of life that contest or exceed its order and operations. The power of the racial state is not static or given; the naturalness of its power must be made and remade in the mundane as well as the spectacular. Throughout this chapter and others I pay particular attention to the soft, quiet, mundane manifestations of this ongoing insurgency against alternative ways of living, being, and relating, through which the racial state created space for the construction of a "neoliberal utopia." The fugitive and the underground threatened this utopic future and were subsequently targeted for disruption, incarceration, exile, and eradication. One genealogy of the utopic fantasies of neoliberalism lies in the politics of law and order.

While many scholars have turned to the politics of law and order in the 1960s and 1970s to better understand the rise of the carceral state, I want to consider the connections between law and order and an ascendant neoliberalism.[8] In what follows, I connect neoliberalism and law and order by noting the ways that law and order produced the freedom of the individual and the market through discourses and practices of racialized imprisonment and policing. I argue that the politics of law and order connected the regulatory freedom of individuality to the freedom of the market and the incapacitation and death of new policing and penal technologies. Neoliberal discourses of individualism, freedom, and choice emerged, in part, out of the discourses used to justify the expansion of the prison. And the discourses used to justify the intensification of incarceration were also discourses about time's progressive unfolding into the future. In this way, the prison and neoliberalism collude at the level of the population and body but also at the level of discourse, temporality, and affect. We can witness this relationship in the ways Nixon and Goldwater connected the prison to the freedom of the market and the individual (what we might think of as a proto-neoliberal subject). Race and white supremacy were central to this process. For example, in Goldwater's 1964 acceptance speech for the Republican presidential nomination, we can see an early connection between the liberation of the individual and the need to contain the insurgent and fugitive black body:

> We must, and we shall, set the tide running again in the cause of freedom. . . . Freedom balanced so that liberty lacking order will not

become the slavery of the prison cell; [freedom] balanced so that liberty lacking order will not become the license of the mob and of the jungle. . . . The growing menace in our country tonight, to personal safety, to life, to limb and property . . . particularly in our great cities, is the mounting concern. . . . Security from domestic violence . . . is the most elementary and fundamental purpose of any government.[9]

Goldwater ended his speech by speaking of the future: "In our vision of a good and decent future, free and peaceful, there must be room, room for the liberation of the energy and the talent of the individual, otherwise our vision is blind at the outset."[10]

Goldwater spoke at the precipice of the rise of a variety of social movements that, as *Business Week* put it in 1968, were going to crumble the social and economic order.[11] Like Nixon four years later, Goldwater argued that there must be a countermobilization by the state against this threat if the individual was to be free. Personal freedom would require the unfreedom of the carceral state and its attendant methods of policing and security. Critically, this vision was a racial project of undoing antiracist liberatory movements in order to clear space for the (white) individual. Dylan Rodríguez has argued that law and order was a project of "white liberation" against U.S.-based, third world, black, and indigenous liberation movements and their accompanying urban insurrections.[12] It was not only the deployment of carceral violence that was deeply racialized, but also the attendant use of individuality.

Within the Western liberal imagination individuality is the constitutive sign of civilization, while "the mob" signifies a condition of barbarism, degeneracy, sexual excessiveness, lawlessness, and blackness. The individual is governed by choice, autonomy, reason, democracy, and consent, while the mob is ruled by violence, culture, religion, intolerance, and immorality.[13] In Goldwater's speech, individuality and the freedom of the market are the raisons d'être for an unprecedented expansion of the prison system. Many scholars have observed that individuality is foundational to neoliberalism and is constructed as arising from the governance of the market. As Stuart Hall observes, "However, anachronistic it may seem, neo-liberalism is grounded in the idea of the 'free, possessive individual.' It sees the state as tyrannical and oppressive. The state must never govern society, dictate to free individuals how to dispose of their property, regulate a free-market economy or interfere with the God-given right to make profits and amass personal wealth."[14] Or as Margaret Thatcher succinctly put it, "There is no such thing as society. . . . There is only the individual and his family."[15] The processes of deregulation, deindustrialization, and privatization beginning in the 1970s required the production of an "exhaustively rational" subject whose value was measured by a capacity for self-care and personal responsibility.[16] Neoliberalism produces a subject who is regulated by a strict adherence to individuality. Individuality is marked as the sign of freedom, choice, and power, but the neoliberal subject is open to regulation, governance, and domination through the freedom it is offered and avows. The neoliberal subject is at once required to make its own life and is always already regulated in this making. This is what biopower and discipline realize together and what neoliberal governmentality achieves beginning in the 1970s.[17] Thus, the power of neoliberalism appears not just in moments of spectacular repression or brutality. The invitation of inclusion or the warm embrace of recognition, freedom, and choice are also technologies of power's subjection. That is to say, power may feel like a fist or a bullet—it might be shocking or dull, numbing or terrifying—but it will also feel soft, loving, affirming, or like the exhilaration of freedom and liberation.[18] Power wraps the subject in its embrace, "intensifying areas, and electrifying surfaces."[19] It does more than discipline or torture the body in order to reproduce its capacities: it titillates and seduces, it caresses the body, it sets one free, it says yes, and it asks for more. Neoliberalism seduces the subject with promises of uninhibited freedom and choice, even as the seduction is performed in the name of management and regulation.

According to Goldwater, the absence of order inherent in the mob produces "the slavery of prison" for those subjected to the mob's tyrannical power. Within this formulation the prison and slavery signify the constraining force of black liberation on the freedom of whiteness.[20] The racial nightmare of urban uprisings—represented by the mob and jungle—threaten white lives, bodies, and property. Significantly, under the rule of the mob violence is the norm rather than the exception. This intrinsic violence is in need of the liberating force of liberalism, since violence is not constitutive of liberal rule but is its exception. In this way, the mob and the jungle invoke a radical alterity to liberalism and also represent the enemy within liberalism and the enemy to civilization.[21] This is an enemy in need of containment. The threat of the jungle and mob are also threats to time, to the "good and decent" future that was Goldwater's promise to a white electorate. Goldwater promised to stave off the "slavery of prison" that was the dystopic future of whiteness. He warned that the freedom of whiteness—of health, body, and property—was under threat, and its future rested on the containment of "domestic violence" or political rebellion. He vowed to protect the future of the individual and the market from the threat of the mob and the racial nightmare of the jungle: "We Republicans seek a government that attends to its inherent responsibilities of maintaining a stable monetary and fiscal climate, encouraging a free and a competitive economy and enforcing law and order."[22] As Goldwater made clear, the free market needed the racial power of the prison and police. The freedom of the individual and market would require new policing and penal technologies. The age of the prison would set the market and the individual free.

In his 1968 acceptance speech as the Republican nominee for president, Nixon expanded Goldwater's argument that individuality needed a massive policing apparatus by connecting the need for law and order to the failures of the welfare state. After declaring, "Just as we cannot have progress without order, we cannot have order without progress," Nixon called for the end of the welfare state in order to inaugurate an era governed by private enterprise and personal responsibility:

> For the past five years we have been deluged by Government programs for the unemployed, programs for the cities, programs for the poor, and we have reaped from these programs an ugly harvest of frustrations, violence and failure across the land. And now our opponents will be offering more of the same—more billions for Government jobs, Government housing, Government welfare. I say it's time to quit pouring billions of dollars into programs that have failed in the United States of America.
>
> To put it bluntly, we're on the wrong road and it's time to take a new road to progress.[23]

Goldwater made a similar argument: "Telling people again and again that the federal government will take care of everything for them leads to the decline of personal responsibility which is the base cause of the rise in crime and the disregard for law and order."[24] By connecting the need for new policing and penal technologies to the dismantling of the welfare state, Nixon and Goldwater argued that the state should protect those valuable to the accumulation of capital and dispose of those resistant or surplus to the new regimes of extraction, production, and distribution.[25] These backward populations produced as surplus to the nation's future were "left queer," abandoned to the anachronistic space of the prison.[26] The state's capacity to assist those vulnerable to premature death (through poverty, hunger, homelessness, illness, etc.) would be abolished, while its apparatuses of regulatory and disciplinary violence (police, prison, surveillance) would be expanded. By narrating this transition through the discourses of law, order, and progress, Nixon and Goldwater produced an epistemology that could justify and render invisible new forms of racial violence.

Neoliberalism requires systems of knowledge that can reason and rationalize its uneven distribution of life and death. A foundational aspect of this regime of knowledge entailed producing disposable people as nonnormative; by queering surplus people, their suffering could be narrated into the naturalness of pathology and individual failing. In his study of law and order, Michael Flamm describes this when he writes, "Above all, [law and order] enabled many white Americans to *make sense* of a chaotic world filled with street crime, urban riots, and campus demonstrations."[27] By helping white people make sense of a changing political and cultural landscape, law and order created an epistemology that monopolized force by erasing state violence while constructing nonstate violence as illegitimate; it also took hold of rationality in order to naturalize, normalize, and render invisible the violences of abandonment and imprisonment. Suturing state violence to the failures of the individual would normalize these structural forms of violence. Law and order provided a new framework with which to view a massive and unprecedented wave of carceral state violence that went hand in hand with the marketization of social, cultural, and political life.

The racial violence of law and order and the governance of the market were naturalized through their attachment to the temporality of progress. Nixon constructed the welfare state as irrational, backward, and inhibiting the teleological development of the nation. Progress made the prison and the market seem inevitable; the future was impossible without them. Under state time the discourse of progress rendered permissible the violence of the market and the terror of the prison. In other words, the future as the inevitable endpoint of progress helped justify new formations of racial violence. Under the logic of law and order, social and biological death were the constitutive and necessary byproducts of the future's progress. Whole populations were constructed as queer; they dragged the nation's future away from progress and thus were worthy of abandonment, containment, and death. By connecting the welfare state and political rebellion to the unfreedom of individuality, law and order made the violence of the market and the prison a new norm. And temporality was critical to this maneuver.

Central to Nixon's call for a penal state that could oversee the dismantling of the welfare state was the specter of antiracist and anti-imperial rebellion. In fact Alan Greenspan, Nixon's coordinator of domestic policy and future chairman of the Federal Reserve, told Nixon privately at the time that the riots, uprisings, and rebellions that swept the country were at heart a "rallying cry for an attack against America's system of free enterprise and individual rights."[28] This sentiment would emerge in Nixon's campaign rhetoric. For example, in a 1968 campaign ad titled "The First Civil Right," Nixon narrates the following as a montage of bloody protesters, gun-toting police, and burning buildings flashes across the screen: "It is time for an honest look at the problem of order in the United States. Dissent is a necessary ingredient of change, but in a system of government that provides for peaceful change, there is no cause that justifies resort to violence. Let us recognize that the first civil right of every American is to be free from domestic violence. So I pledge to you, we shall have order in the United States." The screen then fades to black, and bold white letters state, "This time vote like your whole world depended on it."[29] Nixon's ad appropriates antiracist rhetoric in order to justify the violent suppression of movements opposing the post–civil rights revival of the racial state. Nixon deploys a new form of state antiracism to inaugurate the discourse of law and order.[30] This official antiracism, under which Nixon narrated the order produced by policing and penal violence as a "civil right," incorporated and defused the much more radical and revolutionary antiracisms of the period.[31] These movements theorized the state, and particularly police and prisons, as a site of profound (sometimes unspeakable) violence. But for Nixon, the supposed safety and security produced by a more militarized police and an expanding prison regime was not just *a* civil right but *the first* civil right. Thus, security and order became preconditions for the freedom of the individual, liberal, rights-bearing subject—an individual loyal to the nation and its necessary regimes of white supremacy, heteropatriarchy, and systems of policing and warfare. Nixon's rephrasing erased the failures of civil rights legislation and replaced it with a state antiracism concerned with abolishing white fear of political rebellion. Following the doublespeak of southern segregationists, Nixon made law and order the new name for the militarized containment and liquidation of any threat to the property of whiteness. The ad jettisoned the violence that is foundational to the functioning of the state, making the state the site of safety and security while promoting the rights and freedom of the individual. Violence under this epistemology emanates from the white radical or the black or third world or Native insurgent, not the daily operations of corporate and state power.

The also ad narrates the late 1960s and early 1970s as a struggle with profound biopolitical and temporal ramifications. For the white subject hailed by the ad, to allow the disorder (or the "domestic violence") of the antiwar and third world liberation movements to continue would mean an end to the coherency of one's symbolic and physical world. In other words, as the slogan "Vote like your whole world depended on it" suggests, the era's liberation movements had apocalyptic intentions for the white world. The end of the future was coming. Nixon did not want you to vote as if *the* world depended on it, but *"your"* world, and *"your"* world was not *the* world. "Your world" was the world threatened by the success of the chaos and disorder aimed at the integrity of the state. For millions of people the political violence occurring across the country and around the world was the sign of new possibilities and new worlds. If many imagined the end of the world as it was, Nixon was afraid of their success. But he was not concerned with the fate of *the* world but "your world," your way of life—what Frank Wilderson calls "white life."[32] Nixon declared that for the white subject, life was under threat, and the law would realign the racial order of things.

Nixon believed the social movements of the 1960s and 1970s were a threat to the future. If they were successful, "your world" would disappear and your future with it. For example, in another ad from his 1968 campaign, titled "The Child's Face," a montage of smiling children flashes across the screen as Nixon speaks the logic of what Lee Edelman calls "reproductive futurism" by stating that it is the responsibility of politicians to put children first: "I see the face of a child. What his color is, what his ancestry is, doesn't matter. What does matter is he's an American child. That child is more important than any politician's promise. He is everything we've ever hoped to be, and everything we dare to dream to be."[33] In the ad, the smiling peacefulness of children is contrasted to the violence, disorder, and chaos of the protesters in Nixon's other ads. The ad implies that the child must be protected from the social movements of the 1960s and that these movements were a threat to the racialized heteronormativity central to the child's future. Black power and anti-imperialism were a threat to the child, and Nixon used the face of the child to argue for the expansion of the prison. Prisons and police would protect the child and thus would secure the unfolding of the future.[34] Progress needed order, and the child as the sign of a future yet to come authorized police and penal violence. The future of the civil and social order required the prison. The prison's historical role of containing life deemed excess, disposable, rebellious, and monstrous to the nation, state, and capital was central to its resurgence as a solution to the social and economic crises in the 1970s. Law and order was a form of state insurgency that resurrected this relationship to a new level of dominance. It used the prison to take hold of the future.

I am arguing that the prison did not become central to neoliberalism after deregulation, privatization, and deindustrialization left wastelands where neighborhoods and cities once stood; instead the prison was imagined as central to the future of a "neoliberal utopia" before the legal liberation of the market and the rise of the carceral state in the late 1970s and early 1980s.[35] Law and order made the security and order produced by the prison preconditions for the freedom of the market and the individual, liberal, rights-bearing subject. In short, *neoliberalism is itself a carceral project*. In chapter 3 I argue that for many poor (queer) women of color in the 1970s, the market looked like, felt like, mimicked, and colluded with the prison. Many 1970s activists did not see the prison and the market as separate systems of power but as deeply connected—if not, at times, indistinguishable. The queered surplus populations that were the waste of the market fueled the expansion of the prison, while the market's governance of life and death sometimes looked like the curtailment of mobility and life chances produced by the prison. In short, the containment of racialized and gendered populations was imagined as central to the rule of the free market. Proponents of law and order saw the prison as foundational to the future, the reign of the free market, and the freedom of the individual. Neoliberalism was (and is) a carceral project, while law and order was a neoliberal project. Critically this new formation of carceral state violence was narrated into existence by a discourse that connected the future of the social order to the violence of the prison. The prison would secure the future of things as they were by disposing those resistant to the continuation of the present as it was. Thus, those on the blunt end of law and order's project of liberating the market and the individual offer a productive site from which to understand the changing logics of economic and penal power in the late 1960s and early 1970s. One site that arose in response to law and order was the revolutionary underground.

The Ghosts of Law and Order

As the politics of law and order took hold and the FBI's Counter Intelligence Program (COINTELPRO) systematically dismantled the radical and revolutionary left in the United States (through disinformation, murder, sabotage, incarceration, and forced exile), a large network of underground groups emerged alongside the 1960s aboveground student, civil rights, gay liberation, feminist, antiracist, and antiwar organizations.[36] In order to evade state repression and engage illegal tactics, thousands of activists disappeared into safe houses, under-the-table jobs, and transportation channels that kept them hidden in plain sight. They dyed their hair, forged documents, and took on new names. Some of the better-known groups, such as the Black Liberation Army, splintered off from the Black Panthers and other black power groups, while the Weather Underground departed from the student and antiwar movements of the New Left. Still other groups, including the George Jackson Brigade, emerged out of the culture and politics of the era's antiprison activism.[37] Other underground groups of the period about which much less is known include Fuerzas Armadas de Liberación Nacional, the Chicano Liberation Front, Red Guerilla Family, Emiliano Zapata Unit, Iranian Liberation Army, United Freedom Front (or the "Ohio 7"), Sam Melville–Jonathan Jackson Unit, Nat Turner/John Brown Brigade, and the New World Liberation Front.[38] Many of these groups remain historically obscure because invisibility was their condition of possibility. Underground organizations survived by incessantly erasing the subtle traces every life leaves behind: the detritus of bodies—fingerprints, hair, and skin—but also memories, stories, and documents that could lead to recognition and capture. Therefore a major aspect of their history will never be known: what they did, who they were, where and how they lived. In fact, for three years beginning in 1974, the New World Liberation Front committed over fifty bombings in the San Francisco area (of banks, power stations, corporate offices, the San Francisco stock brokerage, and the South African Embassy) without injuring one person and without a single member being identified or apprehended.[39] A controlled lack of knowledge, "an endorsement of willful forgetting"—you will know what you need to know when you need to know it—was required for the continuation of the underground.[40] In this way the underground was a space structured by a politics of unknowing. This invisibility and illegibility contrasted with the regimes of hypersurveillance, regulation, and policing central to the law-and-order state. By remaining invisible the underground and the fugitive haunted the law-and-order state with the threat of queer ways of being, thinking, and living that were outside normative biopolitical formations.

The underground is not a place but rather an alternative time-space paradigm, a "parallel universe," a shadow world that exists within but negates the normative time of the nation, state, and capital. The underground is a space where one hides in the "expectations of others," fashioning survival along different dimensions that mobilize "timing and synchronization, the thoughtful use of light and shadow, rhythm and pulse."[41] One went underground by cutting off all ties to one's former life or in some cases by following complicated directions to somewhere familiar: "Rita dictated a complicated set of directions, including bus lines and transfer points that zigzagged throughout the south of the city. Janine wasn't in a security mindset: 'I can just drive there, if you like,' she offered. 'No, you can't,' Rita corrected. The circuitous route ended at the Safeway on Rainer Avenue. Rita picked Janine up and drove her in a disorienting manner through the curving, one-block streets of Renton and Skyway. Even if compelled, Janine would not have been able to find her way back to the [underground] house."[42]

The underground was a way of thinking, seeing, moving, speaking, and listening. Many fugitives recount that once underground they would walk past former friends and not be seen. A few were arrested and then let go because the police did not recognize them—even when they were on the FBI's Most Wanted list. The fugitive became a ghost by disappearing into the routines of the everyday, their speech structured by silence, visible but unknown, there but nowhere at all.[43] The fugitive could not be there, in front of you, because she was somewhere else. New lives and identities were constructed by piecing together fragments collected while on the run: new styles, clothing, voices, histories, and names. David Gilbert, a member of the Weather Underground and later a group associated with the Black Liberation Army, recounts that fugitives even had to learn to walk differently because gait and carriage sometimes are more recognizable than hair or clothing. However, "the most essential tool for staying underground was ID." Bill Ayers, a founding member of the Weather Underground, recounts how political fugitives often scoured rural cemeteries for the graves of dead children born between 1940 and 1950 and who died five to ten years later. With a name and birth date, the fugitives would acquire a birth certificate from the local courthouse and apply for a social security card that had never been issued.[44] They could then get jobs, buy cars, and open bank accounts. The newly disappeared resurfaced as the resurrected dead.

The underground existed in a time and space structured by the technologies of the prison, the police, and the law. Put another way, the underground was made necessary, and brought into being, by the ways the state rendered certain forms of resistance illegal, exceptional, violent, backward, irrational, and beyond politics. In addition, the underground emerged as a direct response to the racial politics of law and order, imperial aggression in Vietnam, and the violence of global capitalism. Simply, the underground was a space brought into being by legal and extralegal state violence. Following James Scott's analysis of "state and non-state" spaces, we can position the underground as a nonstate space that is enmeshed with state space. State space is measurable, visible, legible, and thus open to manipulation, regulation, and control, while nonstate spaces exceed the state's systems of knowing and seeing. As Scott puts it, "Legibility is a condition of manipulation."[45] State space (or disciplinary space) encloses what it encounters; it normalizes the disorder and illegibility of its outside.[46] By exceeding the state's epistemological and visual regimes, nonstate spaces critique the norms that make state space possible.

We can extend Scott's analysis by noting that state space necessitates state time. In a discussion of "the temporal elaboration of the act" Foucault describes temporality as carceral state power. When disciplinary power regulates the micro-movements of individuals in space—how one raises one's hand, sews a stitch, assembles a gun, or takes a step—"time penetrates the body and with it all the meticulous controls of power."[47] Time as a mechanism of power possesses the body, so that time accumulates within the body. By inhabiting the body, a building, or a discourse, power uses time to contort the world in its image. Power's object becomes its double, and time is one of the mechanisms used in this process. In short, power's regulation and management of space requires the contortion and control of time. By escaping this spatial disciplining, nonstate spaces exceed state power but also transcend state time. The underground was a nonstate space that also produced nonnormative experiences of (and epistemologies concerning) time. Thus we can understand the fugitive and the underground as political formations from which technologies of state power that normally operate in obscurity become hypervisible. By unmasking state space and state time, the underground is a rich site from which to understand the rise of the neoliberal-carceral state.

Earlier I argued that law and order produced an epistemology that rendered carceral state violence necessary and invisible to the liberation of the individual and the market. Here, I argue that the underground generated forms of knowledge that could see and name this process by theorizing it through a nonnormative engagement with time. The fugitive is able to see what goes unseen by virtue of its normality and banality. Ayers illustrates this when he writes, "We developed a doubleness. More than a secret identity or double life, we saw the world through a distinct lens. . . . We were split, and we could not be whole again."[48] Ayers describes a connection between space and knowledge that is echoed by many others who were underground. Angela Davis writes in her autobiography that going underground felt like "being alone in the dark" because "fugitives are caressed every hour by paranoia." Living as a fugitive meant "resisting hysteria," deciding which ghosts were figments of an imagination on the run and which would bring "machine guns breaking out of the darkness."[49] In the nowhere and everywhere that was the underground, space and time took on new meanings; one always looked for the brown shoes of the FBI, had an escape route, and was ready to be disappeared into a prison or start a new life in a new city under a new name. Going underground meant other nonnormative analytics emerged to narrate the operations of power. It is from the underground that new ways of knowing power and subjection emerged that exceed the logics of the nation, the market, and the law-and-order state.

The Fugitive, Feminism, and the Temporality of Violence

On May 21, 1970, the all-white revolutionary group The Weather Underground declared war on the United States of America. Just one year after splitting off from the largest antiwar organization in the United States, Students for a Democratic Society, the Weather Underground announced its existence and stated, "Within the next fourteen days we will attack a symbol or institution of American injustice." Twenty days later the group claimed responsibility for bombing the New York City police headquarters in response to the murder of Fred Hampton by Chicago police and the "torture of Joan Bird," a member of the Panther 21.[50] David Gilbert credits the delay in their threat to a "hippie sense of time" that stretched fourteen days to nineteen.[51] Over the next five years the group would commit more than twenty bombings of state and corporate infrastructure, including the

U.S. Capitol, the Pentagon, corporate headquarters, police stations, and a variety of state infrastructure.[52] The bombings were mainly in response to the war in Vietnam and penal and police violence in the United States. For example, bombings were committed in response to the murder of George Jackson; the massacre of prisoners after the uprising at Attica Prison; the police shooting of a ten-year-old black boy, Clifford Glover; the sterilization of women of color; the suppression of a rebellion at the Queens House of Detention; new drug laws; and the U.S.-supported neoliberal coup in Chile. It is worth noting that these bombings account for only a small percentage of the more than five thousand bombings that occurred during that period. From the late 1960s to the late 1970s radicals across the country targeted universities, corporations, police, and the military with acts of property destruction. It is also worth noting that unlike contemporaneous leftist armed struggles in South Africa, Ireland, West Germany, Palestine, Peru, Uruguay, and Vietnam, the U.S. left largely did not target human beings. The only people killed or injured by the Weather Underground were three of the group's own members, who died while building a bomb that accidentally exploded inside a New York City townhouse. (Two women escaped the bombing and promptly went underground.)[53] From that point forward the group took great care to destroy only state and corporate infrastructure. It is not the fact that they were underground or committed bombings that makes the Weather Underground unique; what makes them significant is how they understood the time of the post–civil rights state and the space of the underground.

Early on, the group stated the power of the illegibility of the underground: "We're not hiding, but we're invisible."[54] Unlike claims to civil rights, inclusion, and visibility, the fugitive deployed invisibility and illegibility as methodologies to challenge the naturalness of the racial state. By going underground the fugitive claimed there was no way under the state's laws to make a more livable world, so she made visible the violence of the law. The law was not refuge from the exceptional violence of an otherwise benevolent state. Instead, the most mundane operations of the law were theorized as sites of profound racialized and gendered violence. Fugitivity was an epistemology that opened up other ways of thinking about power. The state's routine operations were forms of capture, hunting, caging, and torture. However, the invisibility of fugitivity was more than knowledge; it was also a tactic. The Weather Underground later taunted, "They guard their buildings and we walk right past their guards. They look for us—we get to them first."[55] The group mobilized the invisibility and presumed innocence of whiteness so effectively that when they placed a bomb in the U.S. Capitol that failed to go off, they reentered the highly secure building and placed a second bomb on top of the first. That bomb destroyed a bathroom (bombs were often placed in toilets or ceilings), the congressional barbershop and dining room, and an "expensive painting of George Washington."[56] While the group's rhetoric claimed they were "bringing a pitiful helpless giant to its knees," in reality they were, like the George Jackson Brigade, engaging in "armed propaganda." Both groups hoped that the violence of the state and capital would be rendered hypervisible by "bringing the war home." In so doing they challenged normative notions of activism, common sense, space, and time in order to deploy a politics of knowledge that attempted to epistemologically unravel the logics of the law-and-order state and U.S Empire. The group named white supremacy as invisible but foundational to a new formation of global capitalism and an emerging penal state. In other words, they did not theorize the market as replacing or negating the primacy of race in the distribution of life chances; rather they consistently argued that race (and antiblackness in particular) was *the* animating force behind the necropolitics of the modern state—under the market, in the prison, and on the street.

For the Weather Underground, the prison was "part of a strategy of colonial warfare being waged against the black population."[57] Like many of their politics, this idea was inspired and animated by the black power and third world liberation movements of the period. Prisons were "machines for breaking men and women" with "filth, rats, isolation, brutality, and torture. They [were] instruments of genocide against the black and Latin community."[58] The prison as repressive apparatus aimed at population management and control was also structured by and relationally connected to empire and imperialism: "Like in Vietnam, where 'rebellious' populations have been 're-located' to strategic hamlets and tiger cages, the rebels of Watts, Harlem, Detroit . . . have been shipped to places called San Quentin, the Tombs . . . and Cook County Jail."[59] As the group continually articulated, the violence of the prison was not isolated or exceptional. Many of their communiqués theorized an expansive regime of biopolitical power that connected the antiblackness of the prison, the malnutrition and premature death of Latino children, and the forced sterilization of Puerto Rican women. They made clear the connections among the seemingly disparate operations of the state's deployment and manipulation of race, gender, and sexuality. While law and order attempted to advance the violence of the police and the prison under the freedom granted by the post–civil rights state, the Weather Underground named this process a modification and intensification of past forms of racialized and gendered subjection. For example, after a New York City police officer shot and killed Clifford Glover, the group bombed a patrol car outside the 103rd precinct. In the accompanying communiqué they called penal and police violence against black children and adults the "street level of Nixon's policies."[60] Glover's murder was the constitutive underside to the order, peace, and safety of law and order. The Weather Underground argued that law and order was the continuation of past forms of white supremacy that were supposed to have ended with the civil rights legislation of the 1960s. Glover's murder made visible the connection between law and order and what was imagined to have been an older mode of white supremacy. His death was not an isolated accident but part of the remaking and resurgence of the racial state under the intentionally neutral rubric of law and order. The Weather Underground and so many others saw the future in Glover's murder, a future rushing forward if the present did not end.

This communiqué, and the group's writing more broadly, attempted to make visible the violence necessary to the state's production of itself. For example, women members of the group questioned how the state defines terrorism in a poem:

They call it terror
if you are few
and have no B-52s
if you are not a head of state
with an army and police
if you have neither napalm
nor tanks. . . .
Terror is if you are dispossessed
It is not terror
if you are New York's finest
and you shoot a ten-year old Black child in the back. . . .
 Only those who have nothing
can be terrorists.[61]

The poem names the routine operations of the state and calls them terror—terror that must be made visible and profoundly unnatural. In their underground writing and fugitive praxis—evading and destroying the state's technologies of capture—the Weather Underground questioned the legitimacy of the state and challenged the invisibility and normality of its violence. As Nikhil Singh writes, "Violence threatens to undo the state, but it is also its very condition of possibility."[62] The poem written by fugitive women attempted to name the state's use of terror when its violence is normal and invisible to dominant ways of knowing and seeing.

The police, border control, courts, federal and state prisons, public schools, military, and other state bureaucracies prove the existence of the state in everyday life, but they all require people to believe there is a legitimate state in the first place. The notion that the state exists requires the repetitive action of countless heterogeneous institutions.[63] These institutions capture the legitimate use of violence and incessantly deploy that violence against a variety of threats to the security of the nation, the stability of capital, and the integrity of the social order.[64] Law and order was an insurgent method of state building, and the Weather Underground attempted to disrupt, distract, weaken, and make visible this process by slipping past the state's methods of surveillance and by attacking its infrastructure. The underground and fugitive illuminate the unnaturalness of the state by showing that there is an outside to its regimes of power inside those same systems. By making the state give chase, the fugitive shows how the state creates itself by trying to capture ways of living that escape its structuring of the everyday.

Despite the incredible feat of evading the FBI for over a decade, one of the most profound shortcomings of the group was its inability to structurally integrate a critique of heterosexism, homophobia, and heteropatriarchy into its writing and organizing.[65] In response to sexism, "male supremacy," and heterosexism within the group and the broader left, many women of the Weather Underground started a "women's brigade." This was a way for women who were underground to "be 'free' of the couple form"; conceive, organize, and execute bombings and protests without men; form reading groups; "make love with our sisters"; and write a book of poetry, *Sing a Battle Song*.[66] In 1973 the group wrote a public letter to the women's movement. Detailing their thinking as fugitives and "women underground," the letter sought to clarify their thinking about gender and sexuality and its relationship to the racial state: "Since going underground there have been few times that we have communicated about our internal process. The risk of revealing too much about ourselves to the state is ever present, but we also felt an urgent need to overcome these difficulties and to share our lives with our sisters. The nature of unity among us is the secret thread of clandestine organization. This is what the state is searching out."[67] Here again the group states the power of the underground; it threatens the state with a way of living as escape. In response, the state worked to make the fugitive perceptible, to uncover her secrets, to understand how she operates.[68] Despite the risk of making themselves detectable, the Women's Brigade wanted to clarify their politics.[69]

The Women's Brigade apologized for polarizing a division between feminism and third world liberation by denying the centrality of "women's demands for power over their own lives" as central to any "revolution we would care to make." At countless meetings across the left, women's brigade members felt they had to position themselves as either antisexist or antiracist. They apologized for contributing to this split by siding with a masculinist version of black liberation and third world anticolonial struggles while denying the legitimacy of the U.S.-based women's movement. They feared feminism would mean not fighting for the imprisoned men at Attica or abandoning male members of the Weather Underground whom they refused to defend or reject. Following the ways "third world women were opening up similar questions in their own terms," they realized there was another way of thinking that the underground could open up.[70] Out of this epistemological struggle they connected an underground politics to a revolutionary feminism.

The statement attempted to construct a feminist politics that could theorize how white women were "assaulted, underpaid, brainwashed . . . [and] raped, like women everywhere," while also centering state violence against people of color at home and abroad. By attending to the "common enemies" that connected women across multiple forms of difference without erasing difference, the group constructed a politics of relationality. They worked to move beyond a politics of judging individual people for how they understood their own oppression: "Which [oppression] is more important, or far reaching, or painful . . . is the wrong question." Unlike their earlier politics, they defended white feminist demands and concerns. Yet, they also argued that women's liberation was impossible under the racial violence central to U.S. imperialism: "This is why our movement will have to take on the question of state power." Their feminist politics stipulated, "Everything that chokes our lives and freedom living under imperialism is a women's issue." As they recognized the "legitimacy of white women's demands" they also argued that "the struggle against sexism requires the destruction of the American state," and so they urged the continuation of a "humane" armed struggle.

The statement appealed to white women to see that concerns about free day care, sexual harassment and assault, wage disparities, and health care were intimately tied to the "liberation of the Third World" and to "the fight by black people for their freedom." This required a politics whereby women could "struggle lovingly about our differences, leaving room for change and growth." Indeed, the statement exists because the fugitive authors took flight from their previous ways of the thinking. The statement outlines a trajectory by which feminism led to the underground and the underground led to an insurgent form of feminism that centered relational difference under white supremacy and imperialism.[71]

The struggle over theorizing gender and sexuality in relation to racialized state power coalesced for the women's brigade in 1974, when they bombed the office of the Department of Education and Welfare in San Francisco in response to the forced sterilization of thousands of women of color. The communiqué issued to explain the bombing is worth quoting at length:

The Department of Education and Welfare is an enemy of women.

This action is for all women who:

- wait in lines for too few food stamps and brave food distribution lines because our families have to eat;
- worry through degrading forms and humiliating rules and regulations;
- are kept out of paying jobs because there are no child care programs;
- struggle to raise our children while we're called "pigs at the trough" and "lazy parasites" by reactionary politicians;
- send our children to schools where illiteracy is taught;
- fight to get health care in emergency rooms and county hospitals where our bodies are used for experiments and as practice for doctors;
- go mad, go crazy, locked up in prisons and mental institutions;
- live in projects;
- are patronized, cast away and ignored because we are old;
- resist!!

And especially for Minnie and Mary Alice Rolf, blackwomenchildren, from Montgomery, Alabama, sterilized by HEW at 14 and 12.[72]

The communiqué connected an emerging neoliberal discourse of personal responsibility, under which politicians called poor women of color "pigs at the trough" and "lazy parasites," to the rise of the prison as a technology for managing rebellious and unruly populations. According to the women's brigade, "being on HEW is like having a sexist tyrant for an old man" because HEW "blames women for poverty, and then punishes them."[73] Unions, public schools, health care, social security, and birth control were mobilized by the state as racialized and gendered methods of management and containment. The ordinariness of standing in line and filling out bureaucratic documents is understood as one of the state's methods of enforcing gendered and racialized control. These practices were ways to isolate and individualize women across racialized and class lines, thus preventing a collective, mass-based, multiracial, cross-class rebellion led by women. The state's intuitions for providing care were technologies used to make poor people of color more manageable, isolate and discipline populations potentially disruptive to the social order, and create targets for new forms of knowledge and governance.[74] The prison was not isolated or localizable but was part of a dispersed, flexible, and mobile regime of power. In contrast to the Weather Underground's earlier writings, this communiqué centers gender and sexuality in its analysis of a racialized field of knowledge, containment, and immobilization. For example, it links the forced sterilization of women of color to the gendered production of poverty under a rapid and expanding deindustrialization. Thus, it subverts the epistemological constraints of the law-and-order state as well as the gendered and sexual regulations of the revolutionary left (including the Weather Underground itself). Although it does not name neoliberalism or the prison-industrial complex, the communiqué theorizes the "circuits of control" that traverse multiple institutionalities and spatialities to manage racialized and gendered populations in the early 1970s.[75] In short, the communiqué is a feminist and antiracist theorization of the neoliberal-carceral state at the very moment of its emergence.

In addition to theorizing the racialized and gendered violences of the state, this statement is also a theorization of temporality. The women's brigade engaged the ways the prison and the market produced premature death and what Lauren Berlant calls "slow death," which names "the physical wearing out of a population" so that its deterioration "is a defining condition of its experience and historical existence."[76] Slow death does not occur in spectacular events like military aggression or genocides, but in the temporal space of "ordinariness itself."[77] Slow death does not arise from discipline, but from the security practices of the (neo)liberal state. For example, the communiqué went on to argue that the mundane bureaucratic practices of the state—waiting in line, filling out forms, and learning arbitrary rules—were a form of violence against women.[78] Waiting in line was the racial state's theft and colonialization of women's time. It also entailed the slow degradation of women's bodies in the form of sore feet, an aching back, a dull pain in the temple. These banal acts were a way for the state to allow racialized and gendered populations to exhaust themselves. Slow death was cloaked under the rubric of choice: one made a decision to endure the stress and anxiety of standing in line or filling out a form.

State violence did not look like state violence; there were no guns, soldiers, camps, or bodies. Just women worn out from waiting and worrying, women living outside the confines of the market—on the border of death, insanity, illness, and incarceration. As Elizabeth Povinelli observes, these "quasi-events" or "quiet deaths" confound response because it is hard to say exactly what happened and who caused it. How does one measure the physical, psychological, and emotional cost of learning a rule? How do we measure the toll of filling out a form? Worrying about the next meal? Being ridiculed by men in power? Slouching into the soft curve of a plastic chair in a waiting room one too many times? What is the proper response to the sterilization of a little girl? How does one even comprehend such an event? What is the cost of living with it, trying to think about it? What does it do to one's mind and body to reckon with such mundane horrors that are never named as such? The events catalogued in the communiqué are forms of lethality composed of "an agentless slow death" in which the everyday drifts toward a premature ending: one more drink, another malnourished meal, an unexpected sickness, two hours less sleep, a small pain in the chest. Slow death follows a temporal rhythm that seems natural. By naturalizing slow death, the banality of gendered state violence is individualized, "survival questions are treated as individual problems."[79] The women's brigade attempted to name these processes as forms of state killing (that did not look like state killing) by connecting this routine violence to the much more visible violence of the prison and sterilization.[80]

The communiqué is also a vision of the future, one that understands the future (and the present) as what Denise Ferreira da Silva calls a "horizon of death."[81] For example, the brigade declared that sterilization is a form of "genocide against the future, through the bodies of women."[82] The statement's theorization of slow death is intrinsically a critique of state time as a temporality of psychological and corporeal wearing out. This intimacy with death queers normative conceptions of temporality with its linear progression of school, career, marriage, reproduction, retirement, and death.[83] The statement names the temporality of violence central to the market and the prison as a time of brutal banality and in so doing critiques the progress of law and order while making visible the slow deaths obscured by new epistemological norms. For the Weather Underground, the multiple events named in the statement were an extension of racial and gendered logics of nineteenth-century chattel slavery and colonialism; thus the group was making a claim about the power of the past, but, they argued, the production of premature death was also a way for the state to annex the future. The state ensures the future can be extracted from the present by managing, contorting, and eradicating the future before it arrives. It deploys preemptive action (war, assassination, sterilization, incarceration, policing, administrative violence, and surveillance) to make its "imagined future come to pass."[84] The prison was one way the state solved the "problem of black resistance," thereby ushering in a future that could replicate the past and present.[85] Beyond the prison but connected to it, administrative lines and bureaucratic forms were a form of counterinsurgency against the possibilities of insurrection led by poor women of color that would usher in a future when the racial state and the terror of the market were memories of a way of life that could no longer be thought. In many ways this is the same argument Nixon and Goldwater were making about the civil rights, black power, and antiwar movements of the time. The epistemological and physical force of these movements threatened the future of things as they were. Law and order was a way to secure the future of the liberal individual and the market by disrupting and eradicating the movements and forms of knowledge that saw other futures beyond the racial violence of the market, the prison, and the state.

By diagnosing the present as a replication and intensification of what were supposedly historically aberrant modes of racialized and gendered violence, the Weather Underground challenged normative visions of the future. For them, the future of the social order meant race would continue to collude with gender, class, and sexuality in the unequal distribution of life, death, and dying. The group knew what the future held. They knew what was coming because it had already happened—in the past that was the future that already arrived. White supremacy and heteropatriarchy meant that death was all the future held. The women's brigade understood themselves as inhabiting their future deaths and expected to be killed or captured at any moment; they also argued that if the present had a future, the future would never come. A future under the colluding rule of imperialism, white supremacy, heteropatriarchy, and the neoliberal-carceral state was a future the Weather Underground attempted to undo by trying to bring an end to the present. If there was to be a future, the present could no longer be. The state, the prison, and the market were able to capture time in an attempt to determine the future before it arrived. This is how the Weather Underground critiqued the temporalities of progress used by the state to justify new mechanisms of containment, control, and management.

By describing the centrality of the prison and capital to the unequal distribution of premature death in the 1970s, the Weather Underground produced a theory of time and history that displaced the fantasy of progress that sustained and supported law and order. As they articulated in their writing, the future of the social order meant the accumulation and expansion of premature death and dying. In addition, they challenged the discourse of "national redemption" and "moral regeneration" that underwrote the teleological project of the New Left and civil rights movement.[86] The Weather Underground was not trying to make the nation better or live up to its imagined founding ideals. The future did not require the recuperation of the state and nation. Indeed, central to the critique of HEW was a critique of reform: "Under imperialism, reforms are turned against us. Especially black and Third World women."[87] Reform was not a stepping-stone on a linear road to a better world; it was a mechanism by which the state could reorganize and recalibrate its methods of management, containment, and control. By critiquing reform, the group theorized progress as a way for the racial state to modify, mutate, and intensify its systems of regulation. The discourse of (racial) progress and its attachment to the ideal of the nation-state effaced ongoing racial violence and acted as the horizon for the reanimation of racialized and gendered subjugation and subjection. This was the power of law and order. By using time to justify and obscure the restoration and intensification of formations of violence aimed at liberating the individual and the market, law and order took hold of the past, present, and future with the names *progress*, *safety*, and *order*. In other words, progress is a temporal fantasy that must necessarily construct the wreckage of the past as a historical aberration, while the future is an infinitely open space of possibility and potential. Yet, for the women's brigade, the wreckage of the past keeps piling up, so that what the liberal imagination hopes it has left behind is actually what makes the present and the future intolerable and unlivable.

As a space that subverted the state's regimes of surveillance and visibility, the underground produced forms of knowledge that existed in a temporal economy that contradicted the state's discourse of progress. The underground was spatially and physically unintelligible to the state—the FBI could not and did not find thousands of fugitives—at the same time that the knowledge produced from the underground subverted normative regimes of rationality and time. This subversion produced alternative notions of freedom amid the profound unfreedom of the neoliberal-carceral state.

2. LIFE ESCAPES NEOLIBERAL ECONOMICS,
THE UNDERGROUND, AND FUGITIVE FREEDOM

On the contrary, to flee is to produce the real, to create life, to find a weapon.
—GILLES DELEUZE, "On the Superiority of Anglo-American Literature," *Dialogues II*

But running, as we will see, is not finally reducible to an escape from capture; instead, it names an autonomous force that precedes capture.
—MICHELLE KOERNER, "Line of Escape"

In 1968 the Catholic priest Daniel Berrigan went underground after he and eight other Catholic protesters used homemade napalm to destroy 378 draft files in the parking lot of the Catonsville, Maryland, draft board. In a public letter written while in hiding, Berrigan argued for the creation of a new system of knowledge that would emerge from the space between the prison and the underground: "We have to develop new modes of operating, based on new realities before us, the underground, the imprisoned. Both can be 'at large' in a new way. Both have to confront the rules of the game which society has developed to keep men under lock and key that commonly go by the name 'law n' order.'" This new epistemology, created by the fugitive and the prisoner, produced a disorientating estrangement from normative ways of seeing. "Anyway, for the present . . . I (and others) have the unimaginably exciting chance to explore from the other side of the mirror, those constricting images that waver about the edge of the imagination, terrorizing, policing, clubbing, shadowing, exacting submission, diminishing man in his best parts and thereby creating the race of inventive dwarfs that, from university, church, home, club, domestic bliss, professional status, march from here to Saigon, to keep the game going. Is it possible to march in a different direction?" For Berrigan, living underground consisted of "an obscure twilight existence" that was "neither prison nor freedom" and was "somewhere between crime and punishment." The underground was a space where he became an "invisible man" who lived "just under the crust of the planet." He was in "exile" in a country he once imagined was his.[1] Berrigan experienced the underground as a space of rupture with what Lauren Berlant calls "the good life," a set of "moral-intimate-economic" fantasies that keep people attached to relationships, families, jobs, political systems, institutions, and markets even though the instability, ineffectiveness, failure, and harm of these connections are always already evident.[2] The underground provided Berrigan access to a visual and epistemological regime that saw beyond the good life to "the other side of the mirror"—a space beyond the disciplining violence of the home, the university, and the professional world. As a fugitive, Berrigan could see what he could not see before; invisible things became glaring in an absence they no longer inhabited, and what had always been visible became strange and unfamiliar. This break in vision and knowledge resulted from inhabiting space in a new way; the underground opened up previous impossibilities and placed others in a dead space between prison and freedom. Berrigan found that the underground functioned as a queer space, a space productive of alternative forms of knowledge, living, and seeing that escaped the normativities central to the functioning of the everyday. Most critically, an alternative system of knowledge arising from the symbiotic spaces of the prison and the underground led away from the steady march forward of things as they were toward something unknown.

Central to Berrigan's conception of the underground's relationship to knowledge was an understanding that escape (or being "at large") unlocked alternatives to the impossibilities of the present. Escape was a way of repudiating and undoing the good life because running away, as Sandro Mezzadra writes, "has been one of the basic tools to refuse [the] banality and repetitiveness of everyday life and its suffocating restrictions."[3] Similarly, Michelle Koerner has argued that the fugitive's refusal to adjust to the state of things as they are "implies an active force that has its own values, makes its own conditions, and affirms its capacities for invention and transformation."[4] For Berrigan, this meant contesting the practices and logics of imperialism, the prison, and white supremacy. In this formulation, the fugitive is a figure we can turn to as the site of an immanent critique of the state's policing and penal powers—a figure produced by those same formations. The fugitive points away from the normative to unthought and sometimes unimaginable alternatives. One alternative epistemology produced by the fugitive is a nonnormative conception of freedom. While freedom is traditionally understood as the static space produced by the "absence of coercion by other men," many political fugitives conceptualized freedom through metaphors of movement.[5] A life of hiding, running, taking flight, fleeing, and changing identities exceeded the power of the law by outrunning it. The spatial and temporal rupture that was the underground produced alternative systems of value, knowledge, and freedom that slipped past the regulatory mechanisms of the neoliberal-carceral state. In this way, we can turn to the underground as a critique of the changing contours of capitalism and the prison system in the 1970s United States. In particular, the underground offers a space from which to understand antagonistic notions of freedom that were paradigmatic of the era: one notion argued freedom required the prison and the market, while another understood freedom as the very act of escape, the process of fleeing, the feeling of running away.

In chapter 1 I argued that law and order was symbiotic with and productive of neoliberal discourses that emphasized the relationship between the freedom of the individual and the freedom of the market. The prison as a discursive field, a set of fantasies, and a regime of dispersed institutional technologies aimed at policing and racialized incapacitation became constitutive of the freedom of the market and individual. In this chapter I place the underground and the fugitive in relation to an emerging neoliberal conception of freedom. I continue to explore how penal and policing technologies were imagined as central to the life of the free market, but instead of analyzing the culture and politics of law and order, I turn to the writings of early neoliberal thinkers, in particular Milton Friedman's 1962 *Capitalism and Freedom*. Friedman was a Nobel Prize–winning American economist, statistician, and author who taught at the University of Chicago for more than three decades. As a leader of the Chicago school of economics, he has been perhaps the most important opponent to Keynesian economics and is considered central to the emergence of neoliberal thought and policy. Despite his significance to neoliberal policy across the globe, scholars of neoliberalism and late twentieth-century capitalism have largely ignored Friedman's writings. I analyze *Capitalism and Freedom* to argue that the emergence of "neoliberal freedom" was, in part, a response to the demands of the liberation movements of the 1960s and 1970s. As a discourse neoliberal freedom created epistemologies that normalized new forms of racialized state violence and made this violence necessary to the institution of neoliberal economic policies. I then examine the underground as a space that escaped—and critiqued—the forms of knowledge central to the constitution of neoliberal freedom. While feminist, antiracist, and queer liberation movements made demands that exceeded the material and epistemological possibilities of the social order, neoliberal freedom confined and restricted what freedom could be within the relations between the individual and the market. Neoliberal thought deployed freedom as a system of regulation and discipline. In other words, the language of neoliberal freedom captured ways of thinking and organizing life that attempted to escape new and emerging modes of subjection. The fugitive and the underground are formations that escaped this process. The production of neoliberal freedom thus colluded with the racialized and gendered power of the police and the prison. The prison captured bodies, and neoliberal thought captured epistemology.

Neoliberal Theories of Race and the Capture of Freedom

In *Capitalism and Freedom*, Friedman argues that political freedom, "the absence of coercion by other men," requires economic freedom, "the voluntary cooperation of individuals." Freedom is destroyed by the concentration of state power in the economic realm so that state regulation of economic activity prevents political freedom in the social world. Each chapter of the text describes how state regulation occurs and why it should not in education, trade, finance, discrimination law, licensing, and welfare. Friedman submits basic rules for the governance of the free market: "Co-operation is strictly individual and voluntary provided: (a) the enterprises are private, so that the ultimate contracting parties are individuals and (b) that individuals are effectively free to enter or not enter into any particular exchange, so that every transaction is strictly voluntary." In the free market the consumer and worker are protected from harm by the presence of other businesses and employers, so "the technique of the marketplace" produces freedom in the form of the "voluntary co-operation of individuals." Political freedom follows where economic freedom flourishes, or as Friedman puts it, "exchange can . . . bring about co-ordination without coercion."[6] The imagined absence of coercion and force in the economic realm means freedom will proliferate in the realm of the political. In short, freedom advances when power disappears. And power is a possession held by the state, while freedom is a localizable space that is more absence than form.

Friedman's theorization of freedom emerged out of a three-decade-long struggle by a transnational affiliation of economists to respond to the economic crises of the 1930s and the rise of totalitarian state power in Europe. The term *neoliberalism* was first used by participants of the Colloque Walter Lippman in Paris in 1938 to argue that more than a simple return to laissez-faire economics was required to respond to the crises of the era. This group of thinkers, including Friedman's friend and mentor Friedrich Hayek, feared that the state power central to Nazism would take other forms, such as the New Deal and a spreading communism. Hayek and Friedman "saw in the encroachment of state intervention on every aspect of social and economic life a creeping totalitarianism." Early forms of neoliberal thought saw state regulation of the economy as a way for totalitarianism to corrupt the "paradigm of Western civilization." Through the regulation of the economy newer forms of totalitarianism targeted the freedom of the individual's wants, needs, and desires. Thus social and political freedoms were not enough; the freedom of the market had to be protected to ensure the freedom of the individual. Two decades later Friedman's Chicago school expanded this thinking through a kind of "economic imperialism," which argued that all areas of life, including the law, sex, the family, and welfare, should be analyzed from a market framework.[7] The colonization of life by the market is particularly evident in Friedman's arguments about the free market and racism. In addition to showing how neoliberal economics responded to the radical and revolutionary movements of the mid-twentieth century, an examination of his arguments about race demonstrates that white supremacy is not an aftereffect of neoliberalism but is foundational to its articulation before it became policy in the post-1970s. White supremacy does not haunt neoliberalism; it possesses it, determining its movements, contours, and directions.

In a fascinating chapter, "Capitalism and Discrimination," Friedman argues that the free market and capitalism have been the "major source of opportunity for Negros" and have allowed them to make "greater progress than they otherwise could have." Throughout the text he argues that the neoliberal individual is not tethered to the past nor encumbered by the movements of power. Because the free market considers only "economic efficiency," all are equal within its gentle embrace. Freedom will prosper when the market is liberated from the regulations of the state—the market is where racism will be undone. In the world of *Capitalism and Freedom* the subject is abstracted from history and the social world. "Individual freedom" and economic freedom will produce political freedom. According to Friedman, the West (and the United States in particular) is exceptional in world history because the free market produced freedom in the nineteenth and twentieth centuries, a time when much of the world was lost to "tyranny, servitude, and misery."[8] The free market is central to the imagined freedom foundational to U.S. exceptionalism. This story is made possible by what it forgets. The discourses of personal responsibility, individuality, and choice produced by Friedman require the expulsion of the past from the present. Friedman's text, and the neoliberal discourses it inspired, quiet the whispered demands of the dead and cover the tracks that link freedom to white supremacy, settler colonialism, and heteropatriarchy. The discourses of personal responsibility, individuality, and choice produced by Friedman necessitated the silencing of the past; they effaced the enormity of the ravages and affiliations of history and placed the weight of freedom on the actions of the individual. A new form of subjectivity and state power rested upon the forgotten and the erased. The theory of neoliberal freedom cannot exist without a willful erasure of the possessive power of the past. This is most evident in Friedman's discussion of racial discrimination.

According to Friedman, the free market separates economic efficiency from "irrelevant characteristics" like race and gender. If an individual prefers not to hire people of color, than he imposes a "higher cost" on himself than other individuals who do not share his preference: "The man who objects to buying from or working alongside a Negro . . . thereby limits his range of choice. He will generally have to pay a higher price for what he buys or receive a lower return for his work." Within the all-expansive market logic of Friedman, a person who discriminates "pays a price for doing so." The individual racist is simply exercising his "taste" (just as he has a taste in music) since it is economically efficient to hire workers based on skill, not color. In Friedman's logic, outlawing racist hiring practices would be like making it illegal to listen to Frank Sinatra. Rather than using the coercive power of the state to "enforce my tastes and attitudes on others," the correct course of action would be for one individual to persuade the racist individual to hire people of color.[9] Friedman understands racism as a question of individual taste that might inconvenience other individuals.

By individualizing racism in the era of unprecedented uprisings against structural apartheid and systematic white supremacy, the neoliberal theory of freedom rested on a liberal conception of racism that was a response to black freedom movements of the 1950s and 1960s.

Not once throughout his discussion of racism does Friedman name or consider the effects of racist hiring practices on black workers. While he argues that the market could abolish racism, Friedman cannot comprehend the effects of white supremacy on black life. He is unable to name the forms of systemic and institutionalized racial violence that collude with and enable the actions of the individual racist, even at a time before the civil rights laws of the mid- to late 1960s.[10] Racism, for Friedman, is an individual preference isolated from state and economic power. And its power does not harm black people. In fact, in a remarkable moment when he almost considers how a racist white business might harm the black workers it refuses to hire, he quickly redefines *harm* so as to exclude racial discrimination. According to Friedman, there are two types of harm: positive harm, which is caused by physical force, and negative harm, which is indirect (for example, the effects of pollution downstream or, in this case, the black worker denied employment).[11] Physical force, or coercion, violates the voluntary cooperation of individuals and thus must be outlawed.[12] However, negative harm results from a mutual agreement over a voluntary contract, and since voluntary cooperation between individuals is the essence of freedom, outlawing "negative harm" would reduce freedom and "limit voluntary cooperation."[13] Within the neoliberal theory of freedom, the effects of a racist economic system do not register as harm. Black people are not harmed by white supremacy since harm only looks like physical force. Thus, in the neoliberal theory of freedom, blackness and white supremacy are unthinkable even when they are thought. Friedman invokes racism only to efface its power. The price of neoliberal freedom entails silencing the conditions of poverty, degradation, and subjection produced by white supremacy—processes neoliberal freedom claimed it could abolish. Neoliberalism's antiracism is the mark of white supremacy's continuation. If racist hiring practices do not constitute harm in the theory of neoliberal freedom, then neoliberal thought cannot name the forms of subjection and unfreedom that must end for black freedom to be realized. Friedman's theory that the market can end white supremacy works to police the demands of the period's liberation movements. Yet it accomplishes this through what it forgets, through the forms of racial violence it cannot name or comprehend.

The centrality of race to neoliberal thought is evident in the writing of a group Friedman belonged to with Hayek and Ludwig von Mises called the Mont Pelerin Society.[14] In their founding "Statement of Principles" from 1947 they write:

The central values of civilization are in danger. . . . Even that most precious possession of Western Man, freedom of thought and expression, is threatened by the spread of creeds which, claiming the privilege of tolerance when in the position of a minority, seek only to establish a position of power in which they can suppress and obliterate all views but their own.

The group holds that these developments have been fostered by the growth of a view of history which denies all absolute moral standards and by the growth of theories which question the desirability of the rule of law. It holds further that they have been fostered by a decline of belief in *private property and the competitive market; for without the diffused power and initiative associated with these institutions it is difficult to imagine a society in which freedom may be effectively preserved.*[15]

The Mont Pelerin Society argues that the freedom of "Western Man" is produced by the existence of private property and the diffuse operations of a free, unregulated market. Freedom, civilization, and Man are threatened by state intervention, welfare, and the chaos that follows the absence of law. A free market is not just freedom for the circulation and accumulation of capital; it is the condition of possibility for the freedom of Western Man. Friedman et al. understand the market to be a regime of dispersed power that will produce freedom. Written in 1947, the statement precedes the hegemony of neoliberal policy that would begin in the 1970s and 1980s, yet the document indexes the racialized anxieties and amnesia that institute neoliberalism as a theory and biopolitical project. Although neoliberalism is commonly understood as a class project to restore power to a capitalist ruling class, the "Statement of Principles" shows that this process was also always already a racial project to stabilize and restore the power of whiteness.

Civilization and Western Man are discourses that necessarily invoke, require, and invent the barbarism, savagery, backwardness, and sexual depravity of the racial Other. The definition of freedom deployed by the Mont Pelerin Society is parasitic on an unspoken but present Other. As Christina Sharpe writes, "The desire to be free requires one to be witness to, participate in, and be silent about scenes of subjection we rewrite as freedom."[16]

The invocation of freedom rests upon an inheritance that relies on (and a performance that reproduces) unfreedom. Liberal freedom is routinely defined against unfreedom, where unfreedom is spatially and temporally outside the realm of civilization and Western man.[17] Freedom is also defined against the prison and the prisoner (who is also a racial Other), as evident in the Thirteenth Amendment. In other words, the white body's investment in freedom is constructed against (and through) the social, civil, and living death of people of color. This is the symbiosis between the political ontology of white life and the social death of blackness, or what Saidiya Hartman calls "the complicity of slavery and freedom," where freedom found its authority and dignity in the symbol of slavery, while slavery extended itself into the limits, excesses, and subjections of freedom.[18]

The "Statement of Principles" is structured by an anxiety about losing the freedom of whiteness. It argues that the market is *the* technology that must be mobilized to protect and secure the sanctity of white life. The authors understand that the market is a racialized mechanism that protects Western Man. The powers of the market collude with the powers of race, relegating some people to spaces of prosperity, safety, and security, and others to spaces of disposability, death, and dying. Without the dispersed powers of the market, the freedom that Friedman et al. seek to preserve—a freedom that has always been produced by racialized and gendered subjection and terror—will disappear. The statement implicitly argues that the racial subjection produced by the market must continue if freedom is to live on. Unspoken (but necessary) in this process is that the Others to Western Man will be relegated to spaces of unfreedom and death. The "Statement of Principles" thus rests upon a willful forgetting of the forms of racial terror and subjection that make freedom possible. It is through an "economy of affirmation and forgetting" of the genealogies of racial terror that make capital and the nation possible that the market can be theorized as a technology of freedom.[19] In addition, when proponents of neoliberalism pushed for the freedom of the market, they also expanded the market's powers of racial subjection. The authors acknowledge this fact when they argue that the market will free Western Man and presumably leave those who constitutively haunt the category of Western Man *unfree*. Thus, the freeing of the market gave new life to white supremacy at the same moment it was existentially threatened by global and domestic anticolonial and antiracist movements. If the market frees Western Man while leaving Others unfree, then there is another genealogy of the market that leads us not to freedom but to the slave ship, plantation, coffle, and auction block—a genealogy that undoes the neoliberal narrative of freedom and progress. (I explore this genealogy in the next chapter.)

Neoliberal Freedom and Law and Order

While the state, in Friedman's theory, should be weak enough to free the economic from any and all constraint, it must also have the force necessary to eliminate "domestic and foreign enemies." Throughout his book Friedman emphasizes that the state must maintain "law and order to prevent physical coercion of one individual by another and to enforce the contracts voluntarily entered into, thus giving substance to the 'private.'" Law and order is the precondition for "voluntary exchange." The state violence of police and prisons is required to give shape to the private sphere. The market's freedom needs to be protected; freedom requires containment and control: "[The state's] major function must be to protect our freedom from the enemies outside our gates and from our fellow-citizens: to preserve law and order, to enforce private contracts, to foster competitive markets."[20] Within this formulation the free market is not actually free; the state must regulate the freedom of the market. As Nikolas Rose has observed, constructing a free market seems to necessitate innumerable interventions by "accountants, management consultants, lawyers and industrial relations specialists and marketing experts in order to establish the conditions under which the 'laws of supply and demand' can make themselves real."[21] The free market is not to be left to its own devices; its freedom must be fostered by a powerful regulatory state. The market's freedom must be regulated and disciplined in order to provide governance to a social world "dismembered by liberal individualism."[22] In essence, Friedman's notion of economic freedom inaugurates the unfreedom it seeks to escape; economic freedom must be fostered and enforced by state power.

The brilliance of Friedman's use of the phrase *law and order* was that it could name blackness as a threat to the market without ever mentioning race. As a racial liberal Friedman could deploy the race-neutral language of law and order while still invoking a racialized Other—the "domestic and foreign enemies" who threatened the free market and freedom itself. In fact Friedman was very clear about what must be done to the Others of neoliberal freedom: "Freedom is a tenable objective only for responsible individuals. We do not believe in freedom for madmen or for children. The necessity of drawing a line between responsible individuals and others is inescapable, yet it means that there is an essential ambiguity to our ultimate objective of freedom. Paternalism is inescapable for those whom we designate as not responsible."[23] The compromise for the liberal is to accept that "paternalism" is necessary in some aspects of life, for some people. The fictional coercion-free exchange that occurs between two individuals is made possible by the force of the law and the racial violence of the police.

Life and freedom as Friedman conceptualizes them are the products of what he calls "paternalism." He made clear the mutually constitutive relationship between the prison and the free market: paternalism and law and order meant the policing powers of the state must be expansive and robust. By naming certain populations "not responsible" enough to be free, neoliberal thought fabricates populations that must be policed and imprisoned. Ruth Wilson Gilmore succinctly describes this when she writes, "Convicts are cities' working and workless poor."[24] The free market and the prison require one another: the carceral controls the waste of the market, while the market produces surplus populations that will be immobilized within the prison.[25] The fabrication of freedom within the governing realm of the market necessitates the racialized and gendered unfreedom of the prison. The "burden of conscience" constitutive of the liberal individual facilitates self-discipline but also produces resentment toward (and justifies the punishment of) those who cannot prove themselves worthy of freedom.[26] The subject deemed not responsible is caught between the failures of self-reliance, the racialized criminalization of poverty, and the premature death produced by low-wage labor. As the freedom of the market expands, so do systems of incapacitation. While the free market spreads the insecurity of abandonment, the prison offers the illusion of security to those not captured and caged. This relationship between the market and the prison was made even more explicit by followers of Friedman.

In his 1985 article, "An Economic Theory of Criminal Activity," the lawyer, judge, and economist Richard Posner describes the relationship between the prison and the market: "The major function of criminal law in a capitalist society is to prevent people from bypassing the system of voluntary, compensated exchange—the 'market,' explicit or implicit—in situations where, because transaction costs are low, the market is a more efficient method of allocating resources than forced exchange. . . . The market is, virtually by definition, the most efficient method of allocating resources. . . . Attempts to bypass the market will therefore be punished . . . by a system bent on promoting efficiency."[27] Posner was part of a cohort of economists who, following Friedman and Hayek, started the "law and economics movement."[28] This intellectual movement used an emergent neoliberal economics to analyze crime and punishment. Posner's argument that punishment shapes and is required by the free market was inspired by a 1968 article written by his colleague Gary Becker, "Crime and Punishment: An Economic Approach." Becker used Chicago school economics to argue that criminality was not biological but the outcome of a simple cost–benefit analysis: people committed crime when the benefits outweighed the costs. Foucault found Becker's theory that everyone was a potential criminal refreshing in the face of genetic, behavioral, and psychological theories of crime.[29] Posner extended Becker's economic analysis of crime to include all aspects of social life. Thus Posner's near obsession with using the efficiency of the market as an analytic for measuring all human action, including sexual violence.[30]

By centering the governmentality of the market in a theory of the social good, Posner argued for the disciplining of those who deviated from the market's natural governance. Ways of living that exceeded the voluntary freedom of the market and thus deviated from the natural order of the market's self-perpetuating cycle were subjected to the social, civil, and living death of imprisonment.[31] Posner insisted that the carceral should target behaviors that escape or surpass the rule of the market.[32] What remains unspoken is that the market is a form of punishment in and of itself: whether one deviates from its demands or is forced outside its protection, one risks hunger, homelessness, illness, and premature death. To say that people will be punished if they "bypass" the market means that the market has borders, both metaphorical and physical. To escape or exceed its grasp is to risk imprisonment. It's not just that the market requires the prison; as Posner argues, the market is a type of prison. An entire apparatus of policing and penal technologies is mobilized to punish and capture the fugitive from the governance of the market. In a near mirror image of law-and-order politics discussed in chapter 1, this conception of neoliberal freedom constructed punishment and policing as the necessary corollary to the liberation of the individual and the freedom of the market. As Posner and Friedman made clear, the free market relies on state-sponsored systems of punishment in order to maintain its dominance. Neoliberal freedom was productive of the construction of the individual as a regulative ideal while also immobilizing those resistant or excessive to new economic, social, and political regimes that prioritized the market. In this way neoliberal thought reproduces the very configurations and effects of power it seeks to vanquish. Discipline is inaugurated in the name of freedom; a prison state rises where state power is supposed to crumble; and the regulation of difference escalates under the banner of equality.

Fugitivity and Freedom's Biopolitics

The language of neoliberal freedom provides an ideological screen that obscures the unfreedom necessary to the free market. While it produces a fantasy, its function is not to hide a deeper truth but to create new capacities for control. Freedom, in other words, is not only ideological but is also biopolitical. The language of neoliberal freedom produces the forms of knowledge and subjectivity required for freedom to operate as a system of regulation and discipline. Freedom becomes a way of administering populations not through the deception of a myth but by making freedom a system of governance and management.[33] The power of Friedman's text lies in its ability to produce new forms of subjection with an argument concerning the expansion of freedom. Neoliberal thought made subjection look like its opposite by creating new methods of control and regulation coded by the language of freedom. Gilles Deleuze and Félix Guattari call this materialist understanding of language "incorporeal transformation." This term names language's ability to transform materiality—it is the "material power" of language. They write, "The incorporeal transformation is recognized by its instantaneousness, its immediacy, by the simultaneity of the statement expressing the transformation and the effect the transformation produces."[34] As they theorize it, the incorporeal mediates the relationship between the statement (or discourse) and its object. In a broader sense the incorporeal is what makes an object an object; it is how language alters that which it describes and names. Incorporeal transformation describes language's ability to reign in the errantness of life; it is how a word captures what escapes systems of meaning and governance: criminality takes hold of blackness, madness arrests what exceeds reason, terrorism renders senseless the violence of nonstate actors. Mel Chen refers to this process as the "alchemical power of language" since language "animates" (or possesses) bodies and things.[35] As Deleuze and Guattari note, language "gives life orders."[36] Language limits, contains, controls, and captures what it describes. Similarly Rose writes that neoliberal freedom implants "ways of calculating and managing that will make economic actors think, reckon, and behave as competitive, profit-seeking agents," turns workers into motivated employees who will "freely strive to give their best in the work place," and transforms "people into consumers who can choose between products." Neoliberal freedom transforms materiality through the power of language. It alters desires, feelings, attitudes, affects, and values. It creates subjects who manage themselves through responsibility and individuality. Freedom is more than a discourse; it is a mechanism of biopolitical governance actualized by the power of language. As Rose emphasizes, people and markets cannot be set free; "they have to be *made* free."[37] Freedom is discipline, a notion Friedman's mentor Hayek evinced when he wrote, "Man has not developed in freedom. . . . Freedom is an artifact of civilization. . . . Freedom was made possible by the gradual evolution of the discipline of civilization which is at the same time the discipline of freedom."[38] Hayek argues that freedom must be controlled, regulated, and managed. Regimes of power do not distort freedom and falsify subjectivity.[39] Instead freedom and individuality are modes of subjection that look, and may feel, like liberation. And as Friedman and Posner make clear, for those subjects not responsible enough to be guided by the discipline that is liberty, law and order will capture those who escape freedom's grasp.

Friedman's articulation of neoliberal freedom in the 1960s and 1970s occurred alongside multiple demands for a freedom or liberation that were unthinkable within the confines of neoliberal thought. Like the politics of law and order, neoliberal freedom is a response to the "freedom dreams" articulated by the liberation movements of the 1960s and 1970s.[40] The neoliberal language of freedom worked to control, manage, and capture the notions of freedom produced by the left by rendering them unthinkable and impossible. Unlike the ways that freedom and liberation were articulated in the 1960s and 1970s by activists who were aboveground, underground, and locked down, neoliberal freedom was predicated on a contingency that could be named: the state, economic regulation, and physical coercion.[41] But the forms of political, social, economic, and ontological undoing required for freedom, as articulated by groups like the Student Nonviolent Coordinating Committee, Black Panther Party, Young Lords, Gay Liberation Front, Black Liberation Army, Third World Women's Alliance, Combahee River Collective, and so many others, escape the logic of neoliberal thought. They are not contingent, but infinitely expansive, open, and always already taking flight. This impossible understanding of freedom is fugitive. Freedom for the groups I discuss required the end of white supremacy, the police, prisons, the military, the state, the country, modern subjectivity, and, in the case of black feminist notions of freedom, heteropatriarchy, sexism, misogyny, and on and on. Neoliberal thought functions to manage and contain the demands that would make fugitive freedom possible by rendering them unthinkable. The arguments and language that sustain *Capitalism and Freedom* are made possible by an epistemology that cannot see or understand anything beyond the abstract individual. Thus neoliberal freedom transforms the biopolitical organization of life and death into individual problems with market solutions. Since freedom is tied to individuality, neoliberal freedom cannot see or name the biopolitical distribution of life and death neoliberal freedom requires and inaugurates. The neoliberal theory of freedom sustains the forms of devaluation and unfreedom it purports to abolish.

The language of neoliberal freedom inaugurated a world wherein abandonment would be managed by the prison and a new form of state domination would come into being, not through centralization but through deregulation and privatization.[42] Yet while neoliberal freedom was tightening its grasp on the possibilities of thought and world-making, a space came into being that tried to escape everything that freedom had been and was becoming. The underground and the fugitive offered alternatives to the epistemological and ontological norms produced by the discourse of neoliberal freedom. While Deleuze and Guattari assist with understanding the crushing weight of language's power, they also point to lines of flight and modes of escape that can aid thinking about the relationship between neoliberal freedom and the underground. Embedded within their theory of language as a form of capture is an articulation of the ways that language stutters, stalls, and fails, thereby leading to rupture and undoing. For Deleuze and Guattari, within every moment of capture there are also possibilities of fleeing: "The question was not how to elude the order-word but how to elude the death sentence it envelopes, how to develop its power of escape, how to prevent escape from veering . . . into a black hole, how to maintain or draw out the revolutionary potential of the order-word." If language can take hold of its object in the spirit of order, control, and regulation, then for Deleuze and Guattari there are ways to turn "order into . . . passage," rupture, and flight.[43]

In her analysis of how the writings of the imprisoned black revolutionary George Jackson affected the thought of Deleuze and Guattari, Koerner provides a useful example of this process: "Jackson's use of language could be understood as a 'weapon' precisely because Jackson's lines were shot through with such violent hatred of the 'words and syntax of his enemy' that he 'has only one recourse: to accept this language but to corrupt it so skillfully the whites will be caught in his trap.' In corrupting the 'words and syntax' of domination, one directly attacks the 'conditions that destroy life,' because language is here considered a mechanism by which one's thought, agency, relations, and subjectivity are 'caught' by Power." Jackson understood language as a technology of capture coextensive with police and the prison, but he also saw it as a means of escape. The regulatory norms of grammar and style include and validate certain usages while devaluing others, which for Jackson meant the destruction of life. Yet by corrupting what captured him, he produced alternative forms of knowledge, feeling, and seeing since the production of "resistant subjectivities always involves a dismantling of the dominant order of language."[44] We can include the underground within this understanding of flight from the "death sentence" of language, knowledge, and power. The underground was, of course, a space where fugitives evaded the law, but it was also a place where they escaped dominant regimes of governance, ontology, and epistemology. In fact the underground was brought into being by the forms of violence neoliberal freedom could not name. It emerged to document, contest, and undo the forms of state violence that acted as the condition of possibility for the rise of the neoliberal-carceral state. The underground was a space where the ghosts of neoliberal thought refused to remain imperceptible, where what was forcefully forgotten returned, and where freedom took on unimaginable and impossible meanings. Where neoliberal freedom deadened and captured the possibilities of thought, being, and living, fugitive freedom ran toward unknown and unthought variations of life itself.

The Fictions of the Fugitive

In my engagement with the underground, a world where facts were fabricated and fictions shaped the contours of daily life, I read the memoirs of political fugitives alongside Susan Choi's novel *American Woman*. The novel explores the "lost year" of the Patty Hearst kidnapping, when Hearst was living underground with Wendy Yoshimura. The daughter of the publishing mogul William Randolph Hearst, Patty Hearst was kidnapped by the Symbionese Liberation Army in 1974. After a few months as their captive, Hearst ending up joining the group and was a fugitive with them for close to two years. A few months of this time was spent with Yoshimura.

Yoshimura was born in a U.S. internment camp during World War II and was active in the antiwar movement beginning in 1969. In the early 1970s she became a member of the Symbionese Liberation Army and went underground. She was captured with Hearst in 1975 and became something of a minor celebrity among the Asian American left.[45] Yoshimura's racialized and gendered erasure from the story of the Hearst kidnapping, and the history of the left more broadly, is aptly described by the title of a documentary about her life, *Wendy . . . Uh . . . What's Her Name*.[46] *American Woman* is a fictional account of a historical event that "isn't part of the story" and was "never inscribed into the record."[47] Choi explores the underground from the perspective of Jenny Shimada (the character who stands in for Yoshimura) and thus explores the gaps and erasures that are the refuse of history—that in the end are just "static and lint."[48] Choi also intentionally departs from history by giving Jenny and Pauline (the character who stands in for Hearst) a full year together instead of the few months Hearst and Yoshimura shared. Jenny and Pauline develop a "queer intimacy" in which they cultivate a sexual relationship, fall in love, start an underground feminist reading collective, offer weapons trainings to women, rob a bank, run, hide, and are eventually captured.[49] *American Woman* and the memoirs demonstrate that the fugitive embodies a nonnormative epistemology and practice of freedom that negated the regulatory powers of neoliberalism. While neoliberal economics argues that freedom is the outcome of the market's capture of life itself, fugitive theories of freedom center escape, forgetting, erasure, and running away.

In order to explore the underground and before discussing *American Woman* I turn to memoirs written by former political fugitives. One of the fascinating contradictions of this body of literature is that its promise (issued by the authors and publishers) is that it will reveal a hidden world composed of secrets, lies, and violence. The genre promises to make visible the unknown while also explaining the presumably unthinkable, irrational, and exceptional violence committed by former or captured outlaws. Yet the genre itself cannot live up to its promise because to tell the truth (who, what, when, where) of underground life would betray the fact that "underground means out-of-sight."[50] Diana Block, who spent close to a decade as part of the underground Puerto Rican independence movement, writes in her memoir, "Just because we were now back in sight didn't mean that the nuts and bolts of how we functioned should be available on the printed page."[51] To tell the truth, or make the underground visible, would jeopardize a space thousands of people spent decades building, in addition to risking the lives of those still on the run.

Block writes of her memoir, "This is a 'true' story, but that doesn't mean every aspect of it is exactly how it happened." The genre's condition of possibility is the deployment of fiction in order to convey the truth of a world shaped by lies, deceit, and "a web of factual fabrication."[52] Like the underground itself, for these texts to exist they must wrap themselves in gaps, silences, and half-truths. By remaining imperceptible, the genre, like the space, pushes us to think past history as the disciplining, production, and "determination of the visible."[53] Indeed, even after arrest many fugitives kept the underground concealed. In his court statement, Jaan Laaman, a member of the United Freedom Front, which committed twenty bombings and nine bank robberies in the Northeast, spent pages and pages outlining his political history to the court. The last words of his statement are, "My [prison] sentence expired a few months before the historic Attica uprisings and I was released, but soon I was mourning the murders of some of my close comrades in that rebellion. I returned to full time political work, but with the government already keeping close watch on my activities, I went underground . . ."[54] The statement of his personal history ended where a new way of living began. The ellipses stand in for close to a decade of fugitive life. This is history as a gesture, a knowing glance, a silence the law will never make speak. How do we come to understand a practice of freedom that can't be described, a world that had to be invisible, a place that always moved, a way of living that could not leave a record of itself, a trace of its existence, or even a fingerprint?

During the same time as the release of a number of memoirs written by 1970s political fugitives, a number of novelists explored the underground in more detail through the use of fiction.[55] Fiction is able to describe, detail, and recover what cannot be spoken by the genre of the memoir and the discipline of history. In order to theorize fugitive notions of freedom in relation to the emergence of neoliberalism, I too must turn to fiction. Literature, Koerner writes, "is driven by a desire to liberate what existing conditions seek to govern, block, and capture; as such, it asserts a force in the world that existing conditions would otherwise reduce to nonexistence."[56] The novels defy the historical conditions of their production, a social order defined by the regulation, criminalization, and capture of forms of gendered, sexual, and racialized life that escape the state of things as they are. Fiction itself, like the fugitive, becomes a form of flight from the constraint of existing conditions that are intolerable and uninhabitable. Fiction becomes a way to release feelings, forms of knowledge, and affects that might otherwise remain underground, obscured by a system of policing, imprisonment, and marketization that is always already seeking their capture. Fiction describes what the memoirs cannot due to the ongoing criminalization of former (and current) radical and revolutionary movements.

Choi's attempt to recover the history of the underground through fiction apprehends the fact that the archive of underground life is necessarily incomplete because an archive is evidence. If we understand an archive to be "the institutions that organize facts" and "condition the possibility of existence of historical statements," then we can include the law and police as key sites that shape what can be known as history.[57] The unrecorded history of the underground allows us to see that the production of history is always a story about power. Avery Gordon reminds us of this when she writes, "Our stories can be understood as fictions of the real. . . . The real itself . . . and its sociological representations are also fictions, albeit powerful ones that we do not experience as fictional, but as true."[58] In the case of the underground, racialized regimes of capture shape what we can know—and what remains unknown—about the past.[59] Thus we can add the systems of policing that targeted the fugitive and the underground to the forms of power that select and determine what enters the archive and the knowable.[60] In this context fiction documents the fugitive memories and forms of knowledge that could not be otherwise recorded.[61] It exceeds the "historical intelligibility" produced and regulated by the archive.[62] Block's memoir describes this by detailing the fact that running away also required erasure. Escaping meant erasing a life's detritus that might normally be left behind to be recorded and remembered.

In the beginning of her memoir Block and her comrades must flee their underground home after an FBI surveillance device is discovered in her their car. The device caused panic, but the family had to appear normal so the discovery of the device would remain unknown to the FBI. Block and her comrades continued to meet in coffee shops, in malls, and in parks. They continued to "watch for cars that were watching" them and never used the telephone. In their maintained normality they planned an escape to a new space of the underground. Escaping again meant destroying everything that could lead to their new lives: "Did we need to get rid of all our books on the chance that a stray fingerprint of a friend found on a random page could somehow associate them with us. But how would we get rid of the books? By burning? By shredding? By hauling them off in suspicious sacks to a dumpster?" Block decided that all of their papers and writings should be burned, destroying their only "written history." All that was left behind was a small pouch of her mother's earrings "sitting in their lacquered box, waiting for the FBI to finger and file."[63] For Block, an archive of fugitive life meant visibility and the threat of capture. History had to be erased because its erasure was central to escape.

Block's memoir is composed mostly of dreams and poems that extend this erasure, ensuring the unknown remains so. The memoir's gaps and silences are a trace of the ruins of this history; memory fills in for what had to be destroyed to avoid capture. Poetry and dreams are a way for Block to convey in writing the reality of underground life while flirting with the "admissible and inadmissible" in an "acrobatic language that captured the essence of what I was experiencing, if not the specific details." The law, the prison, and the police structure this genre of writing; all three forces are the condition of necessity for the existence of the underground. A poem or a dream became a way to continue escaping, to remain illegible, even while visible, to an apparatus of capture that continues to track, detail, and imprison those who contested the state of things in the 1960s, 1970s, and 1980s. Block's memoir explores the ephemeral borderline between the underground and what she calls "normal life" by taunting reality (and the police) with the truth of a dream. While she was underground, poetry became a way for Block to write about her life without leaving everything behind: "I could freely paint the eccentric details of my childhood because these truths were not verbatim and would not, in this cloaked poetic form, tie Pat Hoffman [her underground name] to Diana Block."[64] Writing became a way to hide in plain sight; she shared her poems publicly, even publishing a few under different names. Poetry allowed memories—ones that could lead to recognition and arrest—to move beyond the confines of the secrecy and invisibility central to the underground. Dreams, fiction, and poetry were not forms of evidence legible to the state and were thus a way for Block to evade technologies of policing and capture. Fiction is a way of keeping alive memories of forms of life that are not supposed to exist. It is also a weapon, a counterattack. Fiction thus was central to the underground's fugitive notions of freedom.

Novels about the underground record what cannot be written down and also what cannot be remembered. While Block describes the underground as a place that must remain unknowable through erasure, Angela Davis saw the underground as a space of forgetting produced by stress, terror, anxiety, and fear. The underground was a state of emotional duress where fact and fiction become indecipherable and memory disappeared. Davis's autobiography begins with an uncertainty, a doubt, an assertion of forgetting in a text that is supposed to remember: "I believe I thanked her but I'm not sure." She continues, "Perhaps I simply watched her dig into the shopping bag and accepted in silence the wig she held out to me." Even if her memories were not criminal, Davis was unable to record underground life because it was impossible to remember the truth through the terror and debilitating anxiety of "hunted life."[65] Her use of the word *perhaps* is a register of this forgetting—a trace left behind by a life taking flight. Davis describes how being hunted changed her appearance:

> I walked toward the bathroom and stood before the mirror trying to fit the ends of my hair under the tight elastic. . . . When finally I glanced into the mirror to see whether there were still bits of my own hair unconcealed by the wig, I saw a face so filled with anguish, tension and uncertainty I did not recognize it as my own. With the false black curls falling over a wrinkled forehead into red swollen eyes, I looked absurd, grotesque. . . . I had to look normal; I could not arouse the suspicion of the attendant in the station where we would have to gas up the car. I didn't want to attract the attention of someone who might drive up alongside us and look in our direction while we waited at an intersection for the light to turn green. I had to look as commonplace as a piece of everyday Los Angeles scenery.[66]

Davis's assertion that she does not know and could not remember because the underground was a space of "anguish, tension and uncertainty" filled with the "unknown perils of being a fugitive" produces an epistemology that escapes the state's ability to render visible and knowable those under its systems of governance.[67] Forgetting was a way to remain illegible, to evade, and to escape. Choi writes that even in the present moment of the underground, the now was "barely remembered," and in the near future it would be a "half-grasped fever dream."[68] The record of the underground lies with the erased and the forgotten. Exploring its politics, meaning, and legacy requires engaging the ashes of books, letters, and diaries; it means staring at a spotless, empty room and trying to imagine the lives once lived there: "She packed her bag, put on her cleaning gloves, and wiped everything in the house. It took hours. She went through the kitchen drawers and wiped every fork, knife, spoon and utensil. She wiped the spices in the spice rack and the Tupperware containers in the fridge. . . . She saved the bathroom for last. When she arrived there she stood over the toilet she had cleaned once a week on her knees. She felt as if she'd never really seen this toilet before. Then she wiped it, for the last time, and left."[69] Erasure, forgetting, lying, and deceit were ways for the fugitive to distort the confines and creation of state memory and history. This contortion of truth and memory was central to fugitive understandings of freedom; forgetting and deceit were foundational to the practice of running, and running away is what it meant to be free.

Block and Davis describe the underground as what we might think of as a fictional space—as space that exists only through the fabrications required for someone to disappear into the openness of the world. Block writes, "But it was becoming clearer that my overground life was a temporary phenomenon, and each day it was yielding space to my underground life that was soon to become my only life. I was learning to juggle different modalities of daily communication, language, and clothing. I was learning how to invent a story that could serve as a bridge between the two worlds." Language, clothing, and stories become central to inventing a new world inside of the old. The underground was not outside of power but was folded inside the contours of everyday life, a way of escaping without ever leaving. The underground was a space brought into being by a series of performances but also a rigid set of rules: "Never call each other's houses from our home phones, never take a direct route from one person's house to the other, never give our real home addresses to our jobs or our friends at our jobs, always watch the rearview mirror to keep track of cars that could be following us—our rules proliferated and became internalized as part of our daily routine."[70] The underground was a way of deforming power's vision; by erasing one's personal history, identity, and appearance (Block went so far as to avoid colors that might be associated with her old self), the fugitive body became illegible to an expansive policing apparatus. The fugitive replaces a politics of visibility and a legible subjectivity in favor of a way of being that is always moving, always running, always escaping.[71] This practice allowed the fugitive to make visible what law and order and neoliberal economics produced and then effaced by throwing "the building of a national past into relief."[72] It was by being imperceptible that the fugitive could make visible the forms of racialized, gendered, and imperial violence necessary to the formation of the neoliberal-carceral state. This was evident in my readings of the communiqués of the Weather Underground and George Jackson Brigade in chapter 1 and the introduction. However, *American Woman* apprehends what these documents could not: how the underground rearticulated neoliberal freedom through the mundane movements of the fugitive.

Escaping Freedom

Split into four parts, *American Woman* describes post-1960s radicalism from the perspective of Jenny, a twenty-five-year-old Japanese American wanted for a series of anti-imperialist bombings. While she went underground, her boyfriend and co-conspirator, William, was captured and imprisoned. Living alone in upstate New York as "Iris Wong," Jenny works restoring the home of a wealthy woman. Part 1 of the novel is told from the perspective of Frazer, a former political ally who tracks Jenny down to convince her to use her "underground know-how" to care for three fugitives: Juan, the arrogant, sexist, trigger-happy leader; Yvonne, his devoted girlfriend; and "princess" Pauline, an heiress who was kidnapped and converted to her captors' cause.[73] Part 2 explores the banal details of underground life and the clashes that take place between Jenny and her comrades. When it becomes clear that they need money, Juan and Yvonne decide to rob a grocery store, and Jenny and Pauline act as getaway drivers. When the robbery goes wrong, Pauline and Jenny flee. While on the run in part 3, Jenny and Pauline strengthen their bond, which leads to their feminist and queer awakening in San Francisco, where they are eventually captured. Part 4 finds Jenny imprisoned after being betrayed by Pauline. This last part of the novel looks backward to Jenny's father, Jim, who was imprisoned in the internment camp at Manzanar and later at a camp for "incorrigibles." The novel ends with Jenny and Jim traveling to a reunion for former internees.

American Woman begins with Frazer's attempt to go underground and find Jenny. As he drives around in circles, he realizes he is "looking too hard at the wrong thing, and missing the point." Finding Jenny means thinking and seeing like a fugitive: "He should have realized that she wouldn't live here; she wouldn't want to be too near the post office. Yet she wouldn't want to travel too far." The novel thus opens with Frazer's disorientation; he is lost because Jenny does not want to be found by him or the state. Throughout the novel Jenny is on the run from the police and the law; as a queer woman of color, she is also fleeing from the racialized and gendered regulations of the radical left. Jenny is hiding from the complicity between the policing power of revolutionary nationalisms and the police themselves. Her underground life is a never-ending negotiation with the carceral apparatuses of the state, as well as the mundane interpersonal and institutional racialized sexisms that make the fatal encounter always already present. Frazer is lost because he has entered an unfamiliar space, a space outside the formal register of the nation, where the conventions of the social order no longer apply. Since he is "looking at the wrong thing" he cannot comprehend, let alone see, Jenny and the world she has made. Frazer struggles to find Jenny because she is illegible within the dominant order of things. Unlike the politics of the racial liberalism that guide Frazer, Jenny's invisibility refuses a politics of legibility where the "performance of ethnicity [is] the key to liberatory politics." In fact she becomes invisible within the visibility of her racialization—to be visible as an Asian maid is to vanish.[74] Jenny disappears through her racialization, but her racialization is also what erases her from the record of events considered worthy of remembering by the state and the left.

At the end of the novel a reporter named Anne researches Jenny and her father in an attempt to make sense of them in relation to what she knows will become history and what will be left behind: "None of this is the story. There's no good place to put it. In the end it's just static and lint." *American Woman* attempts to tell a story that is almost impossible to imagine as a story because "Jenny is nobody's story."[75] Jenny exceeds the boundaries of historical narrative because she embodies connections that go beyond the confines of normative thought. She is unthinkable because she exceeds all answers and the epistemological borders within which questions are asked.[76] As Patricia Chu explains, "Choi's frustrated and wandering 1970s reporter belies the exemplary, legendary, and tightly narrated *All the President's Men* (1974), Bob Woodward and Carl Bernstein's account of the Watergate cover-up that supposedly defined an era, by trying to fathom how the 'static and lint' of the history of race in America is part of the story of Pauline and the cadre, rather than considering the upheavals of white and ethnic politics separately."[77] By making connections that aren't supposed to connect, the novel remembers the neoliberal-carceral state's connection to U.S. imperialism in Vietnam and the internment of Japanese citizens in the 1940s. In this way the neoliberal-carceral state is always already the "warfare state" and the "racial state."[78] *American Woman* remembers the haunting effects of internment on the banality of the everyday, a history disavowed by neoliberal thought and forgotten by the revolutionary left. This history is remembered in the novel's attention to the spatial politics of life underground. For instance, Jenny's father was imprisoned at an internment camp as a teen, but he never told Jenny about his experience because what he went through was unspeakable. Instead of telling her about captivity, he passed on the survival skills he learned: "Maybe that was his way of describing internment to her. He'd always brushed off her questions, but maybe he'd been telling her things all her life. This is how you make a horse stable into a home, and burlap sack into bed. This is how you pack one little bag, though you're going so far for so long. . . . Her father had expected her to sleep well anywhere and under all circumstances. On the ground, in the back of a car. Across chairs in the bus station waiting room."[79] Jenny recalls these lessons inherited from her father's life in captivity as she performs the mundane rituals of being a fugitive: packing a bag, sleeping anywhere, moving constantly, finding a home everywhere. The fugitive acts she and her father perform are historical registers of racialized state power that escape the epistemological boundaries of liberal thought. These connections are expunged from neoliberal theories of freedom. They are the silences and gaps that make neoliberal freedom possible. The underground and the fugitive are formations that confront the silences that are constitutive of the racial state and capital. Internment's connections to the neoliberal-carceral state are registered in the affective connections passed on from a life in captivity to a life on the run. Yet these connections are too tangled across time and space for Anne to comprehend; it all looks like lint or dust quietly floating within the archives of memory.

The alternative notion of freedom embedded in *American Woman* emerges from Choi's critique of the historical erasures central to racialized and gendered state power, but also her critique of the revolutionary left. For example, part of Jenny's responsibility in taking care of Juan, Yvonne, and Pauline is to ensure that they write a book about their group, the People's Army, that Frazer will sell to raise money for the underground. In this way, Choi gives the reader a firsthand look at how the revolutionary left attempted to write its history. Pauline is allowed to write a section about how she came to revolutionary consciousness, and she reads this aloud to the group as part of the editing process. She describes how, after she was first kidnapped, a member of the People's Army assigned to care for her would read aloud to her through the closet door that separated them: "More and more I longed to see the face of this kind and wise person, this brother who was trying to teach me. I begged him to take off my blindfold. 'Can't I just see you?' I said.

'The words matter, not me,' he explained."[80] After Pauline is finished reading, Juan intervenes to ensure that the group's history is written properly:

Juan interrupted.
"No blindfold."
"No blindfold?"
"I already said to get rid of the blindfold."
"You already said I can't be in the closet."
"For the last fucking time, you were not in a closet."
"Was it a pantry?"
"It was a *room*. Maybe not like the nice rooms you're used to."
"Well what do I know," Pauline said, "I was wearing a blindfold the whole fucking time."
. . . "Get rid of the blindfold. It's bullshit."
"It's true."
"It's not true to the point of the story. There's things that are facts that in context don't help make the point."[81]

Jenny is shocked by this exchange because in their communiqués the group claimed that they were treating Pauline within the guidelines of the Geneva Conventions: "You said you let her exercise and read the papers and eat with you."[82] In a novel obsessed with the erasure of history, here Choi describes the complicity between the revolutionary left and the state as both work to produce what can be known and what should be forgotten. Like the history of Jenny and her father, Pauline's story is unusable because its truth "doesn't help make the point." While the cadre frequently emphasizes eradicating all forms and institutions of racism, sexism, ageism, classism, and fascism, their structure, behaviors, and practice effectively naturalize, reproduce, and reinstitute these forms of subjection within their revolutionary politics.[83] This is evident in Juan's paternalistic rewriting of Pauline's memory, but also in his understanding of race and gender.

Throughout their time together Juan (who is white) consistently fetishizes Jenny's skin color. He tells her that her "Third World perspective is a privilege" and says, "You must be a good shot. Oriental people always have exceptional aim." In an effort to degrade Pauline by essentializing Jenny's body and mind, Juan says, "She's still got to learn that there's no substitute for a Third World perspective like yours. Brown, yellow, black, red: those are four things she'll never be. And she isn't just white, she's a filthy rich white. Y and I are from the Midwest, and I'm not saying our town wasn't racist, or that we don't have a taint that we'll never repair. But at least we're blue collar. . . . That's why you're a good lesson. She sees your reality and knows she won't ever know it." Like Friedman's deployment of the black body as a fungible commodity to be used for his own ends, Juan turns Jenny into what he needs her to be. When Jenny tells him he's racist, he responds, "You can't say I'm racist. . . . I've always wished I was black. Not just wished it, but willed it."[84] For Juan, knowledge is connected to phenotype, and thus he rebiologizes the form of power he claims to want to abolish. Juan naturalizes race because knowledge supposedly arises from the imagined essence of the racialized body. Penny Vlagopoulos suggests, "Juan's understanding of racial identity adopts the colonizer's view of origins."[85] Juan stands in for the heteropatriarchal and racist regulations of the left that were complicit with the state that the left claimed to oppose. While neoliberal freedom reproduced the forms of degradation and subjection it imagined it would undo, Choi outlines how the revolutionary left replicated the racialized, gendered, and heterosexist regulations it declared dead. Juan effectively sustains and reinforces the forms of racialized and gendered subjugation central to the rise of the post–civil rights racial state and late capital. The left was not solely oppositional to the new forms of state power that would emerge after the revolutionary upheavals of the late 1960s and early 1970s—the left was the alibi of the racial state when it reproduced its heteropatriarchal regulations.

As Choi makes clear, even as Jenny is running from the police, she is continually captured by Juan's complicity with dominant thought and practice. In fact, Jenny is caught between the heteropatriarchal regulations of the left and the state earlier in the novel, when she has to flee the home of a liberal couple who have agreed to house her. After the couple make Jenny dinner, which includes a toast "to freedom," she awakens to find the husband "in her room, leaning into her bed, his old cheese-and-tobacco breath hot on her neck."[86] The next morning, after erasing her presence from the house, Jenny runs away, taking flight from freedom's grasp. And after Juan's arrogance leads to the death of a storeowner during a poorly conceptualized robbery, Jenny and Pauline flee from Juan. Throughout the novel Jenny is running from more than just the law. She also escapes formations of power that are not restricted to the state or the police, the forms of power that possess everyone and everything, that come in the form of a kind, liberal rapist and a freedom fighter on the run. Unlike the politics of the left or the state, Jenny begins to practice a politics of difference that can make sense of the histories erased by the multiple forces she is fleeing. This fact is at the heart of the novel's theorization of freedom. It is an understanding of power that Deleuze and Guattari describe when they write, "It's easy to be antifascist . . . and not see the fascist inside you, the fascist you yourself sustain and nourish and cherish."[87] Similarly, Foucault claims that the "challenge is to refuse what you are," to exorcise "the fascism in us all, in our heads, and in our everyday behavior, the fascism that causes us to love power, to desire the very thing that dominates and exploits us."[88] Or as Chela Sandoval writes, "The major enemy to face during our own time has infiltrated every citizen-subject's body."[89] What Jenny discovers, and what *American Woman* demonstrates, is that freedom for the fugitive did not come from hiding or engaging in armed struggle—it came from running.

Running from Freedom

Freedom is a mode of biopolitical control that cloaks coercion as consent while simultaneously making freedom the product of incarceration. In short, freedom is not something one possesses—one is possessed *by* freedom. And to escape its grasp one must keep running and never look back. To be intimate with running, to have had to run, and above all else to *desire* to run expresses the "politics of fugitivity" at the heart of Jenny's flight.[90] When I argue that the fugitive and the underground escaped neoliberal epistemologies and produced alternative conceptions of freedom, I am following Foucault's assertion that the capture of life by power is never total: "It is not that life has been totally integrated into techniques that govern and administer it; it constantly escapes them."[91] Fred Moten has referred to these moments of escape as a "fugitive mode of life" produced by a "runaway inheritance."[92] Thus the neoliberal-carceral state's ability to capture life (bodies, subjectivities, psyches, knowledges, and affects) is never total. If neoliberal freedom was one way to govern thought and populations, then its power was not complete. To be possessed does not mean one is lost to what has taken hold; something remains: an excess, a remainder, a surplus that escapes a structure that appears to be (and feels) total. In many ways this escape is inherent in the operations of power. The technologies used to produce life always push against the raw material necessary to the process. Something is left behind by the encounter between power and its object. The technologies used to construct materiality constantly produce "embodied life and unintegrated life at the same time. There is always a shaping and an errantness."[93]

The errant names what escapes power's operations. Errantness is when something slips off the shaping of an object, when an object pushes back, or when the act of making the object changes what is doing the making. Errantness names the fugitive potentiality embedded in every moment of power's operation. The conditions of excess parallel the conditions of capture so that the possession of life is never complete. Throughout *American Woman* Jenny runs toward the errant and away from the forms of capture reproduced by the state and the revolutionary left.

Moten describes this potential excess when he addresses Foucault's notion that resistance precedes power: "To say that resistance is prior to power is for me bound up with the notion that the object is in some ways prior to the discipline that is set in motion in order to regulate it. Marx talks about this specifically in terms of the ways in which worker insurgency actually calls the disciplinary techniques of capital into existence."[94] There is an insurgency inherent in that which is regulated, disciplined, and governed. A number of scholars have argued that "the resistance of the object" offers a way out of the unimaginable expansiveness of contemporary biopolitics.[95] For example, in trying to answer the question "How does life persist in escaping the grids of biopower?," Lynne Huffer argues that we escape biopower by "living our lives as works of art."[96] Antonio Negri similarly sees the production of new forms of life as *the* site of resistance to contemporary biopower. When life is subsumed under capital, the sites of power's rupture are generalized to all levels of society. Biopower is not simply power over life but also "the power . . . of life as the response to these powers." Negri adds, "When capital invests the entirety of life, life reveals itself as resistance."[97] This politics is described by Koerner when she rewrites Althusser's notion of interpellation in the description of a black teenager running from the police. Recall that for Althusser one becomes a subject when one responds to the hail of the police ("Hey, you there!"): "The hailed individual will turn around. By this mere one-hundred-and-eighty degree physical conversion, he becomes a subject." By stopping and facing the police, "the subject quite literally captures himself or herself."[98]

Althusser acknowledges that some "bad subjects" will not respond to the hail of the police and will simply flee the scene. Yet he never mentions how running away affects interpellation; thus Koerner characterizes Althusser's example as a structuralist scene because it cannot conceptualize movement. We are left to wonder *what of the subjects who don't turn around to meet the call of the police, but instead escape?* For Koerner fugitive descriptions of fleeing the police challenge Althusser's theory of interpellation. Indeed Jenny is always running away because in her experience, power is, at its heart, predatory. Yet she does not run toward a (neo)liberal subjectivity that aspires to the liberty of the market or freedom promised by the nation or the state. Nor does she make her way toward a reformed form of citizenship or leftist conception of a new nation. She runs toward something that is left unspoken and unimagined. If Jenny could see where fugitivity leads she would already be captured. One must continually take flight from what is already coming—from the past that captures the now, the future that is already here, and the everyday of the present that is already possessed. It's not that one escapes freedom—freedom is the practice of running away.

3. POSSESSED BY DEATH BLACK FEMINISM, QUEER TEMPORALITY, AND THE AFTERLIFE OF SLAVERY

In the wake, the past that is not past reappears, always, to rupture the present.

—CHRISTINA SHARPE, *In the Wake: On Blackness and Being*

In her 1978 essay, "Women in Prison: How We Are," the imprisoned Black Liberation Army member Assata Shakur wrote, "For many, prison is not that much different from the street. . . . For many cells are not that different from the tenements . . . and the welfare hotels they live in on the street. . . . The fights are the same except they are less dangerous. The police are the same. The poverty is the same. The alienation is the same. The racism is the same. The sexism is the same. The drugs are the same and the system is the same."[1] Shakur centers gender and sexuality in an analysis of a racialized field of knowledge, containment, and immobilization that manages populations subjected to "assigned disposability."[2] By repeating that the prison's power is "the same" within different spaces, Shakur outlines a massive system of biopolitical governance animated by antiblackness, heteropatriarchy, and capitalism. This system cannot be apprehended by "ideologies of discreteness" or universal knowledge.[3] Indeed, this is Shakur's point in writing about the particularities of the experiences of incarcerated women of color and queer women of color. She claims the regulations of a burgeoning neoliberal-carceral state possess life in ways that render the free world an extension of the prison. An assemblage of race, gender, capital, sexuality, policing, and penal technologies creates an intimacy between the deindustrialized city and the gendered racisms of emergent regimes of capture and caging. Diffuse structural networks of racism and sexism mimic the steel bars of a cage. This is the complicity between freedom and captivity, the entanglements between the living and the living dead, and the hemorrhaging of a buried past into the imagined progress of the present. To Shakur, prison looks like and *feels* like nineteenth-century chattel slavery: "We sit in the bull pen. We are all black. All restless. And we are all freezing."[4] Affect continually forces the past to open directly onto the present. The sensations and feelings of frozen skin speak in a way that words cannot. In prison, shivering black flesh weighted with chains looks like slavery. As a fugitive who escaped prison, went underground, and now has political asylum in Cuba, Shakur sees herself as a twenty-first-century runaway slave, a "maroon woman."[5]

Although Shakur's essay does not name neoliberalism explicitly, we can read it as a black feminist theorization of neoliberalism at the very moment of its emergence. It is a narration of the drastic racialized and gendered restructurings of social and economic life in the 1970s United States from the perspective of someone detained for resisting those changes. Written by a captured member of the underground black liberation movement, the text names the discourses and state violence neoliberalism requires yet erases. Neoliberalism is most certainly an economic doctrine that prioritizes the mobility and expansion of capital at all costs, but its mechanisms exceed the liberation of the market from the repression of the state. Shakur indicates that one of the conditions of possibility for the emergence of the neoliberal state is the kinship shared between the free world and the prison—an affinity structured and produced by a gendered antiblackness inaugurated under chattel slavery. Technologies of antiblack, heteropatriarchal violence queer time by making the separation between past and present look and feel indecipherable. This queer time is intimately connected to a queering of space where the division between free world and prison is indiscrete. By theorizing the neoliberal-carceral state's forceful effect on time and space, Shakur argues throughout the essay that technologies of immobilization specifically target black women. By reading black feminist texts from the 1970s as implicit theories of neoliberalism, we can come to understand the formation and implementation of neoliberalism in a new light. Shakur not only connects an emergent neoliberalism to a rapidly expanding prison regime; she also links the contemporary prison to chattel slavery, an institutional, affective, and discursive connection apprehended by Angela Davis's phrase "From the prison of slavery to the slavery of prison."[6]

The connections made by Shakur between the prison and neoliberalism, and between slavery and the prison, have been thoroughly explored by many scholars.[7] During the past two decades a growing body of scholarship has affirmed and extended Shakur's analysis of blackness, slavery, and the prison by exploring what Saidiya Hartman calls "the afterlife of slavery."[8] By centering racial terror in a genealogy of the prison, scholars have come to understand the barracoons, coffles, slave holds, and plantations of the Middle Passage as spatial, discursive, ontological, and economic analogues of modern punishment that have haunted their way into the present.[9] If the carceral becomes a functional, but not identical, surrogate for slavery's production of social and living death, then Shakur's text also hints at another connection that has garnered less attention: slavery's haunting possession of neoliberalism. While the prison's connection to slavery and the market has been well explored, the contemporary market's relationship to chattel slavery has largely been overlooked. If slavery's antiblack technologies inhabit and structure the prison, how do they live on in the operations of the market? What is the relationship between an antiblackness inaugurated under the Atlantic slave trade and the methods of population management used under neoliberalism? How does the absence, death, and loss left behind by slavery connect to the formation of the contemporary neoliberal-carceral state? What is the connection between the necropolitics of chattel slavery and the biopolitics of neoliberalism?

To answer these questions I analyze three texts written by captive and fugitive black women in the 1970s United States: Shakur's "Women in Prison: How We Are"; Safiya Bukhari's "Coming of Age: A Black Revolutionary"; and Davis's "Reflections on the Black Woman's Role in the Community of Slaves." All three texts were composed at the very moment of the neoliberal-carceral state's emergence and index the ways that black feminism developed under and critiqued this formation. I examine how Shakur, Bukhari, and Davis theorize the relationships among the carceral, the market, the population, and the body. While Davis's essay explores black women's experiences of terror and resistance under chattel slavery in order to contest the contemporary discourse of the black matriarch—a discourse foundational to neoliberalism—Bukhari's and Shakur's essays describe black women's experiences of gender, sexuality, race, violence, and incarceration in the early

1970s. I also include a discussion of Sherley Anne Williams's 1986 novel, *Dessa Rose*. Although the novel was written in the mid-1980s, in the author's note Williams cites Davis's essay—and the rise of the prison in the 1970s—as the inspiration for the novel. Williams uses fiction to recover the histories of enslaved fugitive black women Davis could not discover in the written record. Williams turns Davis's brief description of an uprising on a slave coffle led by a pregnant black woman into a novel that theorizes the racialized, gendered, affective, and economic politics of chattel slavery and its regimes of incarceration, torture, and terror. All the texts emerge from the late twentieth-century prison (and an emergent neoliberal state) in order to theorize chattel slavery as a history of our social, political, and economic present. They index how the neoliberal-carceral state queers normative notions of temporality as progress by highlighting how the past lives on in the present. Yet the texts do not queer time by deploying the conventions of fact; rather they use fiction, memory, and imagination to connect the forgotten, the lost, and the dead to the now. These texts insist that the absence of memory shapes the contours of the present. While many projects on the legacy of slavery utilize demographic data to measure slavery's extension into our present in positivist terms, I attempt to engage the past through its forgetting. I connect the powers of the market across time and space through nonnormative epistemologies that rely on affect, memory, and imagination. Indeed, it was the reason and rationality of mathematics, demographics, and insurance that produced millions of corpses in the service of making millions of commodities.

This chapter has three goals. First, it connects the powers of the market under slavery to the powers of the market under neoliberalism by exploring how imprisoned black feminists made sense of the afterlife of slavery in an emergent neoliberal state. Second, it uses black feminist engagements with loss to assert that death and loss undo the progress of time so that the past lives on within and possesses the present. By engaging death, loss, and forgetting, I connect penal and economic technologies in the 1970s United States to the carceral nature of the market under chattel slavery. I examine the power of contemporary regimes of marketization and capture not as a historically linear, mirror image of the economic and carceral systems foundational to chattel slavery but as forms of power possessed by a past that is not past—a past that possesses the present. As Christina Sharpe describes the "still unfolding aftermaths" of slavery, "Black subjection may have changed, but the fact and structure of that subjection remain."[10] Third, by constructing a critical genealogy of the market through the writings of black feminists working within and under the neoliberal-carceral state, I argue that the neoliberal-carceral state queers space and time by creating a regime of power whereby the market supplements and mimics the prison.

Possession, Death, and the Afterlife of Slavery

In *A Map to the Door of No Return: Notes to Belonging*, Dionne Brand writes of the Middle Passage:

> The door [of no return] signifies the historical moment which colours all moments in the Diaspora. It accounts for the ways we observe and are observed as people, whether it's through the lens of social injustice or the laws of human accomplishment. The door exists as an absence. A thing in fact which we do not know about, a place we do not know. Yet, it exists as the ground we walk. . . . Where one stands in a society seems always related to this historical experience. Where one can be observed is relative to that history. All human effort seems to emanate from this door.[11]

Brand argues that the Middle Passage and chattel slavery compose the original template for modern power. The door of no return is the site from which all disciplinary and biopolitical regimes emanate. It (and not it alone) determines the way people are regulated, visualized, mobilized, positioned, and organized. Yet the deathly touch of terror and the warm embrace of inclusion are not just stained from the original scene. What began at the door is also transmitted, transformed, renewed, and repositioned in our present day.[12] This is what Hartman calls the "afterlife of slavery," when premature death, incarceration, limited access to health care and education, and poverty are structured by the logics and technologies of chattel slavery.[13] Under this analytic the past does not give way to the present, slowly dissolving under the bright shining light of progress; slavery's afterlife is the past's possession of the present. The past holds the present captive—structuring, surrounding, and inhabiting it. The fabrication of concrete and compartmentalized conceptions of time and space dissolves under the crushing weight of the blood-stained gate. But this possession does not just take the form of the tactile, visible, and known. Part of the afterlife of slavery emanates from an absence that cannot be recovered or repaired. The door of no return is not a place; it is a gap that founds the now; it is history as the unknown.

The present rests upon this rupture, upon the unknowable, upon the forgotten, upon the dead.

In this chapter, I use the term *possession* as a modification of the concept of haunting. In *Ghostly Matters: Haunting and the Sociological Imagination*, Avery Gordon argues that haunting describes how that which seems to be *not there*—that is absent or missing—is often a "seething presence . . . acting on and meddling with taken for granted realities." A ghost is one way something lost, disappeared, or dead makes itself known. Engaging a haunting requires considering the apparitions lingering outside the frame of disciplinary knowledge, to make contact with the reality of fictions and the fictions of reality, to reckon with "endings that are not over" and past events that "loiter in the present."[14] If haunting names the lingering presence of the dead in the realm of the living—the present absence of what is there and yet hidden, the feeling that there is something in the room with you even when your eyes tell you otherwise—then *possession* is when the ghost does not haunt but takes hold. Possession is when the ghost inhabits and controls. To be haunted is to see the ghost that has been waiting for your field of vision to change. Possession is not so passive and patient. Unlike a ghost, possession does not wait; it grabs hold of you first, perhaps without your knowledge. What seizes you are not the murmurs of the oppressed or the whispered demands of those killed by state violence and terror; possession is the deathly grip of the dominant. Possession is a "psychological state in which an individual's normal personality is replaced by another," "domination by something (as an evil spirit, a passion, or an idea)," or "something owned, occupied, or controlled."[15] To be possessed is to be under the control of something more powerful than the imagined free will of the liberal individual. Possession is a name for the queering force of temporality; it is the present captured and shaped by the events we call the past.

We can witness possession in the relationship between race, gender, and death as theorized under the rubric of black feminism in the 1970s. For example, in her 1968 essay, "The Black Revolution in America," included in Toni Cade Bambara's collection *The Black Woman: An Anthology*, Grace Lee Boggs argues that American capitalism was born out of the labor of black slaves and has since used white workers to "defend the system and . . . keep Blacks in their place at the bottom of the ladder, scavenging the old jobs, old homes, old churches, and old schools discarded by whites . . . thereby contributing to the overall capital of the country." She goes on to outline a regime of biopolitical management animated by this history: "They [black youth] also recognize that although a particular struggle may be precipitated by an individual incident, their struggle is not against just one or another individual but against a whole power structure comprising a complex network of politicians, university and school administrators, landlords, merchants, usurers, realtors, insurance personnel, contractors, union leaders, licensing and inspection bureaucrats, racketeers, lawyers, policemen—the overwhelming majority of whom are white and absentee, and who exploit the black ghetto the same way the Western powers exploit the colonies and neo-colonies in Africa, Asia, and Latin America."[16] In a theory of power as possession, slavery's relationship to the present is more than the haunting of a ghost. Slavery's social, political, economic, and legal regimes are not lurking behind contemporary formations of power. Instead the "complex network" of biopolitical regulation and management outlined by Boggs is given life by an antiblackness as old as liberal freedom. Contemporary biopolitics is possessed by discourses and technologies produced under slavery that were carried into the future (our present) by a "concentric/accumulative" temporal economy of power.[17] Extending Ruth Wilson Gilmore's definition of racism as "state-sanctioned or extralegal production and exploitation of group-differentiated vulnerability to premature death," we can understand race and death as a possession born out of the genocide of conquest and the racial terror of slavery.[18] Being placed at the "bottom of the ladder" by an expansive network of racialized management and control is Boggs's way of describing the uneven distribution of value and disposability produced by slavery's ongoing force in the present. Although death is normally conceptualized as a natural biological phenomenon, it is more often manufactured and distributed by regimes of power far removed from one's last breath or slowing heartbeat. Race is one such technology; it is a mechanism for distributing life and death, and it is animated by a past of subjection, subjugation, torture, terror, and disposability that has changed shape and name but has not ended. Race possesses life in both the biological and biopolitical sense, ending or extending biological life for individuals and populations. While race sometimes haunts, it more often forcefully inhabits—and death and life are the outcome.

The relationship between race and possession is also evident in the writing of prisoners and activists in the 1970s who connect the contemporary prison to chattel slavery. Within this body of work the contemporary prison is animated by logics, technologies, and discourses constructed under nineteenth-century U.S. slavery. For countless prisoners and activists, race (and antiblackness) were instruments that transcended space and time so that the past could invade and contort the present in its image. For instance, in his best-selling collection of prison writing, Soledad Brother, published in 1970, George Jackson describes how the prison's connection to slavery reverses, compresses, and undoes the progress of time: "My recall is nearly perfect, time has faded nothing. I recall the very first kidnap. I've lived through the passage, died on the passage, lain in the unmarked shallow graves of the millions who fertilized the Amerikan soil with their corpses; cotton and corn growing out of my chest, 'unto the third and fourth generation,' the tenth, the hundredth."[19] Jackson describes the relationships among memory, time, and possession. His captive body is metaphorically infested with the cotton and corn grown in the prison of the plantation. Time did not wash away the horrors of slavery; it modified and intensified them. Jackson both lives the past and continues to live its afterlives. He feels possessed by the forms of death produced under slavery. Throughout his larger body of writing he connects this undead past to his "living death" in prison. This possession is not temporally constrained; neither the law nor the state can exorcise this death sentence. Instead, Jackson argues that the United States "must be destroyed" and that anything less would be "meaningless to the great majority of the slaves."[20] His theories and declaration that "I am a slave to, and of, property" were not unique among members of the black liberation movement.[21] The work of Shakur and Davis is one of the lines of flight that proceed and depart from the thought of Jackson and the black liberation movement. Indeed, Davis dedicates "Reflections" to Jackson's life (cut short by his murder by prison guards) and his struggle against his own misogyny.

Although the connections between slavery and the prison are important to my thinking in this chapter, I am also interested in more expansive understandings of the afterlife of slavery. For instance, Sharpe argues that our very subjectivity is indebted to and born out of the "discursive codes of slavery and post-slavery." Engaging and analyzing a "post-slavery subjectivity" means examining subjectivities constituted by transatlantic slavery and connecting them to present (and past) "mundane horrors that aren't acknowledged to be horrors."[22] Omise'eke Tinsley describes one contour of this: "The brown-skinned, fluid-bodied experiences now called blackness and queerness surfaced in intercontinental, maritime contacts hundreds of years ago: in the seventeenth century, in the Atlantic Ocean."[23] This is one of the main projects of black feminism, as exemplified by Hortense Spillers's classic essay, "Mama's Baby, Papa's Maybe: An American Grammar Book," where she connects slavery to the life of the symbolic world: "Even though the captive flesh/body has been 'liberated,' and no one need pretend that even the quotation marks do not matter, dominant symbolic activity, the ruling episteme that releases the dynamics of naming and valuation, remains grounded in originating metaphors of captivity and mutilation, so that it is as if neither time nor history, nor historiography or its topics, show movement, as the human subject is 'murdered' over and over again by the passions of a bloodless and anonymous archaism, showing itself in endless disguise."[24] Like Jackson and Shakur, Spillers argues that slavery ruptures the progress of time. The ways meaning and value are institutionalized have been determined by the violence and terror of slavery. Slavery's centrality to racial capitalism manufactured a death sentence enacted across generations, one that changes name and shape as time passes. Freedom presupposes and builds on slavery so that postslavery subjectivities are shaped by forms of power that resemble and sometimes mimic power under slavery (force, terror, sexual violence, compulsion, torture), while they are also confined by the postemancipation technologies of consent, reason, will, and choice.[25] Frank Wilderson summarizes this more expansive understanding of the afterlife of slavery: "The imaginary of the state and civil society is parasitic on the Middle Passage. Put another way, No slave, no world." According to Wilderson, slavery connotes an ontological (not experiential) status for blackness, one that is shaped not by exploitation and alienation but by accumulation and fungibility (the condition of being owned and traded).[26] Slavery does not lay dormant in the past but is attached to the political ontology of blackness and whiteness.

As freedom navigated the late nineteenth and twentieth centuries it was not innocent and it did not come alone. Something from the past held on to freedom as it maneuvered time and space. Freedom was possessed by a ghost wished away by (neo)liberal thought that did not so easily disappear. Time does not erase what has happened, dissolving terror and violence into the progress of the future, nor is the past passively sedimented in the present. Rather the past returns to the present in expanded form so that the present "finds stored and accumulated within itself a nonsynchronous array of past times."[27] In the 1970s, when the market produced the freedom of capital mobility, individuality, and choice and the prison manufactured the freedom of safety and security, the spirit of slavery dictated the movements and meanings of that freedom. Today the spirit of slavery lives on in more ways than one can imagine: in the shade of tree-lined suburban streets, in definitions and measures of human value, in the prosperity and health of some, and in the hail of the police as one walks down the street. It guides bullets and bombs, makes visible what we see, and vanishes what is right in front of us. It is laced in the cement and steel of the prison, solidified in dreams of liberation, and embedded in psychic life. Although it is sometimes recognizable, it also lives on in what we do not know and cannot remember—in the lives erased, expunged, ended, or that were simply never recorded to begin with. Whether it comes as spectacle or something one cannot see or feel, it is always there. The spirit of slavery does more than meddle in the present; it has intensified, seduced, enveloped, and animated contemporary formations of power. Possession names the ways the operations of corporate, state, individual, and institutional bodies are sometimes beyond the self-possessed will of the living. Something else is in control, something that may feel like nothing even as it compels movement, motivates ideology, and drives the organization of life and death. Slavery is not a ghost lingering in the corner of the room; its spirit animates the architecture of the house as a whole. The past does not merely haunt the present; it *composes* the present. As Toni Morrison writes, "All of it is now, it is always now."[28]

Black Feminism and an Unthinkable History of the Present

In the closing section of Shakur's essay, "What of Our Past? What of Our History? What of Our Future?," she seamlessly connects the past, present, and future in an attempt to develop the psychological force needed to build a "strong black women's movement."[29] Black feminism is a movement that emerged amid the crises of global capitalism, white supremacy, heteropatriarchy, and state power that spanned the 1960s and 1970s. Neoliberalism is the state and corporate response to these crises.[30] Black feminism also emerged out of the failures of white feminism to center (or even consider) race and white supremacy and the inability of the black nationalist and black liberation movements to theorize and analyze gender, sexuality, and heteropatriarchy. Thus some white feminist and black nationalist movements were complicit with the forms of power they imagined they opposed. When white feminism failed to critique the white supremacy of the state, and black nationalists were unable to critique heteropatriarchy, both formations so-lidified racialized and gendered discourses that contradicted (and undid) their aspirations for freedom and liberation.

We can place Shakur's and Davis's black feminist essays within the larger epistemological formation "women of color feminism" that arose in the 1970s and 1980s to mark the contradictions of late twentieth-century U.S. capitalism. Women of color feminism emerged and expanded alongside the neoliberal-carceral state and, in the case of Shakur's and Davis's work, from within the prison and the underground. By analyzing race, gender, class, sexuality, and the state as interlocking and colluding mechanisms of power, women of color feminism can name the ways multiply determined difference is simultaneously central to and yet incessantly disavowed in the production and reproduction of capital. Most critically, it understands race, gender, and sexuality not as static categories of identification but as pro-cesses that produce value and disposability for individuals, populations, and forms of knowledge.[31]

For Grace Kyungwon Hong women of color feminism names that which cannot be apprehended under normative ideals or hegemonic epistemolo-gies. As a way of knowing, women of color feminism names the repressed, the erased, and the expunged at the very moment of their formation and articulation. For longer than we can know, black feminists have argued that slavery is central to the economic, political, and social present, in contrast to dominant epistemologies, which relegate slavery to a quarantined and dor-mant past. Therefore black feminism is one epistemological formation that is able to challenge the ways that the normal and banal are mobilized to ob-scure violence, terror, and death. By showing how slavery's afterlife shapes the present, black feminists have made visible forms of violence that are hidden by their normality. Black feminist scholars and activists have worked tirelessly to make visible what often goes unseen and unsaid, to reckon with the endings that are not over, and to make connections between past and present that are unthought. Black feminism engages "the shadows and what is living there," naming what has never entered the archives that constitute evidence and fact.[32] As we will see, the work of Davis, Shakur, and Williams analyzes what is unthought, unknown, or illegible in dominant forms of thought.

If chattel slavery's foundational relationship to the contemporary distri-bution of life and death is often undertheorized, overlooked, or erased in normative epistemologies (and in progressive, radical, feminist, and queer formations), its connection to capitalism is an epistemological impossibility. Under the historical terms that frame the Western political economy, understanding slavery as capitalism is unthinkable because there are no adequate epistemological instruments available to make sense of such a connection.[33] According to Walter Johnson, in both Smithian and Marxist economics slavery is an untheorized foundation of the history of capitalism, "an un-thought (even when present) past to the inevitable emergence of the present."[34] Slavery is understood to have a temporal relation to capitalism instead of a spatial one. That is, slavery is theorized as precapitalist, as opposed to animating, colluding with, or being indistinguishable from capitalism.[35] The problem of slavery's status as the unthinkable history of capitalism is not isolated to the shortcomings of economic theory; it stems from Western liberal epistemologies.

As discussed in chapter 2, proponents of neoliberalism are not alone in the forced forgetting of slavery and racial subjection. Slavery's status as an unthinkable history of the present is also evident in critical scholarship on neoliberalism. More specifically, slavery as the unthought structures the way critical theories of neoliberalism understand the relationships among the economic, the social, the population, and the body. For instance, in his book *Neoliberalism: A Short History*, David Harvey argues that neoliberalism produces the "financialization of everything" by intensifying the market's hold over daily life.[36] Harvey and many other scholars understand neoliberalism through a historical teleology in which capitalism is regressing to a point never before witnessed. For instance, Harvey writes, "Neoliberalization has unquestionably rolled back the bounds of commodification and greatly extended the reach of legal contracts."[37] Neoliberalism has broken the liberal divisions among the social, economic, and political so that the economic reaches beyond its supposed isolated domain. Under "neoliberal governmentality" market-driven truths and calculations infiltrate the domain of politics.[38] Within this narrative, the 1970s signal a change in the relationship between the market and life.

Foucault proposes that an economic rationality became a way of producing knowledge about (while also regulating) marriage, raising and educating children, health, and criminality. The economic was mobilized to make sense of the social; at the same time the market was promoted as the appropriate device for production of the social good.[39] Under 1970s neoliberalism, everything could be filtered through the scientific rationality of the economist. The market became a mechanism and a paradigm for regulating all aspects of life. The economic became a model of "social relations and existence itself, a form of relationship of the individual to himself, time, those around him, the group, and the family."[40] Foucault claims that neoliberalism pushes the economic into the social so that they become indistinct. Under neoliberalism, according to Wendy Brown, "market principles frame every sphere and activity, from mothering to mating, from learning to criminality, from planning one's family to planning one's death."[41] When neoliberalism converts the social into the economic, when the market infiltrates the political and life itself, we witness "the end of liberal democracy" and the "twilight of equality."[42]

Marxist theories understand neoliberalism to be a countermobilization by the state and capital against the labor movement. Within this narrative neoliberalism is a global strategy of accumulation that funnels capital back to the ruling class. This narrative of the primacy of class and capital over race and white supremacy holds even when slavery is considered. In "Neoliberal Political Economy, Biopolitics and Colonialism: A Transcolonial Genealogy of Inequality," Couze Venn argues that a genealogy of neoliberalism's biopolitics must account for colonialism and slavery. Yet even when slavery is thought, it still disappears. Venn writes, "The Triangular Trade is but one among a host of other examples that demonstrates that, underlying the process of accumulation, we find the deliberate and planned establishment of dispositifs to ensure wealth transfer to the rich and powerful."[43] Venn insists that slavery, like neoliberalism, is a transnational project of wealth accumulation. It is a global project for the production of a ruling class. The body of the slave is theorized as a form of wealth abstracted from race and gender. Slavery is about class and wealth, not the production of a transnational racial ontology. But Hartman cautions, "However, representing the slave through the figure of the worker (albeit unwaged and unfree), obscures as much as it reveals, making it difficult to distinguish the constitutive elements of slavery as a mode of power, violence, dispossession and accumulation or to attend to the forms of gendered and sexual violence that enable these processes."[44] By equating slavery with other mechanisms mobilized to redistribute wealth, slavery's heteropatriarchal antiblackness is expelled from capital's operations, even as, in the words of Spillers, "the socio-political order of the new world" is inaugurated by approaching the black body with a structuring logic of force, accumulation, and death.[45] In short, slavery's connection to neoliberalism often remains unthinkable even when it is addressed.

The predominant narrative about the relationships among the market, the body, population, and life under neoliberalism rests on the unthinkability of slavery. That is, the theories and epistemologies mobilized to make sense of neoliberalism are incapable of connecting slavery to neoliberalism's biopolitics. My argument is not that slavery is *like* neoliberalism but that the racialized and gendered logics, discourses, and biopolitical power of the market under slavery possess and structure the market under neoliberalism. Indeed if "neoliberalism is merely the most recent [form of] governmentality that relies on market knowledge and calculations for a politics of subjection and subject-making," then what is the role of slavery's production of global capital, race, and technologies of subjection in this process?[46] If neoliberal freedom requires the expulsion of the past from the present, how can a genealogy of neoliberalism that centers slavery alter how we understand neoliberalism's operations? What histories of the market and the economy can black feminism provide so that we tell a different story about neoliberalism?

If slavery's relationship to capitalism and the present more broadly is unthinkable and unthought, black feminism is uniquely situated to engage such epistemological impossibilities. Women of color feminism broadly and black feminism more specifically necessarily engage the erasures inherent in regimes of knowledge. As an analytic, it confronts what is unthinkable and unknowable.[47] For instance, in the author's note to *Dessa Rose* Williams writes, "This novel, then, is fiction; all the characters, even the country they travel through, while based on fact, are inventions. [But] what is here is as true as if I myself had lived it."[48] Like the memoirs of underground activists, fiction remembers forcefully forgotten memories and histories.[49] Fiction functions as a type of truth, an "imaginative archive."[50] To fully make sense of the present we must engage this archive. Yet Williams recovers the past not to fill a historical void—the void cannot be filled—but to confront fragmentation, displacement, and loss as processes foundational to the production of knowledge. This is a process that embraces the fictions of fact and the facts buried in fiction.[51] It is a genealogy of loss that leads not to the buried truths of subjugated knowledges but to the unknowable gaps that make possible what we call knowledge. What is foreclosed as unknowable—what we do not and will never know— saturates what can be known and is fundamentally constitutive of what remains. Katherine McKittrick describes this analytic: "Reconstructing what has been erased, or what is being erased, requires confronting the rationalization of human and spatial domination; reconstruction requires 'seeing' and 'sighting' that which is both expunged, and 'rightfully erasable.' What you cannot see, and cannot remember, is part of a larger geographic project that thrives on forgetting and displacing blackness."[52]

Within this epistemological economy, the unthinkable, the unseen, and the unknowable produce the thinkable and the possible. As Hartman asks, "Was the experience of slavery best represented by all the stories I would never know?" and "How does one write about an encounter with nothing?"[53] In her memoir *Lose Your Mother: A Journey along the Atlantic Slave Route*, Hartman returns to the slave dungeons on the Gold Coast hoping to find ancestors and a history. What she finds is the dust and waste of those who entered the door of no return. She finds the emptiness left by slavery's regimes of unimaginable violence and terror, the nothingness left by the deaths of 60 million or more. All that is left is sunlight shining through a barred window. To Hartman, even as slavery's afterlife is crushing, visible, and pervasive, it also looks like dust floating in dead, stale air. Slavery's mark on the now manifests as the prison, as poverty, as policing technologies, in insurance ledgers, and in the organization of space, but it also emerges in the space cleared by so much death. Slavery's afterlife emerges in the gaps between the written down, the forgotten, and the never will be. There is an unspeakable loss left by the relationships, love, knowledge, feelings, and stories disappeared with those who were drowned, starved, murdered, and worked to death. The shape of the world emerges from what we will never know. By engaging the unknowable, black feminism can help make connections between past and present that other epistemologies leave unthought and unthinkable. These are connections that have been lost or that can be remembered only in the imagination. Fugitive in their operation, they are connections that take flight from the constraints of (neo)liberal thought.

Loss, Forgetting, and the Shape of the Now

Written while she was a captured fugitive in the Marin County Jail, Davis's essay "Reflections on the Black Woman's Role in the Community of Slaves" is an attempt at making unthinkable connections across time and space, to give a language to a "subject still awaiting her verb."[54] Davis refutes the liberal and black nationalist concept of the black matriarch by analyzing the ways that black women resisted the social and living death of enslavement. According to Davis, the discourse of the black matriarch emerged under chattel slavery as one form of counterinsurgency against enslaved women's foundational role in leading uprisings, guiding resistance, and making sabotage possible. The concept of the black matriarch was a form of "ideological warfare" used to erase histories of black women's resistance to racial and sexual terror.[55] In addition, it rendered valueless the systems of care they created in order to survive. Finally, the weaponized discourse of the black matriarch made heteropatriarchy a valued norm that possessed the present day.[56]

Like Spillers's theory of temporality, whereby "the dynamics of naming and valuation" are possessed by "captivity and mutilation" so that the present is ossified in the past, Davis argues that by taking the form of the black matriarch, seemingly anachronistic temporalities not only accumulate; they also capture.[57] Her conception of discourse and its relation to temporality means that time is a form of captivity, one that makes her what Spillers calls a "marked woman."[58] Davis is marked by a history of violence, trauma, and terror that alters normative conceptions of temporality. In other words, antiblackness and heteropatriarchy are epistemological and bodily forces, but they are also temporal intensities that structure life itself. The black matriarch thus operates as a "controlling image" that maneuvers time and space in a way that queers the linearity of temporality.[59] As a discourse, it carries the crushing weight of the past into the present and wraps the now in its queer embrace.

According to Davis, the discourse of the black matriarch also produced black women as outside normative gender regimes because in order to "extract the greatest possible surplus from slaves" black women were "released from the chains of the myth of femininity." Enslaved black women were "annulled" from the category of woman and thus shared in the "deformed equality of equal oppression" with black men. Yet the production of black women as gender-nonnormative was central to the creation of fugitive life under racial capitalism and antiblack terror; it made other ways of organizing life amid death possible: "Stripped of the palliative feminine veneer which might have encouraged a passive performance of domestic tasks, she was now uniquely capable of weaving into the warp and woof of domestic life a profound consciousness of resistance."[60] What the market tried to capture—the networks of care, intimacy, sustenance, and love created by enslaved black women—were not exhausted or confined by its operations.[61] Significantly, Davis recovers histories of black women's fugitivity and resistance that are "untranslatable into the lexicon of the political" through an engagement with loss, forgetting, and death.[62] The essay is an act of historical recovery, a gesture of insurgency, but it is also an implicit meditation on loss.

In her note to the essay, Davis apprehends the relationships among her lack of knowledge, the prison, and slavery when she acknowledges the difficulty of writing and researching while incarcerated: "The chief problem I encountered stemmed from the conditions of my incarceration: opportunities for researching the issue I wanted to explore were extremely limited. I chose, therefore, to entitle this piece 'reflections. . . .' It does not pretend to be more than a collection of ideas which would constitute a starting point—a framework within which to conduct rigorous reinvestigation of the black woman as she interacted with her people and with her oppressive environment."[63] The administration would not allow Davis access to the materials she required to produce rigorous scholarship. As a result the essay is partial; her ability to know more completely was rendered impossible. We can read Davis's description of life as an imprisoned scholar as a theorization of the prison as an institution that regulates the production of knowledge. The prison arose as a system of bodily immobilization and a regime of power that produces, manages, and regulates what and how we know. In addition, her incomplete recovery of the histories of enslaved black women speaks to the ways that slavery was a regime of racialized economic exploitation and terror, but like the prison, it was also a regime of power that regulated, produced, disciplined, and eradicated knowledge. Even as Davis was held within the "slavery of prison" she could only reflect—or imagine—the connections between the past that brought her to her imprisoned present. Imagination and reflection were necessary for two reasons: the prison denied her access to research materials, and the facts, testimonies, stories, and records she needed to compose a factual account of black women under slavery were never recorded to begin with. As Jenny Sharpe writes of enslaved black women, "We have much to learn, but can never fully know."[64] In fact Williams was motivated to write *Dessa Rose* because of the necessary partialness of Davis's essay. The novel recovers the histories of enslaved black women Davis was unable to discover; it recovers what does not exist in the written record of slavery. Williams writes in the author's note to *Dessa Rose*:

Dessa Rose is based on two historical incidents. A pregnant black woman helped to lead an uprising on a coffle (a group of slaves chained together and herded, usually to market) in 1829 in Kentucky.

Caught and convicted, she was sentenced to death; her hanging, how-ever, was delayed until after the birth of her baby. In North Carolina in 1830, a white woman living on an isolated farm was reported to have given sanctuary to runaway slaves. I read of the first incident in Angela Davis' seminal essay, "Reflections on the Black Woman's Role in the Community of Slaves" (*The Black Scholar*, December 1971). In tracking Davis to her source in Herbert Aptheker's *American Negro Slave Revolts* (New York, 1947), I discovered the second incident. How sad, I thought then, that these two women never met.[65]

Williams's use of fiction to recover slavery's production of loss is not unique. *Dessa Rose* was published just one year before Toni Morrison's *Beloved*. Both novels remember the past as a mixture of fact, memory, and imagination. Both critique the limitations of realist forms and positivist history to re-cover and circulate the forgotten. They can be considered examples of what Sherryl Vint calls "the postmodern slave narrative," a form that compels us to question the discourses embedded within realistic representations of slavery in dominant history.[66] Slave narratives were often shaped and edited to be palatable for sympathetic white readers. White desire for the horrors of slavery to be "delicate" and "veiled" determined what entered the written record. But even when the truth was altered, there was still doubt. Har-riet Jacobs (Linda Brendt) begins her *Incidents in the Life of a Slave Girl* by assuring readers, "This narrative is no fiction. I am aware that some of my adventures may seem incredible, but they are, nevertheless, strictly true. I have not exaggerated the wrongs inflicted by slavery; on the contrary my de-scriptions fall short of the facts."[67] Jacobs insists she is telling the truth even as her truth is undone by what she leaves out. The absences she produces by amputating pieces of the truth exist to please the white readers who would doubt the veracity of her story had she not left anything out. In other words, had she told the truth, her life would be unreal, so she censers the truth to make her life seem more realistic. The fiction of her fact is produced by the desire for a fiction one can pretend is fact. Truth is evacuated so the story is digestible to the sympathetic white imagination.

Elsewhere Jacobs observes, "No pen can give adequate description of the all-pervading corruption produced by slavery."[68] While some facts are too awful to speak, others are too horrifying to capture in writing. The vio-lence and terror of slavery exceed representation. It is both unspeakable and unknowable. But where facts fail, the imagination steps in. Morrison and

Williams reject conventional distinctions between fact and fiction, arguing that there is a truth of the slave's experience that has been left out of both traditional slave narratives and official discourses on slavery. Morrison calls her imaginings a kind of "literary archeology" that recovers a "truth about the interior life of people who didn't write it (which doesn't mean that they didn't have it)."[69] If we are to truly reckon with the history of slavery and make sense of its afterlife, we must engage the unspeakable and unknowable; one way this is accomplished is in literature. Taking flight from the dominant production of knowledge, fiction is where the truth we must remember lies in wait.

For Davis and Williams prison and slavery produce the absence of memory, or, to paraphrase Jenny Sharpe, a story that was not recorded from the start—a story that only exists as an absence.[70] The epistemological loss that *Dessa Rose* recovers in fiction is central to our ability to make sense of the now. With the recovery of a never recorded past, Williams connects the prison to slavery, but also offers a genealogy of the powers of the market that leads to the coffle, the sweat box, the auction block, and the plantation. It is by engaging what has been lost and how it was left behind that Williams and Davis make sense of the present—a present in which life is lived in loss because abolition did not redress the crimes and horrors of slavery but only located its death sentence elsewhere.[71] The absence produced by slavery is part of the foundation of the present, a process that all three texts engage. For this reason it is worth exploring *Dessa Rose*'s theorization of history and slavery before turning to the market and our neoliberal present.

Dessa Rose addresses the relationships among death, forgetting, history, and slavery by remembering the past through fiction and critiquing the production of knowledge about slavery and enslaved people. For instance, Dessa, the novel's protagonist, is incarcerated in the basement of a sheriff's farm after helping to lead an uprising on a slave coffle in which five white men were killed and for which thirty-one slaves were executed and nineteen branded or flogged. Dessa was sold to the coffle after she attacked her former master for killing her lover (an enslaved person named Kaine). The novel follows Dessa from when she attacks her master to the uprising on the coffle, her incarceration, and her escape and refuge on an old rundown plantation where a white woman lets fugitive slaves live. Dessa's logic for attacking her master inverts slavery's logic of disposability: "I kill white mens. . . . I kill white mens cause the same reason Masa kill Kaine. Cause

I can."[72] It is her reasoning that makes her so terrifying to the police and to a researcher who comes to interview her.

While detained for her participation in the uprising on the coffle, barely visible in the shadow of the cellar, Dessa is interviewed and interrogated by a scholar researching the management of captive populations for his newest book, *The Roots of Rebellion in the Slave Population and Some Means for Eradicating Them*. The scholar, Adam Nehemiah (or Nemi), wants to understand Dessa's history in order to develop more effective methods for quelling rebellion—for making fugitivity impossible. Summarizing the life of his research subject, the "devil woman" who "attacked white men and roused other niggers to rebellion," Nemi writes:

> These are the facts of the darky's history as I have thus far uncovered them:
>
> The master smashed the young bucks banjo.
> The young buck attacked the master.
>
> The master killed the young buck.
> The Darky attacked the master—and was sold
> to the Wilson slave coffle.[73]

Nehemiah's conversion of Dessa's life into five lines, "the facts of the darky's history," represents the form of historical truth that the novel as a whole contests. This is a history in which black will and agency are intelligible only as criminal transgression, in which Dessa's attack on her captor (master), the murderer of her lover, can be understood only as what Nemi calls "a fantastical fiction." Black will, love, and killing rage are not intelligible to the historical record Nemi is composing. The facts are too outrageous—something for romance novels, if novels, as Nemi points out, were about black people. The only aspects of Dessa's life worth remembering are those that explain why she incited rebellion on the coffle. In this way, Nemi mobilizes the power of knowledge for discursive capture and bodily containment. After Dessa escapes from the basement, Nemi becomes obsessed with tracking and capturing her. Here we find the scholar as the captor of fugitive thought and on the hunt for a fugitive slave. The capture of knowledge and the body are demanded by the scholar–slave catcher. When he finds her at the end of the novel, his scholarship becomes proof of who she really is: "I know it's her. . . . I got her down here in my book . . . it's all here. . . . She walks on the insides of her feet from being on the chain. Her hair fit like a cap on her head underneath that scarf. I know her. . . . Science. Research. The mind of the darky."[74] The history Nemi has produced abolishes Dessa's personhood and attempts to (re)capture her body. Chains can be broken and white men killed, but racial knowledge is another prison for Dessa that knows no bounds. Nemi's words are history as an apparatus of capture, a history that is produced by racial torture and terror. Dessa takes flight by contesting his knowledge and the slave system's technologies of capture and caging.

In his pursuit of the most rational and effective methods for population management, Nemi, under the supervision of the local sheriff Hughes, punches, threatens with death, and starves the chained Dessa: "Nonetheless he has prevailed upon Hughes to institute the saltwater treatment: no food and nothing but heavily salted water to drink. They had gotten results; he glanced at where his journal, still open to the day's entry, lay at the makeshift table."[75] Nemi's research journal is full of knowledge gained from torturing Dessa. But what Dessa does not tell him, and thus keeps out of the historical record, is what composes the rest of novel. If Nemi's facts silence and capture the fugitivity of the slave, fiction enables the ghosts of slavery to speak.[76] Reflection and imagination can point to something else that will never be known or that was never allowed to be.

When Dessa speaks, she refuses slavery's politics of accounting and methods of measuring value by naming the forgotten, by remembering what Nemi could not and would not see as having value or significance for the historical record. *Dessa Rose* remembers the dead whose names were never written down and thus registers the absences that shape our present. For instance, in a fight with Rufel, the white woman who lets runaway slaves stay on her farm provided they work her fields for free and who cannot remember the name of the enslaved woman who raised her, Dessa recalls the names of the dead "until speech became too painful":

> Dessa heaved herself to her knees, flinging her words in the white woman's face. "Mammy gave birth to ten chi'ren that come in the world living." She counted them off on her fingers. "The first one Rose after herself; the second one died before the white folks named it. Mammy called her Minta after a cousin she met once. Seth was the first child lived to go into the fields. Little Rose died while mammy was carrying Amos—carried off by the diphtheria. Thank God, He spared Seth." Remembering the names now the way mammy used to tell them,

lest they forget, she would say; lest her poor, lost children *die to living memory* as they had in her world. . . . Even buried under years of silence, Dessa could not forget.[77]

Dessa contests the way racial capitalism's financialization of life produces death and loss. She remembers what Nemi's history and the market's ledgers erase and forget: the names a sympathetic white woman cannot recall. We can contrast Dessa's remembering of names and lives recorded nowhere else with the entanglement of death, knowledge, and the market in the ledgers of slave ships and plantations. According to Ian Baucom, the slaves who died in the hold of a ship or the turbulence of the sea are unknowable: "We know almost nothing of them . . . Not as individuals. As 'types' they are at least partially knowable, or imaginable."[78] An unimaginable number of slaves did not survive the passage. However, their deaths and value live on in the records of an emergent global capitalism and the ontology of an ascending racial order.

February 4	One slave purchased: a man.
February 5	The captain orders the crew to check and clean their guns; purchases one woman.
February 7	One woman.
February 9	One woman.
February 13	Two men.
February 14	Canoe sent upshore for water; one man and one woman.
February 15	One man.
February 17	First child purchased, a boy; the captain also buys a woman.[79]

Or simply the name of death:

Dysentery.
Insanity.
Consumption.
Ditto.
Ditto.
Ditto.
Ditto.[80]

As evidenced by Williams and Davis, an engagement with slavery's afterlife means we must make sense of what we know and how we know it, who we are and how we got here, but it also means making sense of that which never was. It means looking at dust for a trace of the past and connecting the present to the absence of memory. Slavery lives on in what we can see and feel, but also in what feels like nothing, in the absence left by the millions who lie at the bottom of the ocean or under rows of cotton and rice. Within such an analytic—one provided by black feminism—one must see what is not there, feel the trace of a form of power that cannot be named, and as Williams argues, one must remember what was never written down. If one of the purposes of fact is to constrain thought, limit its power to the proof of records and documented events, then imagination is the tool required to confront the unknowable. If history is more than a flash or revelation, if it is a piling up, if time does not pass but accumulates, then one must be able to search the wreckage, but also see what was destroyed along the way.[81]

By remembering the never recorded details, intricacies, and intimacies of the life of a rebel and fugitive slave, Williams positions fiction as an archive of facts that have been disappeared while also mobilizing fact to contest the fictions produced by the neoliberal-carceral state. Williams's fiction and Davis's reflective essay contest the knowledge (and lack of knowledge) produced by Nemi's research and slavery more broadly. By engaging the unthinkable, the unthought, and the forcefully forgotten, black feminism levels a critique of the regimes of knowledge that structure the racial state and capitalism. *Dessa Rose* contests the power of white supremacy, the market, and speculative reason to produce the unknowable by remembering the past through imagination. It apprehends the assemblage of biopolitical and necropolitical power composed by the life of chattel slavery and its afterlife in the prison and beyond. Davis and Williams connect the absence of death and forgetting to the ground we stand on. As the power of the market resurged in the 1970s and 1980s, Williams reminds us where that power came from and what it was able to do. By operating within a fugitive epistemological economy, black feminism is able to make connections between the prison and slavery and, as we will see, neoliberalism and slavery. Davis and Williams offer us a history of the present that does not exist elsewhere. They refuse to let the unknowable relegate slavery to the realm of the unthinkable. They engage the past through its very forgetting—a forgetting that is foundational to the neoliberal-carceral state.

In its engagement with the unknowable and unthinkable, black feminism makes possible a critical genealogy of neoliberalism and biopolitics that can account for chattel slavery. We can then understand antiblackness and heteropatriarchy as foundational to neoliberalism, and we can adjust our understanding of the relationships among the market, the body, and the population. Because black feminism is a formation that makes sense of the management of populations through an engagement with the production of terror and death, it can help us tell a different story about neoliberalism, one wherein the past lives on in the present, one wherein "all of it is now." We can understand the market in a similar capacity because the market functioned as a biopolitical and carceral technology under chattel slavery, and these logics continue to animate aspects of its operation. The market possessed the body, managed populations, and mimicked the carceral. By engaging a black feminist genealogy of slavery and the market—one composed by imprisoned, fugitive black feminists writing within an ascendant neoliberal state—we can understand the necropolitics of slavery as possessing the biopolitics of neoliberalism. In other words, it is not only the slavery of prison that is central to neoliberalism but also the prison of the market.

The Prison of the Market

In the passage that inspired Williams to write *Dessa Rose*, Davis captures the relationships among race, gender, sexuality, terror, and the market that were central to slavery: "During the same year [as the execution of a black woman charged with starting a fire], a group of slaves, being led from Maryland to be sold in the South, had apparently planned to kill the traders and make their way to freedom. One of the traders was successfully done away with, but eventually a posse captured all the slaves. Of the six leaders sentenced to death, one was a woman. She was first permitted, for *reasons of economy*, to give birth to her child. Afterwards, she was publicly hanged."[82] Enslaved black women were subjected to particular forms of racial terror, torture, and discipline. These forms of punishment, and the accompanying racial logics concerning the management of black life, were animated by the rationality of the market. The unnamed pregnant rebel's death was delayed to extract the capital growing in her body. Reproduction was enveloped by the market in order to commodify a life before it entered the world. The future of the child was possessed by the speculative value of the market: a baby was a future dispossessed and open to the fungibility of the economy in human flesh.[83] Slavery commodified life itself, producing what Hartman calls "the subject of accumulation."[84] As Davis shows, slavery's disciplinary and biopolitical regulation of black life was animated by the dictates of the market. For example, she argues that the concept of the black matriarch is a myth because it presumes an enslaved mother had authority over the life of her family and children. The myth of the black matriarch is "cruel because it ignores the profound traumas the black woman must have experienced when she had to surrender her child-bearing to alien and predatory economic interests."[85]

Motherhood was possessed and eradicated by the market; the enslaved female body became a factory that under the law replicated the slave across time.[86] Reproduction, race, gender, sexuality, and death were inextricably intertwined with the terror of the market. The market helped drive the punishment of the insurgent female black body while also taking hold of it with demands for profit. Skin, iron, and capital were linked as race and death created value. Under the logic of the Atlantic slave trade, the market's arithmetic of accumulation was sutured to the flesh, inhabiting the bodies and lives it stripped down to the sum of their biological parts for sale within the freedom of the market. This process marked the violent nexus among the market, discipline, and the production of life. The market was not a zone of freedom, but a zone of death and terror. The historian Stephanie Smallwood writes, "The violence exercised in the service of human commodification relied on scientific empiricism always seeking to find the limits of human capacity for suffering, that point where material and social poverty threatened to consume entirely the lives it was meant to garner for sale in the Americas. In this regard, the economic enterprise of human trafficking marked a watershed in what would become an enduring project in the modern world: probing the limits up to which it is possible to discipline the body without extinguishing the life within."[87] The central aim of this early biopolitical project was not to punish and torture but to slow the depletion of life in the name of economic efficiency. White supremacy and the market produced the shadow life of the slave within the space between life and death. While torture and terror were the outcomes for captives, their pain, panic, dread, and horror were unintelligible in the rational calculations and concerns of the market. The market decided how many rocks a body could ingest, how many bodies a ship could swallow, and where the line between life and death would reside. Out of social, living, and biological death, the human commodity would live so that bodies, value, and a racial order would circulate the globe.

Through this circulation the market more than dictated the slave's living death, more than determined how the most value could be extracted from the frailty of a dying child or the rage of women close to insurrection; it transformed people into money and, in some cases, a form of credit. According to Baucom, "They were not just selling slaves on the far side of the Atlantic, they were lending money across the Atlantic. And, as significantly, they were lending money they did not yet possess or only possessed in the form of slaves. The slaves were thus treated not only as a type of commodity but as a type of interest-bearing money. They functioned in this system simultaneously as commodities for sale and as reserve deposits of a loosely organized, decentered, but vast trans-Atlantic banking system."[88] This is the unimaginable power of the market. The market was mobilized to manage every aspect of life and to transform it so that black flesh was fully fungible with other captive bodies, gold, rum, or animals.[89] Yet the slave was not just equivalent to other commodities, as Baucom argues; she became money. The body and soul of the slave were socially and biologically killed and brought back to life through a possession of the racial powers of the market. Alive or dead, born or unborn, slaves were money.[90]

Economic rationality possessed every moment of life's terror and death's release for enslaved people. Liberal distinctions between public and private and among the economic, political, and social were fabrications, illusions that depended on their erasure from the realm of the human. This erasure made possible the alchemy of the market so that with its social, economic, and discursive mechanisms the market could transform a human being into an object and test the limits of that object's biological life.[91] In *Dessa Rose*, Nathan, a slave who aided in the coffle uprising, narrates the ways value, gender, race, and terror were intertwined when he describes Dessa's punishment after she attacks her master (captor) for murdering her lover:

> I seen her when she come out that sweatbox they put her in. Know what that is, Mis'es? It's a closed box they put willful darkies in, built so's you can't lie down in it or sit or stand in it. It do got a few holes in it so you can breathe, but plenty people done suffocated in em. They whipped her, put her in that, let her sweat out in the sun. . . . They lashed her about the hips and legs, branded along the inside of her thighs. . . . They'd just about whipped that dress off her and what hadn't been cut off her—dress, drawers, shift—was hanging around her in tatters or else stuck in them wounds. Just from the waist down, you see, cause *they didn't wanna impair her value.* . . . I don't know how long they had her in that box. Her face was swolled; she was bloody

and dirty, cramped from laying up in there. I didn't think she could stand up; but she did. . . . She stood up.[92]

Nathan's description apprehends the ways slavery tested the boundary between life and death, torturing the body, murdering the soul, but preserving biological life. The merger of antiblackness, heteropatriarchy, and the market animated the power of the sweatbox. The market and the carceral are indistinguishable in the disciplining of Dessa. Wilson's goal in torturing Dessa was not death; "he didn't believe in damaging goods." Rather "what he done then was mostly for show, impress the mistress with how slaves ought to be handled. . . . He wasn't trying to kill her."[93] Dessa's incarceration in the sweatbox was the performative and pedagogical merging of race, gender, terror, and the market, an assemblage that produced social and living death as it flirted with biological death. Yet death was not the goal because the market set limits on how far white desire for black pain could go. Wilson's production of black suffering for his wife, other slaves, and himself had to be balanced with his longing for the accumulation of capital in the form of a battered body. The violence of chattel slavery was driven not only by the need for capital; the pleasures of terror were also central to the maintenance and reproduction of the social order. But the pleasures brought on by black pain had to be balanced with the production of value. The value of the unnamed pregnant rebel's child trumped the desire for her death: "I had been spared death till I could birth a baby the white folks wanted to keep slaved."[94]

By speaking the unspeakable and remembering the forgotten, this passage shows us that the market was central to slavery's carceral technologies. The market possessed the body with a logic of accumulation, fungibility, and death that determined what form punishment and discipline would take. By indexing a genealogy of the market's relationship to the body of the slave, the work of Davis and Williams can help us understand neoliberal biopolitics in a new capacity. When capital changed from a Fordist-Keynesian regime to a neoliberal regime of "flexible accumulation" in the 1970s, as a number of scholars have argued, we witnessed the transition from the formal to the real subsumption of life and labor under capital.[95] The 1970s mark the moment when capital enveloped life itself. Yet, as evident in the writing of black feminists in that decade, this process goes back to the plantation and is informed, animated, and possessed by this past imagined to have disappeared.

While the economics of slavery possessed bodies and populations with its logic of accumulation and disposability, the market fatally haunted black life, tracking and managing it everywhere fugitives could find a moment of respite. With chattel slavery the market possessed the body but also restricted, controlled, and incarcerated it. The market under slavery was a prison itself. Dessa's freedom did not lie outside the sweatbox, off the coffle, or beyond the plantation. The carceral nature of antiblackness and the market made it so that freedom was unimaginable: "You could scape from a master, run away, but that didn't mean you'd scaped from slavery. I knew for myself how hard it was to find some place to go."[96] There was no place to go because everyplace was a marketplace. Smallwood writes, "Those who managed [to escape] found that, here again, the most powerful force opposing their desperate efforts to return to a place of social belonging was not the physical constraint of prison walls and iron shackles, but rather the market itself."[97] Smallwood, like Shakur and Williams, understands the market as a powerful extension of various technologies of capture: chains, shackles, bars, prisons, and ships. Although penal technologies were central to detaining and immobilizing captive Africans, white supremacy and the market *made* them slaves. Whether they burrowed under prison walls, killed a crew and overtook a ship, or quietly swam away, fugitives were easily recognized as a commodity on the run. An expansive grid of captivity engendered by race and commodification meant there was no outside to the prison of slavery.[98] As Smallwood notes, "The market was everywhere, always shining a light on the captive's 'exchangeability.'"[99] The market fused chattel and blackness together at the level of discourse, skin, and ontology, ensuring the mark of commodification held stronger than iron and steel. The market produced a regime of surveillance wherein black flesh became ontologically inseparable from slavery's chattel logic. The terror of social and living death would follow captives into what was ostensibly the free world. *Blackness* meant *slave*, and the market would follow wherever commodified flesh could hide. This fabrication of blackness as ontological, as more than political, as more than the profound, uneven distribution of death and dying, meant that the necropolitics of race would live on well past the "non-event of emancipation," weaving slavery and subjection into the very texture of freedom.[100] Race and white supremacy carried slavery's chattel logic into the future, queering the time of progress into an anachronistic image of itself. The racial terror of the market could queer time and space so that captivity enveloped freedom and the past captured the future of now, then, and to come.

Chattel slavery is central to the contemporary politics of the market in addition to the politics of life and death in general. Indeed the market's deployment of racialized and gendered terror to produce and manage human beings began on the "floating dungeon" of the slave ship. As a paradigmatic technology of modernity, the slave ship—simultaneously a prison, a factory, a market, and an instrument of warfare—and its social relations inaugurated the economic, discursive, and institutional life of transnational capitalism.[101] The carceral, the imperial, and the industrial were intertwined in the biopolitical regulation of black life, the expansion of capital, and the production of blackness, whiteness, and white supremacy. The slave trade produced methods for controlling populations; disciplining, torturing, and immobilizing the body; regulating health and hygiene; and extending the market beyond the economic. Additionally, it produced regimes of race and racism wherein blackness was subjected to "open and absolute vulnerability," making white life dependent on black (living) death.[102] In short, the slave trade inaugurated methods for ranking life and measuring value that have yet to be undone.[103]

We can position slavery and its various technologies of domination (ship, plantation, sexual violence, management of birth, chains, whip, guns, ledger, etc.) as preceding Giorgio Agamben's argument that the concentration camp is the paradigmatic structure of modernity.[104] In *Homo Sacer: Sovereign Power and Bare Life*, Agamben argues that the juridico-political structure of the camp is a "hidden matrix of the politics in which we are still living." The camp is the "new biopolitical *nomos* of our planet," he concludes, and our future resides in our ability to recognize the ways the camp inhabits and drives the architecture of cities, airports, and the distribution of life and death across the globe.[105] The camp is not a historical anomaly but a temporal and spatial structure that is continually brought back to life. That is, it may change name and shape, but its function remains the same. As with Agamben's call to see space, time, and power in a new way in order to make visible the camp's possession of our everyday, we must learn to see the spirit of slavery in spectacles of racialized violence and death. We must also learn to recognize it in the operations that go by the names *freedom*, *humanity*, and *democracy*. Such a project requires understanding that the biopolitics and necropolitics of slavery are not relegated to an amputated past, nor do they reside in a time progress will soon leave behind. Rather, the slave trade's logics and technologies have intensified, expanded, and accumulated. The past does more than repeat: it envelops, seduces, and multiplies.[106]

Black Feminism and the Terror of Neoliberalism

In many ways Shakur's "Women in Prison: How We Are" is a ghost story, a story of those dead to the law, dead to the world, and living a death in life.[107] It is a story that confronts what goes unseen by virtue of its banality and thinks what is unthought within the analytics of black nationalism, white feminism, late liberalism, and white radicalism. Shakur's essay is about the people who constitutively haunt a new phase in the life of global capitalism. The imprisoned women of color in the text compose the "detritus" of neoliberalism—the human waste necessary to its success.[108] Shakur writes:

> There are no criminals here at Riker's Island Correctional Institution for Women (New York), only victims. Most of the women (over 95 percent) are black and Puerto Rican. Many were abused as children. Most have been abused by men and all have been abused by "the system." . . . Many are charged as accessories to crimes committed by men. The major crimes that women here are charged with are prostitution, pick pocketing, shoplifting, robbery, and drugs. . . . The women see stealing or hustling as necessary for the survival of themselves and their children because jobs are scarce and welfare is impossible to live on.[109]

Shakur describes the effects of this process on the body of a woman named Spikey: "She is in her late thirties. Her hands are swollen. Enormous. There are huge, open sores on her legs. She has about ten teeth left. And her entire body is scarred and ashen. She has been on drugs about twenty years. Her veins have collapsed. She has fibrosis, epilepsy, and edema."[110] Prison, deindustrialization, and welfare animate a network of management and control that specifically targets black women. Throughout the essay Shakur describes the late twentieth-century postindustrial city as a place emptied of jobs, littered with abandoned buildings, and surrounded by policing and penal technologies. The effects of neoliberalism's economic and policing technologies are written on the decaying bodies of Shakur's fellow captives. Yet caged bodies do not decompose of their own volition; they are produced by the regimes of power that detain and envelop them. Shakur sees the open sores and missing teeth as traces of power's touch, marks left by its mundane routines. Her description of bodily disintegration captures the diffuse violence and quotidian routines of domination that order black life but are invisible in their banality. Terror eludes detection by operating behind rational categories—naturalized by social science and the state— such as crime, poverty, and pathology.[111] Neoliberalism's management of life and death, evident in spectacles of warfare, state violence, and mass starvation, sometimes looks simply like swollen hands and scarred flesh.

Shakur posits that the affective, economic, racial, and gender politics of chattel slavery returned under an emerging neoliberal-carceral state. The spirit of slavery animated the bars of prison cells and the coldness that surrounded captured black bodies; it seeped past the razor wire and concrete walls of the prison, structuring poverty on the street, regulatory violence in the welfare office, and the unfreedom that governs an antiblack, heteropatriarchal world. Shakur describes this in her autobiography: "The only difference between here and the streets is that one is maximum security and the other is minimum security. The police patrol our streets just like guards patrol here. I don't have the faintest idea how it feels to be free."[112] Similarly the captured fugitive, Black Panther, and Black Liberation Army member Safiya Bukhari wrote from prison in her 1979 essay, "Coming of Age: A Black Revolutionary," "The maturation process is full of obstacles and entanglements for anyone, but for a black woman it has all the markings of a Minotaur's maze. I had to say that, even though nothing as spectacular takes place in the maturation process of the average black woman." According to Bukhari, unlike stories of spectacular repression and brutality in prison, the forms of subjection and subjugation produced by antiblackness and heteropatriarchy are so banal that metaphors fail to describe them.[113] She argues that everyday life in the free world mimicked and replicated her experience of incarceration. She observes that the world contains "obstacles and entanglements" for everyone but that a relationally different and intensified regime exists for black women. The racialization of gender and sexuality are central to how freedom is imbued with the discipline and control of the carceral. The Greek myth of the Minotaur's maze describes the impossibility of escape that confronts black women and other people surrounded by capitalism, antiblackness, and heteropatriarchy. Yet the analogy fails because the impossibility of escape is not isolated to a maze or a prison—it describes the everyday structures of the world. The prison is embedded in the intimate so that life is prison and prison is life. By naming the shortcomings of normative epistemology to describe the relationship between antiblackness and heteropatriarchy Bukhari demands another way of knowing power—one that can account for the banality of terror in the neoliberal-carceral state.

For example, in Bukhari's writing the prison regime makes itself known in the ways that black women's lives are "a story of humiliation, degradation, deprivation, and waste that [starts] in infancy and [lasts] until death—in too many cases, at an early age." The prison's power is not attached to the law or even to concrete, identifiable structures of discipline or control. Death can only be categorized as diffuse processes like "humiliation, degradation, deprivation, and waste." In other words, death makes itself known in ways that exceed the capacities of language. *Humiliation* describes a fragment of a shadow of something unspeakable, *degradation* a minor aspect of a process that escapes comprehension, and *waste* names the soft contours of something indescribable and unnamable. In this context, the only way to achieve "genuine liberation for black women" is to bring about the "liberation of black people as a whole." Thus the end of patriarchal regulation requires the end of antiblackness, and the end of antiblackness requires the abolition of patriarchy. Bukhari declares that to "slay the beast" that is the racial state, black women (and the black liberation movement) must end "racism, capitalism, and sexism."[114] In this way, antiblackness makes itself known as gender and sexual regulation, and gender and sexual difference are produced by capitalism and racism. Black feminism documents how liberal epistemology and revolutionary politics often share an affinity for the occlusion of the centrality of race, gender, sexuality, and capital to the formation and functioning of the social.[115] To miss one for the destruction of another is to let regulation reproduce itself under the name of liberation.

Shakur connects the diffuse carceral regime she and Bukhari describe to the poverty produced by an emergent neoliberal state and the market's production of poverty: "The rest of the women who weren't doing time for the numbers were in for some kind of petty theft, like shoplifting or passing bad checks. Most of those sisters were on welfare and all of them had barely been able to make ends meet. The courts had shown them no mercy. They brought in this sister shortly after I arrived who was eight months pregnant and had been sentenced to a month for shoplifting something that cost less than twenty dollars."[116] In this passage, Shakur names the connections between carceral and policing apparatuses. By centering women of color in her analysis of this landscape, she apprehends how gendered and racialized methods of survival performed in the empty lots abandoned by capital become crimes to fill prisons, which in turn fill empty spaces.[117] In the late 1970s criminalization became the weapon of choice in dealing with the social problems produced by the globalization of capital and the resistance it engendered.[118] The imprisoned women of color—the "butches," "fems," "bulldaggers," and "stud broads"—centered in Shakur's analysis show the ways that heteropatriarchy, white supremacy, and neoliberalism collude to immobilize poor (queer) women of color. Shakur's writing highlights the centrality of gender, sexuality, and race to the ways the neoliberal-carceral state renders socially and civically dead human beings "who come from places where dreams have been abandoned like the buildings."[119] We can thus understand heteropatriarchy, racism, and the prison as colluding technologies that exist in the shadow of the abandoned buildings that litter Shakur's postindustrial landscape. The very foundations of neoliberalism's theories, techniques, and operations rest upon racialized and gendered logics, even as white supremacy and heterosexism are incessantly disavowed in its distribution of life and death. Although it produces the neutral discourses of equality, diversity, freedom, and opportunity, neoliberalism necessitates force, punishment, warfare, immobilization through incarceration, and the uneven distribution of social and biological death.[120] State violence is not the exception to neoliberalism but its condition of possibility. Simply, the neoliberal state requires the management, regulation, and immobilization of surplus or expendable populations.

When a guard tells her that the Thirteenth Amendment did not abolish slavery but transferred it to the prison, Shakur connects deindustrialization and the market under neoliberalism to slavery and the prison: "Well, that explained a lot of things. That explained why jails and prisons all over the country are filled to the brim with Black and Third World people, why so many black people can't find a job on the streets and are forced to survive the best way they know how. Once you're in prison, there are plenty of jobs, and, if you don't want to work, they beat you and throw you in the hole. . . . Prisons are a profitable business. They are a way of legally perpetuating slavery."[121] Within this analytic the market mimics and colludes with the prison's antiblackness. Through the racialized and gendered production of poverty and criminality, the market functions as a type of prison. It queers normative conceptions of space in the name of capture and caging. If a critical genealogy of the prison leads us back to the coffle, the plantation, the sweat box, and the slave ship, the market also leads back to slavery's economic, ontological, and epistemological technologies.

Because slavery returns to possess the present, for Shakur and Davis it also returns to drive resistance. Davis writes that revolutionary struggle in the 1970s is "identical in spirit" with enslaved women but entails relationally different conditions and tactics, while Shakur uses memory and imagination to recall histories of "fierce determination" and struggle: "I can imagine the pain and strength of my great-great grandmothers who were slaves and my great-great grandmothers who were Cherokee Indians trapped on reservations."[122] Shakur draws on the affective force of the dead to help combat the changing contours of global capitalism, white supremacy, and institutionalized sexism. She remembers "women who delivered babies, searched for healing roots, and brewed medicines. Women who darned socks, and chopped wood, and layed bricks. Women who could swim rivers and shoot the heads off a snake . . . fierce women who could stop you with a look out the corners of their eyes."[123] Shakur is forced to rely on memory and imagination because she has been captured and because histories of slaves and slavery have been rendered unknowable. This is the space produced by stories that were never recorded and lives that never existed beyond the confines of social death.

Using memory and vision, Shakur names and makes visible the disappeared and the destroyed. She apprehends the ways the socially dead of now and then form the foundation of the neoliberal-carceral state. Neoliberalism rests upon the emptiness left by those who have been captured, detained, or killed. Through their absence 2.5 million people in prison and jail order the world. Capital moves freely across space where millions of bodies should be. This space is produced by the demise of the golden age of capitalism and the destruction of social movements militantly pursued throughout the 1970s. The disappeared are the required refuse of neoliberalism.[124] Neoliberalism generates order, choice, freedom, and prosperity through the disappearance of millions of people. Shakur places captive black women at the center of this equation.

By centering racialized genders in her analysis of the 1970s United States, Shakur describes the necessity of regimes of capture and caging to the implementation of neoliberalism. She writes, "My sisters on the streets, like my sisters at Riker's Island, see no way out" because "we were, and still are, in a much more terrible jail."[125] The spaces of the prison, ghetto, and home are neither compartmentalized nor discrete; rather they collude with each other, composing an expansive grid of captivity that immobilizes and disposes of racialized and gendered populations. If Shakur's jail captures some, it also immunizes other bodies from such routine abjection and social death, thus securing capital, whiteness, and white life. The market is central to this regime of power. It is complicit in the process of producing surplus life, life that will be policed and imprisoned. White supremacy, heteropatriarchy, and the market overdetermine the presence of Shakur and her fellow captives in prison. Shakur's conception of jail undoes normative conceptions of space by exceeding the walls of the prison proper. Her conception of power is not just disciplinary but also biopolitical. Power does more than restrict the body; it possesses it. Power manages life, bodies, and populations from the inside; power queers space and time because this jail—this network of management and immobilization—is animated by the spirit of slavery. Slavery's production of social and biological death did not end with emancipation, did not cease with the end of segregation, and refused to heed under civil rights legislation. Its logic and power exceeds the realm of law. The past comes back not just to haunt but to structure and drive the contemporary operations of power.

By centering antiblack and heteropatriarchal technologies and discourses, Shakur queers normative conceptions of space and time to demonstrate that neoliberalism's mechanisms of control are expansive in the spatial and temporal sense. Neoliberal-carceral technologies track, manage, and immobilize rebellious or surplus life, a process that is driven and informed by technologies inaugurated by the Atlantic slave trade. *We were, and still are, in a much more terrible jail.* In her essay those resisting the massive restructuring of capitalism in the 1970s are part of a five-century-long struggle against slavery and white supremacy, while the forces opposing them are part of that same history. Shakur, Bukhari, Davis, and Williams teach us that we do not seize hold of the past in order to make sense of the present; sometimes the past grabs you first. One does not choose what of the past is relevant to the now; possession is not so simple. The spirit of slavery has its own desires that exceed our control and even our conscious thought. But for the demonic to be exorcised, you must first know that you are possessed.

4. "ONLY THE SUN WILL BLEACH HIS BONES QUICKER"

DESIRE, POLICE TERROR, AND THE AFFECT OF QUEER FEMINIST FUTURES

Recognizing the power of the erotic within our lives can give us the
energy to pursue genuine change within our world, rather than merely settling
for a shift of characters in the same weary drama.

—AUDRE LORDE, "The Uses of the Erotic," in *Sister Outsider*

The problem, as I see it, is not sexual liberation, but the liberation of desire.

—FÉLIX GUATTARI, *Soft Subversions*

In their 1971 statement on the occupation of Weinstein Hall at New York
University by gay liberation activists, the organization Street Transvestite
Action Revolutionaries (STAR) asked a profound question concerning the
future of movements for sexual and gender liberation. STAR's statement was
a response to the abandonment of the occupation by protesters "upon the
request of the pigs." To STAR this tactical decision to end the occupation
demonstrated an ambivalence at the heart of the gay liberation movement's
desire for a different ordering of the world. STAR asked, "Do you really want
Gay Power or are you looking for a few laughs or maybe a little excitement.
We are not quite sure what you people really want. If you want Gay Liberation then you're going to have to fight for it. We don't mean tomorrow or the
next day, we are talking about today. We can never possibly win by saying

'wait for a better day' or 'we're not ready yet.' If you're ready to tell people that you want to be free, then you're ready to fight. . . . So now the question is, do we want gay power or pig power?" With this question STAR placed a different type of desire at the center of movements for sexual liberation: a desire that deployed sexuality as a critique of the systems of racialized policing central to the 1970s post–civil rights state. Sexual liberation in this analytic wasn't about fun and excitement that was content for the present to passively remake itself into a more livable future. The statement "Wait for a better day" was an alibi for the intensification of racialized, antiqueer, and antitrans state violence. STAR couldn't wait for the present to be transformed into a better future because they knew the future looked like the unlivability of the present. Sexual liberation required a politics that saw the police as one of the forces that made the future impossible. STAR argued that gay liberation had pacified and captured itself by listening to the demands of the police: "Chalk one up for the pigs, for they truly are carrying there [sic] Victory Flag. And realize the next demonstration is going to be harder, because they now know that we scare easily." The many potential futures of gay liberation lay not in allying with the "pig power" of the police but in remaining oppositional to systems of racialized policing and capture. The statement ended, "You people run if you want to, but we're tired of running. We intend to fight for our rights until we get them."[1]

To STAR, gay power was antagonistic to police power. Indeed the eradication of pig power was the goal of gay power. But STAR saw this antagonism waning even a few short years after the uprising against police violence at the Stonewall Inn. STAR warned of the dawn of a new political horizon when queer activists would work with the police, applaud the police, join the police, argue for more police, and demand harsher forms of state power to be enforced by the police.[2] STAR argued that queer desire didn't have to lead back to the racial state. One could *want* a form of power that superseded the state, surpassed inclusion and equality, and escaped capture by the police. STAR argued for a fugitive form of desire that took flight from systems of policing and capture so that gay power could lead somewhere unknown and unthought.

In this chapter I examine how feminist and queer activists and writers in the 1970s conceptualized the relationships among desire, fugitivity, policing, and police violence. Departing from STAR's argument about sexuality's relationship to policing, I focus my analysis on the poetry of June Jordan and Audre Lorde. In their poetry from the 1970s and early 1980s, Lorde and Jordan theorized the racial politics of police violence and its relationship to desire. Yet this aspect of their work has not been examined as part of a genealogy of queer and feminist antiprison politics. Read together, their poetry comprises a body of queer, feminist, antiprison, and antipolice politics that can help us make sense of the racial, gendered, and sexual politics of the neoliberal-carceral state. This body of work makes visible the violence of the racial state, but it does so by exploring the terrain of desire. More specifically, Lorde and Jordan worked to make sense of an emerging desire for state power and how this desire for subjection authorized and materialized new forms of carceral and economic state power in the late 1970s. Like STAR's statement, their poetry expands a queer conception of desire beyond sexuality to the racial politics of policing and state power. These thinkers warned that the state sought to capture desire to bolster the normative order of things, and policing was one way this was accomplished. At the same time, Lorde, Jordan, STAR, and many other activists and thinkers engaged desire as a form of escape from white supremacy, heteropatriarchy, policing, and prisons. For so many the late 1970s seemed to be a profound turning point: Pig power or gay power? Escape or capture?

In this same period poststructuralist thinkers like Foucault, Deleuze, and Guattari theorized how the state and capital worked to limit and contain revolutionary desires. They were particularly concerned with how desire was structurally directed toward the repressive ends of fascism. This line of thought is perhaps best summarized in Guattari's 1977 essay, "Everybody Wants to Be a Fascist."[3] Analyzing the work of U.S. women of color feminists alongside European poststructuralist philosophers allows us to think transnationally about the emergence of a variety of 1970s movements that took the prison as their object and abolition as their goal. As Chela Sandoval has observed, the work of thinkers like Foucault, Jacques Derrida, Frederic Jameson, and Roland Barthes share "lines of force and affinity" and contain the "decolonizing influences" of the formation she calls "U.S. third world feminism."[4] Sandoval posits that women of color feminists and poststructuralist thinkers in the 1960s and 1970s shared the same "psychic terrain" of a radically changing global capitalism and theorized postmodern configurations of power in profoundly similar but also radically different ways. Part of this shared epistemological terrain is that feminists of color and postwar European philosophers were confronting the expansion of incarceration as a form of population management used against the global revolutions of 1968. This is evident in the writings of Lorde, Jordan, STAR, and other U.S. feminists, as well as the antiprison and antipsychiatry writings and activism of Deleuze, Guattari, and Foucault.[5] Yet while feminist of color and poststructuralist thinkers were confronting desire as one of the conditions of possibility for new formations of power, all of these thinkers also placed desire, or "the erotic" in Lorde's terminology, as central to new forms of knowledge, ways of being, and abolitionist imaginings of a world without racialized and gendered state violence. As Lauren Berlant observes, the study of desire in our current moment would not be possible without the radical upheavals of the 1960s and 1970s that named desire as a site of subjection while also deploying desire as a site of revolutionary possibility.[6]

While other chapters have focused on feminist and queer activists who became political fugitives, this chapter advances a less identitarian conception of fugitivity. I explore fugitivity as an epistemological and affective force, as opposed to a social, political, and legal location. I do so by examining the relationship between desire and the neoliberal-carceral state. I argue that a desire for police and prisons is central to the rise of the neoliberal-carceral state, but that fugitive desires and affects are foundational to undoing the reign of the carceral and the terror of the market.

Desire, Policing, and Neoliberalism

In her 1980 poem "Letter to the Local Police," Jordan writes as an aging husband who recently relocated to Saratoga Springs in upstate New York:

Dear Sirs:

I have been enjoying the law and order of our
community throughout the past three months since
my wife and I, our two cats, and miscellaneous
photographs of the six grandchildren belonging to
our previous neighbors (with whom we were very
close) arrived in Saratoga Springs which is clearly
prospering under your custody

Indeed, until yesterday afternoon and despite my
vigilant casting about, I have been unable to discover

a single instance of reasons for public-spirited concern,
much less complaint

You may easily appreciate, then, how it is that
I write to your office, at this date, with utmost
regret for the lamentable circumstances that force
my hand

Speaking directly to the issue of the moment:

I have encountered a regular profusion of certain
unidentified roses, growing to no discernible purpose,
and according to no perceptible control, approximately
one quarter mile west of the Northway, on the southern
side

To be specific, there are practically thousands of
the aforementioned abiding in perpetual near riot
of wild behavior, indiscriminate coloring, and only
the Good Lord Himself can say what diverse soliciting
of promiscuous cross-fertilization

As I say, these roses, no matter what the apparent
background, training, tropistic tendencies, age,
or color, do not demonstrate the least inclination
toward categorization, specified allegiance, resolute
preference, consideration of the needs of others, or
any other minimal traits of decency

May I point out that I did not assiduously seek out
this colony, as it were, and that these certain
unidentified roses remain open to viewing even by
children, with or without suitable supervision

(My wife asks me to append a note as regards the
seasonal but nevertheless seriously licentious
phenomenon of honeysuckle under the moon that one may
apprehend at the corner of Nelson and Main

However, I have recommended that she undertake direct
correspondence with you, as regards this: yet
another civic disturbance in our midst)

I am confident that you will devise and pursue
appropriate legal response to the roses in question
If I may aid your efforts in this respect, please
do not hesitate to call me into consultation

Respectfully yours.[7]

Jordan's poem places a fugitive queerness prior to state power. The wildness of the flowers—their lack of decency, their promiscuous racialization, their excessive sexuality, and their organization that escapes "perceptible control"—threatens the safety and stability of the normative subject and the security of the city. Yet the flowers do not live in resistance to the state; they did not emerge as a force that threatens the state out of *reaction* to state power. Instead their deviance, their abnormality, their fugitivity is a political ontology produced by the people and institutions that seek their capture. The flowers live in a state of statelessness that challenges the rationality and existence of the state itself. In this case power does not bring fugitivity, resistance, and insurgency into being; these forces exist before and within modern biopolitical formations. Power emerges to capture what escapes.

The flowers can signify a variety of minoritized formations: the multitude, the racialized, the queer, the colonized, the feminine, the anarchic, and the wildness of the natural. In each case the flowers signify the insurgency of life itself. And their fugitivity is contagious: it might spread to children or even to the man, who must assure the police that he did not seek them out. What Jordan observes in "Letter to the Local Police" is that the state builds itself by capturing fugitive ways of living and being. In the poem these forms of life are queer in their racialization; the sexuality and race of the flowers is illegible to normative modes of knowing and seeing, and this makes them a threat that needs to be disciplined and controlled.

The poem documents the fact that the police are not only a repressive force imposing their domination on a subordinated population; simply and profoundly, some people desire the police. Jordan thus theorizes desire as a structural relation generated by and productive of policing and the racial state.[8] The man in the poem is not forced to fall in line with the repressive power of the police; he initiates the "call to order," he yearns for control, he dreams of regulation and discipline.[9] He desires the cleansed visual landscape central to the operation of the neoliberal-carceral state, a landscape without the sexual and racial perversity of the uncontrollable flowers. The poem makes clear that the state, with assistance from neoliberal citizen, works continuously to capture fugitive ways of living, being, and thinking. In describing the desire for police, the poem documents that the neoliberal-carceral state did not only emerge from repressive violence or the soft power of neoliberal and carceral discourses.[10] The poem asks us to consider the desire for state violence, power, and subjection. By analyzing the relationships among the post-1960s neoliberal citizen, the police, and the forms of life that exist before control, Jordan's poem theorizes the production of the modern racial state by the policing of fugitive forms of life, those racialized forms of queerness that exceed and precede normalization, regulation, and discipline. In addition, Jordan highlights the neoliberal subject's complicity with the police so that we might speak of neoliberal subjectivity as a form of "becoming the police." Thus the poem asks us to consider how people in the neoliberal-carceral state "desire repression for themselves and others."[11] The work of Deleuze, Guattari, and Foucault is instructive for understanding how desire operates in Jordan's poem.

In his preface to Deleuze and Guattari's *Anti-Oedipus: Capitalism and Schizophrenia* Foucault writes, "How does one keep from being fascist, even (especially) when one believes one to be a revolutionary militant? How do we rid our speech and our acts, our hearts and our pleasures, of fascism? How do we ferret out the fascism that is ingrained in our behaviors?"[12] Foucault's questions about identifying and eliminating fascism were part of a broader postwar anxiety on the left of replicating the conditions that a generation earlier gave rise to fascism and Nazism. Indeed the Weather Underground in the United States and the Red Army Faction in Germany refused to be "good Germans" amid the violence of U.S. imperialism and global capitalism.[13] Their turn to fugitivity and armed struggle was, in part, an effort to refuse complicity with racialized, imperial state violence. Yet Foucault's questions complicate the notion of a guilty, complicit subject and an innocent, resistant subject. He argues that fascism is ingrained in speech, love, pleasure, and the body; there was the historical fascism in Germany and Italy that was able to "use the desire of the masses so effectively," but also the fascism "in us all, in our heads, and in our everyday behavior, the fascism that causes us to love power, to desire the very thing that dominates and exploits us." Following Foucault, we can ask about the man in Jordan's poem: How and why does he want the police to regulate and discipline forms of life beyond their power? Why does he desire state power and state violence? What draws him toward the police, and why does he behave as if he were the police? Foucault believes the goal of politics should be to track down multiple forms of fascism, "from the enormous ones that surround and crush us, to the petty ones that constitute the tyrannical bitterness of our everyday lives." This means finding "new zones" of political struggle. One such zone is the terrain of desire—but a desire not bound to the vision of Marx or the dreams of Freud. The guide to this new political struggle is outlined in *Anti-Oedipus*, which Foucault calls "an introduction to the non-fascist life."[14]

In *Anti-Oedipus*, Deleuze and Guattari theorize the ways that desire has been captured by psychoanalysis and capitalism and argue that desire is a profound site of new revolutionary possibilities. As opposed to understanding desire as a lack that exists in the isolated realm of fantasy, they argue that desire is productive and material—desire creates the world. They revise Marx's historical materialism by arguing that "history is the history of desire."[15] Desire is primary; it calls power into being.[16] They write, "We maintain that the social field is immediately invested by desire, that it is the historically determined product of desire, and the libido has no need of any mediation or sublimation, any psychic operation, any transformation, in order to invade or invest the productive forces and the relations of production. *There is only desire and the social, and nothing else.*"[17] Desire is not isolated to the confines of the mind; it is not a dream or a fantasy locked away in the psyche. Desire possesses the social, economic, and political sphere.[18] Further, desire is actually a "desiring-assemblage," an ongoing process enveloped with other "desiring-machines." These desiring-machines continuously connect and disconnect, changing but always creating.[19] The proper model of the unconscious is not the theater but the factory, so that "desire is part of the infrastructure."[20] In this way desire is not a subjectivity, a static structure, a feeling, or a thing. It is an event, it is affect, and it flees organization, enunciation, and identification even as its capture is always imminent.[21]

Significantly Deleuze and Guattari's notion of desire is similar to but contrasts with Foucault's conception of pleasure. Deleuze recalled of this difference, "The last time we saw each other, Michel says to me, with much kindness and affection, something like: I cannot bear the word desire; even if you use it in another way, I can't stop thinking . . . that desire=lack, or that desire is the repressed. Michel adds: As for me, what I call 'pleasure' is perhaps what you call 'desire'; but in any case I need another word than desire." For Foucault, desire is invested with Freudian notions of repression and lack that make the productive capacities of pleasure impossible. But for Deleuze pleasure names the normative formation of "strata and organization" that reflect a statist individuation of subjectivity. Pleasure is a way for subjects to find themselves again "in a process which overwhelms them. [Pleasure] is a process of re-*territorialization*."[22] In "The Biopolitics of Pleasure" Timothy Dean argues that pleasure according to Foucault lacks "the psychological depth attributed to desire," and thus "pleasure malfunctions as a reliable sign of subjective truth and this interrupts the smooth deployment of regulatory power."[23] Dean's description of pleasure is similar to Deleuze's of desire. For the purposes of this chapter I am not concerned with taking a side in the debate about pleasure and desire, nor am I particularly interested in pinning down the essence of either word. It's not that desire and pleasure are interchangeable, but that both philosophers were looking for a word that could go beyond identitarian affects; they were trying to describe something they believed was indescribable.[24] In this chapter *desire* describes the myriad ways we might come to *want* power, while *pleasure* describes the effects, or the aftermath, of power's operation. Guattari's definition of desire can help clarify this distinction: "Desire is not, like eros, tied down with the body, the person, and the law; it is no more dependent on the shameful body—with its hidden organs and its incestuous taboo—than to a fascination with and to myths about the nude body, the all powerful phallus, and sublimation. Desire is constituted *before* the crystallization of the body and the organs, *before* the division of the sexes, *before* the separation of the familiarized self and the social field."[25] Like Jordan's flowers that live in a wild, promiscuous, and uncontrollable collectivity prior to policing, desire in this passage exists before structures like the family, individuality, sex and gender, and psychoanalysis capture and convert it into pleasure, sexuality, identity, the law, and the body.[26] As I discuss later in the chapter, this notion of desire as uncontrollable, illegible, and evasive aligns with Lorde's articulation of the erotic. Yet like Lorde's argument that the erotic is liberatory and at the same time can be possessed by racism, capital, and heteropatriarchy, even as desire for Deleuze and Guattari is a line of flight escaping the control of the state, psychoanalysis, and capital, it can also be captured for the most violent, conservative, and repressive ends.

Throughout their individual and collective body of work, Deleuze and Guattari were concerned with how people desire their own subjection and the subjugation of others. How can the autonomy of desire, which can undo the order of things as they are, be remade in the name of that same order?[27] Inspired by the psychoanalyst Wilhelm Reich, Deleuze and Guattari wondered how people become invested in their own subjection so that they sometimes fight for their subordination as fiercely as their liberation. How do people come to support, fight for, and desire forms of power that will undo them in the end? Why are the exploited "not continually on strike: after centuries of exploitation, why do people still tolerate being humiliated and enslaved, to such a point, indeed, that they *actually want* humiliation and slavery not only for others but for themselves?" In this formulation fascism and other forms of power not only arose because of ideology, illusion, or ignorance but because of desire. At some point millions of people wanted fascism, and it is this "perversion of the desire of the masses that needs to be accounted for."[28] Like Foucault's argument that the discipline central to the prison expanded to schools, factories, and hospitals, Deleuze and Guattari argue that "what fascism set in motion yesterday continues to proliferate in other forms," among them the state, unions, racism, the ghetto, the family, and the superego. Fascism, like capitalism, is scattered everywhere in the political and economic contours of the social fabric and it shapes what people want for themselves and each other.[29] Sharon Holland extends this concern with desire's centrality to architectures of capital, arguing that "the psychic life of racism" functions on the terrain of desire.[30] Desire, she says, is intimately constitutive of the mundaneness of everyday racisms. Queer studies reproduces this separation of desire from racism when it casts desire as solely residing in the realm of freedom and transgression. But for Holland desire is a sign of the established order. Desire is thus part of the infrastructure of white supremacy and capitalism.

On the psychoanalyst's couch, in the factory, in the family, and on the street, Deleuze and Guattari see capitalism hunting down fugitive desires in order to have them renounce their unruly objects. Once captured, these desires are forced to reinvest in the powers of the family, the state, and capital. Capitalism as a structure of desire taps into the worker's "potentiality for desire" by infiltrating childhood, the family, and love, so that capital possesses "the very heart of worker's subjectivity and vision of the world." Capitalism functions not only through violence but also by soliciting desire by "modeling individuals according to its preferences." People come to desire the objects the market produces so that they submit to exploitation and hierarchy and come to love it. Capitalism represses, excludes, and neutralizes all desires, sexualities, and affects that do not reproduce and maintain compliance with its "totalitarian organization founded on exploitation, property, male power, profit, productivity."[31] Only forms of desire that bolster the normative order of things are produced as valuable, recognizable, or thinkable. The shapes desire may take are infinite, but physical force and discursive constraint channel these possibilities into recognizable normative outcomes.[32] By eliminating alternative desires, desire for the life of capital and capital as life is all the horizon seems to hold.

The capture of desire has changed radically in the neoliberal era. Neoliberalism demands the complete possession of individuals with its logic. Unlike older modes of capitalism, neoliberalism is not satisfied with externally compelling subjects to display desirable behavior; it demands the "complete surrender of 'interiority.'" Thus one must submit to neoliberal regimes of work, and one must also enjoy work, love work, and desire work. Neoliberalism produces a deeply structured "regime of desire" that captures unproductive and unruly ways of living the present and wanting the future. Neoliberalism produces desire in order to biopolitically compel through desire. One of power's goals, then, is to shape the distribution of the knowable and the sensible as well as the desirable.[33] This regulation of desire is significant because it determines what and who is valuable. Desire is attracted to an already constituted valuable object, and so value is determined by desire. If one can shape desire, one can also shape value, with all its racialized and gendered effects. Thus one way biopolitics functions is by shaping and controlling the desires of a population.

By possessing desire, power can shape what one does, how one thinks, and what one wants. Scholars in queer studies have been at the forefront of observing how neoliberalism has taken hold of desire in the form of a normative sexual politics that Lisa Duggan famously termed "homonormativity."[34] Homonormativity produces a dominant gender and sexual politics connected to a broader queer social and economic order called "queer liberalism."[35] Queer liberalism disciplines and contorts queer desires for a revolutionary undoing of the social order in favor of liberal reforms that align with white supremacy, heteropatriarchy, imperialism, and neoliberalism.[36] Homonormativity is one way that neoliberalism shapes desire to preserve and expand its existence while also abolishing other ways of imagining life that might challenge its future. Neoliberalism says to its subjects, "Desire it yourself, but only as I say; be autonomous but under my guidance."[37] It also says, "Desire within the boundaries of what I deem desirable, think within the confines of what I render thinkable, love how I love, and resist in my name." Yet neoliberalism does more than produce a desire for capital, for life as capital and the life of capital; it also creates a desire for the systems of racialized and gendered violence that make neoliberalism possible: police and prisons. "Letter to the Local Police" documents the management of desire in the era of the neoliberal-carceral state and, further, how the neoliberal-carceral state operates through the terrain of desire.

Desire, Whiteness, and Policing

As he monitors Saratoga Springs, the male protagonist in Jordan's poem polices as if he were the police and expands their disciplinary and regulatory power to spaces that have escaped the state's regimes of capture. He polices what the police fail to regulate. He writes that he discovered the flowers because he has been "vigilantly casting about" for causes of concern or complaint. He has been patrolling, looking for criminal and nonnormative transgressions of the law and order of Saratoga Springs. The police have ineffectively monitored and controlled the flowers, which inhabit a space outside the racialized, gendered, and sexual politics of the state's biopolitical management, so the man steps in for the police and seeks to capture what they have allowed to escape. The man has been policing before he notifies the police of the flowers that need to be policed. His policing precedes the state's policing. But more than that, he desires what he thinks the police should desire: a world wherein unruly, racially perverse flowers are controlled and contained. Thus the man shows the police what to discipline and regulate. His policing sets a template for the state's policing. His desire animates the structures of the state's desire, even as the state's desire enlivens his own. Just as prisons and police capture, cage, and kill those who disrupt and escape the normative order of things, neoliberal subjectivities and discourses police and expunge other ways of being and knowing that do not align with the organization of life and death under neoliberalism. Neoliberal subjectivity has been animated by a regulatory logic that polices those who fail to conform to the racial, gendered, and sexual norms that govern the distribution of life and death. The proper neoliberal subject polices what exceeds the domain of neoliberalism's ordering of life and in this way is one with the police. In the poem the policing performed by the neoliberal subject supplements, expands, and intensifies the policing performed by the racial state.

We can place the man's activities in the almost all-white town of Saratoga Springs within the policing apparatuses that maintain white supremacy, racial capital, heteropatriarchy, and state power. His "casting about" is part of a centuries-long project of patrolling, monitoring, and regulating the enslaved, the colonized, the poor, and the deviant. Policing is shorthand for the multiple mechanisms and institutions that "ensure private property *within* public order including access to the means of violence, their legal narration, and their use." What Nikhil Singh calls the "whiteness of the police" emerged in the age of modern liberalism to maintain white supremacy and racial capitalism through state and extrastate violence. It also includes the accompanying discourses that legitimate and naturalize this violence. As Singh writes, "The specific importance of police power revolves around its ongoing links to colonial and settler colonial methods and relationships including extermination and population transfer, but as importantly its conservation within and utility for the machineries of value creation, capital accumulation, and the economies of violence that these machineries require and develop."[38] In Singh's formulation, policing is material and discursive. It is a mechanism that maintains the organization of the social world through violence, and it produces knowledge to make sense of that same organization. For example, the man in Jordan's poem is alarmed by the physical presence of the flowers, but he is also concerned that they are uncategorized, unidentified, and unnamed. He worries that there is no discourse to govern them. The solution he imagines might require the physical force of the local police, but it also requires systems of knowledge to make sense of and name the wild and unruly forms of life that are not categorized within modern epistemological regimes. The man wants the physical force of the police as well as their epistemological power. He wants to rule the unruly and name the unnamed.

In desiring the power of the police the man also renounces his own potential desire:

> May I point out that I did not assiduously seek out
> this colony, as it were, and that these certain
> unidentified roses remain open to viewing even by
> children, with or without suitable supervision.

The man makes clear that he has no loyalty or connection to the flowers and that he most certainly did not look for them. He was not drawn to their perverse indecency, their wildness, or their collectivity. The insurgency of the flowers is contagious, and the man makes clear that he has not been contaminated. He doesn't want the flowers; he wants their subordination. The process of policing alternative forms of life requires the regulation and disciplining of the self. This extends to the letter writer's wife. She is concerned about the "civil disturbance" of a "seasonal but nevertheless seriously licentious / phenomenon of honeysuckle" at the corner of "Nelson and Main." In this closing section of the poem, desire for the police includes gendered difference. It is not only the masculine neoliberal subject who polices like the police; by including the wife's desire in the letter, Jordan notes the centrality of the white female subject to regimes that police and capture forms of gendered, racialized, and sexual life that disturb civic white life. The wife's desire generates police power and is generated by that same power.[39] In order to achieve this level of solidarity, the neoliberal-carceral state must solicit and seduce subjects to follow, support, and take part in its systems of violence: "If I may aid your efforts in this respect, please / do not hesitate to call me into consultation." Desire is thus structurally generated and institutionally directed. This final line of Jordan's poem offers a dramatic revision to the story of how the United States came to have the world's largest prison system because it centers desire instead of repression. Returning to Althusser's theory of interpellation will help to clarify the significance of the distinction between repression and desire in "Letter to the Local Police."

In Althusser's famous example, a policeman calls out to a passerby, "Hey you there!," and the passerby, recognizing himself as the one being hailed, turns around to be addressed by the policeman. The policeman's call is a demand to align oneself with the law, to see in oneself what the policeman sees, to be recognized by the power of recognition.[40] By turning around and answering the hail of the police, the passerby is interpellated and becomes a subject. Submission to the external call of the police brings the subject into being. Thus the individual's subjectivity is dependent on the call of the police. At the end of chapter 2 I argued that the fugitive rewrites Althusser's theory of interpellation by refusing to answer the call of the police. The fugitive does not capture herself and become a subject because when she sees the police, she does not stop and turn around. She runs away. She hides. She escapes. Like the fugitive's flight, Jordan's attention to the man's desire for policing also helps us to revise understandings of police power indebted to Althusser's notion of interpellation. We can call this the repressive model of policing.

The rise of the neoliberal-carceral state has been narrated through multiple discourses of repression that rightly describe its power as a form of racial warfare, the new Jim Crow, a war on the poor, a war on liberation movements, a new caste system, a war on drugs, a form of new slavery, and a new way to manage disposable populations under a changing racial capitalism.[41] But Jordan's poem asks us to also consider how millions and millions of people want the prison and desire the police. The poem can stand in for a larger neoliberal and carceral imaginary of desire that took hold of political, economic, and social life in the 1970s and after. How did so many people come to see freedom in social death, safety in disappearance, and justice in racialized and gendered state killing? And how did this desire for state violence become so mundane as to be unremarkable for so many?

The form of the poem makes this banality clear. Jordan's poem is a simple, single letter to a local police department of a small city—a minor piece of correspondence written in the proper pleasantries of a liberal, highly educated, concerned citizen. The letter writer does not call for the flowers to be killed or bombed or eradicated in waves of genocidal state violence. Instead he kindly assures the police that he knows they will "devise and pursue / [the] appropriate legal response" to the problem. In this way, the poem names the law as a site of regulatory violence, but one that does not always operate through spectacle. The letter writer desires an everyday violence cloaked in the justice of the law. As I argued in chapter 1, the language of rights in the post–civil rights era (in particular "the first civil right") became foundational to multiple campaigns to expand the U.S. prison system. The liberalization of civil rights came to require the modernization and expansion of incarceration.[42] A forty-year wave of racialized and gendered police and carceral violence emerged not in contradistinction to the law but in the language of rights, safety, freedom, equality, and security. What the man in Jordan's poem calls the "appropriate legal response" is another name for the post–civil rights violence of the racial state. The man writes the letter in a new post-1960s language that is able to speak race without ever saying its name. The racial and gendered violence the man desires is called "rights" and named "the law." And he becomes a subject through this desire for the power of the racial state.

Whether through Althusser's interpellation or Foucault's discursive productivity, the subject comes into being "through a primary submission to power." Subjection names this process of being subordinated to power and becoming a subject through that very same subordination. In Althusser's example the subordination occurs discursively: it is produced by the voice of the policeman who hails the individual. The individual is subordinated by the call of the policeman and comes into subjectivity through this repressive power. Unlike Althusser's analysis of an individual who turns around to answer the call of the police, the man in Jordan's poem is never hailed but instead, we can imagine, calls out to the police, "Hey, come here!" and "You there, call me, I want to help!" The man does not capture himself by turning around. He is not hailed or interpellated while he walks down the street. To the contrary, he contacts the police in order to improve and expand their policing. He doesn't run from the police—he runs *toward* them. Instead of submitting to power, he *wants* power. He calls out to power to come closer, intensify, and expand. He tells power where it is failing, where its gaps and fissures weaken its totality. He sees a fragility that power misses and redirects its sight to what has gone unseen. In Jordan's theorization of police power, the formation of the subject does not happen through subordination to the police but through a desire for the police. Unlike Althusser's theory, the man's turn toward the police occurs *before* the policeman calls out because complicity with the law is the condition of possibility for the emergence of modern subjectivity. It is not turning around to face the police that creates the subject because the turn is prior to subject formation. Judith Butler calls this a "prior desire for the law, a passionate complicity with the law, without which no subject can exist."[43] If the law confers subjectivity, one must desire the law, want the law, and run toward the law. This means the man in Jordan's poem desires the police before they announce their desire for him. He sees himself in the police—his future and the future of normativity embodied by the figure of the child that is the cause of his concern.

The man's concern about the categorization of the flowers contains an anticipatory logic that is central to the temporality of policing. Defending against future uprisings and rebellions—the "riot / of wild behavior"—requires managing the temporality of nonnormative and revolutionary forms of desire. In fact modern policing constituted itself by targeting nonnormative and radical ways of desiring. For example, we might think of the policing of alternative political desires in the forms of black liberation, Native sovereignty, anti-imperialism, socialism, anarchism, sexual and gender liberation, and anticolonialism. Or we might think of the policing of more intimate ways of desiring in the form of gender-nonconforming embodiment, queer sex, interracial sex, and public sex. We might also think of the regulation of the desire to migrate and immigrate, to work, to learn, to feed one's family, to have a home, to live. Even simple desires like wanting to eat, sit down, or buy a cup of coffee with the help of people walking down the street are policed by loitering and antivagrancy laws. *Policing is the disciplining and management of desire.* In particular, policing targets desires that call forth other ways of being, living, and thinking that undermine the future of capital, heteropatriarchy, the racial state, and the police themselves. Recall that the Black Panthers' efforts to police the police were then policed and dismantled by the racial state.[44]

For the man in Jordan's poem, the threat the flowers pose in the present moment concerns the threat they pose to the future. Their way of living threatens the future children who might encounter them and a social order that requires and desires allegiance, decency, identity, racial purity, and normative sexuality. The future the flowers represent overflows into the present. In the past forty years the neoliberal-carceral state has produced a speculative politics of fear and anxiety about the near future so that there is a "generalized and heightened sense of expectancy of what has not yet come."[45] This anticipatory biopolitics is part of an ongoing slippage between population management and warfare that emerged out of the production of a social order that sought to defend and legitimate chattel slavery, genocide, and racial capital.[46] This history possesses the policing the man performs and the future he imagines. When the man looks at the flowers, he anticipates a future. He sees a threat on the horizon and works to police the future before it arrives. The flowers haunt the man's everyday with their presence—with memories of a time before control and governance—but they are also the summoned ghosts of a future that must never arrive. As the man implores the local police, the present must be managed to preempt potential undesirable futures.

Just a few years before Jordan's poem was published, James Baldwin described this emerging desire for prisons and police in an open letter to Angela Davis while she was incarcerated. He wrote, "One might have hoped that, by this hour, the very sight of chains on black flesh, or the very sight of chains, would be so intolerable a sight for the American people, and so unbearable a memory, that they would themselves spontaneously rise up and strike off the manacles. But, no, they appear to glory in their chains; now, more than ever, they appear to measure their safety in chains and corpses." Baldwin went on to argue that so long as white Americans live within that most "monstrous of traps" he called the "refuge [of] whiteness," they would allow millions of people to be killed in their name, would never feel "sufficiently human," and would continue to be exploited and killed in Vietnam, on college campuses, and in factories. In Baldwin's essay whiteness is another name for desire. To "glory in their chains" meant white people wanted whiteness and the death worlds it required more than their own freedom or even their own lives. Whiteness meant white people willfully desired to be "used by a carnivorous economy which democratically slaughters and victimizes whites and blacks alike."[47] Baldwin's conception of whiteness was a way for him to reconcile how white people could tolerate, want, and work for the demise of so many others and themselves.

Where Deleuze and Guattari see desire as central to the formation and functioning of capitalism, Baldwin sees desire as foundational to white supremacy and antiblackness. Nixon's and Goldwater's law-and-order politics channeled this desire for whiteness into a forty-year wave of police violence and mass capture and incapacitation. Neoliberal economics directed this desire into a regime that submitted life itself to the terror of a new structure called "the economy."[48] The cultural politics of homonormativity and homonationalism guided this desire toward hate crimes legislation, marriage, inclusion in the military, imperialism, warfare, and gentrification.[49] Understanding whiteness as desire exceeds an identitarian conception of race that would individualize it within particular people. It can help us understand how whiteness possesses and expands within structures that were intended to bring about liberal equality and freedom. Whiteness as desire also supplants an ideological conception of race that would declare white people lost and confused among a contorted maze of illusions and lies. Whiteness is a mode of habit, perception, and embodiment that developed from the management of settler, slave, and racial capitalism.[50] In other words, whiteness developed as way of manufacturing and desiring slavery and colonization. This desire also animated the rise of the neoliberal-carceral state. The "whiteness of the police" names the apparatuses of state violence that control the always present threat of blackness and other potentially insurgent formations. Further, the whiteness of the police is a way of desiring the present and the future. Yet if whiteness is not an ideology or identity, if it is a structural and structured mode of desire, how can desire lead beyond the police and prison to something else? What becomes thinkable, possible, and desirable if we follow the lead of Jordan's flowers? What other futures can desire open up if it escapes regimes of capture and takes flight? We can turn to Lorde's poetry about police violence and its relationship to the power of desire to help answer these questions.

The Erotic, Racial Terror, and Queer Feminist Futures

In her 1976 poem "Power," Lorde responds to the acquittal of a white New York City police officer, Thomas Shea, in the murder of Clifford Glover, a ten-year-old black boy he shot in the back. As I described in chapter 1, the

Weather Underground attacked the New York Police Department in response to Glover's murder. Lorde's poem is a different type of attack. It describes her attempts to comprehend and manage the unthinkable forms of fear, grief, rage, and terror she felt after the killing. She describes the moment she began to write the poem: "A kind of fury rose up in me; the sky turned red. I felt so sick. I felt as if I would drive this car into a wall, into the next person I saw. So I pulled over. I took out my journal just to air some of my fury, to get it out of my fingertips. Those expressed feelings are that poem."[51]

> The difference between poetry and rhetoric
> is being ready to kill
> yourself
> instead of your children.
>
> I am trapped on a desert of raw gunshot wounds
> and a dead child dragging his shattered black
> face off the edge of my sleep
> blood from his punctured cheeks and shoulders
> is the only liquid for miles
> and my stomach
> churns at the imagined taste while
> my mouth splits into dry lips
> without loyalty or reason
> thirsting for the wetness of his blood
> as it sinks into the whiteness
> of the desert where I am lost
> without imagery or magic
> trying to make power out of hatred and destruction
> trying to heal my dying son with kisses
> only the sun will bleach his bones quicker.
>
> A policeman who shot down a ten year old in Queens
> stood over the boy with his cop shoes in childish blood
> and a voice said "Die you little motherfucker" and
> there are tapes to prove it. At his trial
> this policeman said in his own defense
> "I didn't notice the size nor nothing else
> only the color." And
> there are tapes to prove that, too.

Today that 37 year old white man
with 13 years of police forcing
was set free
by eleven white men who said they were satisfied
justice had been done
and one Black Woman who said
"They convinced me" meaning
they had dragged her 4´10˝ black Woman's frame
over the hot coals
of four centuries of white male approval
until she let go
the first real power she ever had
and lined her own womb with cement
to make a graveyard for our children.

I have not been able to touch the destruction
within me.
But unless I learn to use
the difference between poetry and rhetoric
my power too will run corrupt as poisonous mold
or lie limp and useless as an unconnected wire
and one day I will take my teenaged plug
and connect it to the nearest socket
raping an 85 year old white woman
who is somebody's mother
and as I beat her senseless and set a torch to her bed
a greek chorus will be singing in 3/4 time
"Poor thing. She never hurt a soul. What beasts they are."[52]

"Power" describes Lorde "trapped on a desert of raw gunshot wounds," haunted by a "dead child dragging his shattered black / face off the edge of [her] sleep." The murder and its aftermath possessed her, robbing her of the calmness that accompanies the few moments of respite in an expansive system of racialized and gendered subjection and terror, or what she calls "the hot coals / of four centuries of white male approval." Lorde is drowning in the blood from the child's "punctured cheeks and shoulders," her stomach churning at the "imagined taste" of his blood. Lying in the "whiteness / of the desert where I am lost," she thirsts for his blood as it disappears in the whiteness that surrounds her. She cannot sleep; she is ready to kill or be killed—to drive into a wall, or into the first person she sees. Whereas Jordan theorizes the power of the police in a sterile, emotionless, post–civil rights prose that does not speak race, Lorde theorizes the violence of the racial state in a vivid, animate, and furious poetics. Glover's murder pushed Lorde to a place unfamiliar to normative epistemologies—a place beyond the knowable, toward what Lisa Marie Cacho calls an "unthinkable politics."[53] A place where the desire central to Lorde's black lesbian feminist fury leads.

In "Power," Lorde contests the forms of knowledge and truth produced by the carceral state's antiblackness and works toward a different accounting of the dead, one that does not rely on the imagined truth of the law. For example, in the middle of the poem she notes that the court cannot register or comprehend racialized terror even when there are "tapes to prove" that Shea's partner said, "Die you little motherfucker" and that Shea said, "I didn't notice the size nor nothing else / only the color" after the shooting.[54] "Power" is the name Lorde gives to the ability of the state to determine regimes of truth—the knowable and the unknowable.[55] Yet Lorde does not appeal to the recognition of the state. The poem is not legible to statist epistemologies. It does not demand vengeance or the imagined justice of the law with a new trial. Instead, Lorde wonders how to wage an affective struggle at the level of rage, despair, and desire. These emotions are also what she calls "power." The poem's ending warns of what will happen if the power of her desire is captured and corrupted. Lorde questions how to make "power out of hatred and destruction," how to know the difference between poetry and rhetoric so that her power will not "run corrupt as poisonous mold / or lie limp and useless as an unconnected wire."[56]

In "Power" Lorde outlines a different accounting of racial terror and demands an alternative mode of visionary politics that can see beyond things as they are toward a new form of power that might lead elsewhere—to a place beyond a world that can acquit Glover's killer, tolerate his murder, or even conceive of the conditions that made his death possible. Lorde does not want the power of her desire to "run corrupt" in a wave of violence and vengeance or lie unused and disconnected. She wants another way of feeling so that poetic ways of knowing and desiring can be a methodology for making a new ordering of the world.

Lorde's classic essay "The Uses of the Erotic" can help to clarify the theorization of desire in "Power." Indeed "Power" connects Lorde's black lesbian feminist theory of desire outlined in "The Uses of the Erotic" to the racial violence of the police. In both pieces the power of desire is open to exploitation and corruption at the same time that desire is a potential site of liberation, one that can undo systems of devaluation and violence. Lorde argues that the erotic is a form of "non-rational" power that lies in a "deeply female and spiritual plane, firmly rooted in our unacknowledged and unrecognized feeling." It is a form of "true feeling" that refuses mediocrity and leads one to demand the most from all aspects of life. The erotic is connected to sexuality but also exceeds it. It is a joyful "life force" that refuses to settle for the given order of things. It bridges the emotional and the political and is embodied in the seemingly contradictory figures of the "poetic revolutionary" and "meditating gunrunner."[57] Patriarchal power is ontologically threatened by the disruptive power of the erotic. It thus isolates and contains the erotic within the realm of sexuality and the space of the bedroom.

Deleuze and Guattari too argue that desire is not isolated to the "bedroom of Oedipus." Even when desire does take the form of love and sexuality, it escapes the bedroom to dream of "wide-open spaces."[58] When desire takes flight, it escapes categorization, recognition, identity, and hierarchy. Desire is not only sexuality; however, when it takes that form, it runs toward rupture and disruption. Carried away by desire, sexuality is an occasion to activate all aspects of life by becoming a site of alternative knowledge.[59] When the erotic and desire escape the bedroom they provide energy for radical and revolutionary change against the "numbness" and "horror of a system that defines the good in terms of profit rather than in terms of human need."[60] Lorde specifies that contesting racial capitalism and heteropatriarchy requires activating feelings and the senses in new and previously unthought ways.[61] She sees the erotic as a form of political struggle that uses desire as its path to new possibilities.

Lorde positions the erotic as an unrecognized, unnamed force that is prior to the powers of white supremacy, capital, and heteropatriarchy. These powers are secondary formations that emerge to corrupt and channel the erotic's primary disruptive force. They seek to capture the erotic and make it work toward subjection and subordination. Like desire, the erotic is capable of calling the order of things into question. Both formations are "explosive" because they are revolutionary in their essence.[62] They do not want revolution because they are revolutionary in their own right. Revolution is not their intent; it is their ontology. However, the erotic and desire diverge in ways just as profound as is their similarity. Like the different understandings of pleasure and desire articulated by Foucault and Deleuze, they are part of a larger transnational vocabulary produced in the 1970s that attempted to name the ways power was changing even as it remained the same. Lorde's theorization of desire differs from and exceeds the thinking of Deleuze and Guattari when she situates the erotic within black lesbian feminism and the racial politics of state violence.[63] In other words, the erotic is a form of desire, but desire as it has been theorized cannot encompass the erotic. By accounting for the racialization of sexuality, the erotic leads to where desire cannot go.

In "Power," Lorde calls for an affective struggle guided by the erotic in the form of poetry. Elsewhere she argues that poetry is how the erotic makes itself known. The poetic is a methodology for "naming the nameless so it can be thought." Poetry is the "distillation of experience" whereby dreams and feelings lead to places beyond the liberal epistemologies of the "white fathers." If white, patriarchal rationality operates under the phrase "I think, therefore I am," black lesbian feminism and the poet whisper "in our dreams: I feel, therefore I can be free." The rational thinking of the liberal subject is not the path to a new way of living. The affective powers of feelings and the erotic can create alternative futures that lead to a place "we have never been before."[64] "Power" channels the violent fury Lorde experienced after Glover's murder away from the rationality, whiteness, and policing of rhetoric toward the dreams and visions of the poetic. Lost in a desert of whiteness, she escapes through poetry. "Power" is her attempt to let the erotic lead her away from the violence of the racial state. In this way, the erotic is a fugitive affect—fleeing organization and enunciation even as multiple forces and institutions seek its capture—and poetry is the means for its flight.

The erotic in the form of poetry is a tactic and an epistemology that threatens to unravel the rational rhetoric that is the foundation of the carceral state. Undoing racial terror requires feeling in ways previously unthought and unknown, and this requires new ways of being—a subjectivity that abandons the rationality and visibility of the modern liberal subject who embodies the whiteness of the police. Lorde calls forth a poetic subject illegible to "the white fathers," a subject we can see in Jordan's flowers, which signify an erotic fugitivity that threatens the order and stability of the neoliberal-carceral state. STAR also demanded that desire lead away from the rhetoric and capture of the police—"the request of the pigs"—and toward a poetic mode of desire they called "gay power" that could lead somewhere else. This poetic subject is guided by the erotic so as to desire something beyond the police, heteropatriarchy, capital, and white supremacy. The erotic is a way of wanting more than the given state of things. It channels desire away from the neoliberal-carceral state toward a future that has yet to be articulated. The erotic is a form of fugitivity that leads to something unimaginably different, but already here in moments as powerful as they are fleeting. As we run, the erotic is the fugitive we must follow.

"BEING CAPTURED IS BESIDE THE POINT"

A WORLD BEYOND THE WORLD

To whom do I flee and where?

—JACQUI ALEXANDER, *Pedagogies of Crossing*

Throughout *Fugitive Life*, I have examined the communiqués, literature, memoirs, prison writing, and poetry of underground and imprisoned activists in the 1970s United States to provide an analysis of the centrality of gender and sexuality to a new mode of racialized state power called the neoliberal-carceral state. I've paused on the neoliberal-carceral state's moment of inception in the 1970s to consider how feminist and queer prisoners and activists reorganized their efforts to respond to a rising wave of incarceration animated by a new mode of governance structured by the market. I've worked to document resistance to forms of biopolitical state power that are as new as they are old by examining the alternative modes of life and living produced within spaces of social death and emerging regimes of capture. As Davis and other activists hid, ran, wrote, robbed, and bombed their way toward what they hoped was a better world, they created a vast political and cultural world called "the underground." In the process they produced alternative ways of thinking and being that exceeded how neoliberal and law-and-order discourses defined the livable, the valuable, the thinkable, and the possible. For these activists being a fugitive meant escaping rapidly expanding systems of racialized policing and imprisonment. At the same time, fugitivity produced new forms of knowledge that theorized how the prison and market reshaped what could be seen, known, and thought. Being on the run meant getting away, but also thinking and seeing anew and beyond. I suggest that imprisoned and fugitive women in the 1970s are central—but overlooked—figures in the story of how the United States came to have the world's largest prison system.

In *Fugitive Life* I have searched what has been left behind, forgotten, and erased by changing regimes of state and economic power in an attempt to comprehend neoliberalism and the prison in ways that open new lines of thought when considering the unprecedented changes of the past forty years. If we are to understand the forms of power we find ourselves inhabited by and that gave rise to the neoliberal-carceral state, we must look to spaces and times of expulsion, disappearance, and incapacitation for the diagnosis and the cure. I have analyzed the space of the underground and the figures of the prisoner and the fugitive in order to explore different understandings of freedom, temporality, queerness, race, gender, economics, and incarceration. The underground, the fugitive, and the prisoner are sites of an immanent critique of the state's policing and penal powers produced by those same formations. For example, Bukhari, Davis, and Shakur have all been prisoners and fugitives, and their critiques of the prison and neoliberalism emerged from these two symbiotic positionalities. As fugitives and prisoners they could see what others could not: invisible things became glaring in an absence they no longer inhabited, and what had always been visible became strange and unfamiliar. Running away was a tactic that challenged the power of the neoliberal-carceral state, yet it also opened up new formations of knowledge and politics. I want to examine these alternative ways of knowing and feeling by exploring the major themes of *Fugitive Life* in a discussion of the 1980 edited collection *Top Ranking: A Collection of Articles on Racism and Classism in the Lesbian Community*.[1]

Top Ranking includes essays by some of the more well-known women foundational to the development of black feminism, such as Audre Lorde, Beverly Smith, and Barbara Smith. But it also collects the writings of the imprisoned butch political prisoner Rita Brown, anti-imperialist lesbian feminists, lesbian antiprison activists, and black lesbians who interrogated the policing functions of white lesbian communities. In this same period books such as *This Bridge Called My Back: Writings by Radical Women of Color*; *Home Girls: A Black Feminist Anthology*; and *All the Women Are White, All the*

Blacks Are Men, but Some of Us Are Brave: Black Women's Studies helped re-shape the long-standing project of analyzing race, sexuality, and gender as mutually constitutive forms of power central to the state, institutionalism, and capital. In describing the significance of these texts, Jacqui Alexander writes that they spoke to "refugees fleeing some terrible atrocity far too threatening to engage, ejected out of the familiar into some unknown, still-to-be revealed place. Refugees forced to create out of the raw smithy of fire a shape different from our inheritance, with no blueprints, no guarantees."[2] *This Bridge Called My Back* and the other collections charted a new way to be in the world. A different way of being without direction or promise would leave behind the forceful afflictions and quiet terrors of possession. Alexander outlines the making of an affective epistemology—a fugitive way of knowing that escaped articulation—that would give rise to a way of being beyond ontology. This way of feeling and knowing composes an architecture of the world without a blueprint of who and what should go where. It led to a place where one's arrival was always deferred. This place could be unknowably different from the present because it refused to be modeled on what came before—it was still to be revealed. Perpetually deferred, it nevertheless offered a place to flee to. Like the running of the fugitive, its future was uncharted.

This way of knowing was central to the underground—a world inside the world but also beyond it, a place where what was coming was always unknown. Making such a world necessitated a politics attuned to movement, transformation, and becoming undone. Indeed to go underground one had to first travel in circles, go the wrong way, get lost, and become someone else. For example, in *American Woman* Jenny never knows what the future will bring or where she is headed. She shows that fleeing the police is not enough; power lives not only in the state and its institutions of enforcement. Power is not static, residing in easily identifiable places and people. It circulates, possesses, escapes, and mutates. It exists only in movement because it exists only in relationships. And so Jenny's fugitivity is from the racialized and heteropatriarchal normative modes of thought and living that possess the state, capital, and the revolutionary left, but also the mundane contours of the world itself. Jenny doesn't know where she is going, but she knows what she is running from. It comes in the form of a blue uniform, a bearded revolutionary hero, or the hot breath of a sympathetic man in the middle of the night. For her there might not be a way out, but that does not mean one should stay put.

Alexander also observes that *This Bridge Called My Back* works to recover memories, feelings, histories, and connections that have been lost because "we had forgotten what we had forgotten."[3] To remember is to contest the production of the world through what we don't know that we don't know. Like the project of Davis, Shakur, and Williams discussed in chapter 3, a different future is impossible without calling to the present disremembered memories of the forgotten. Reordering the world means being open to the unknown places fugitivity leads while being guided by memories and feelings one never knew had been lost. The black feminist writings composed by captured fugitives offer us a genealogy of the present composed by loss and the forgotten. Their warning concerning the power of the market and its relationship to the carceral is made possible by their deployment of an epistemology attuned to unknowing. All three offer a genealogy of the prison and of the market that leads to the hold, the coffle, and the sweatbox, but they do so through memory, fiction, and the contingency of feeling. Undoing the terrifying possession of the present by what is dominantly called the past requires alternative ways of knowing outlined by Davis and Shakur, but also the collections discussed by Alexander. We can place *Top Ranking* within this broader world-building project. Yet *Top Ranking* differs from the other collections in its attempt to center an analysis of the prison and its relationship to racial capitalism and heteropatriarchy in the immediate aftermath of the 1970s. Unlike the other collections, it is currently out of print and has been relegated to the footnotes of this period.

In their introduction, "Racism and Classism in the Lesbian Community: Towards the Building of a Radical Autonomous Lesbian Movement," the collection's editors, Joan Gibbs and Sara Bennett, construct a politics of relational difference in which solidarity between different people and communities relies on an understanding of the "differences in our oppression." Like the ways the George Jackson Brigade centered difference in their underground politics, Gibbs and Bennett want lesbianism to be a force of insurgent connection. They see capital, the racial state, and the prison manufacturing nonnormative populations that contain the potential for unlikely and previously unimagined alliances. After showing how slavery and settler colonialism shape the contours of the present, they define *radical* as an epistemology whereby the liberation of lesbians is necessarily connected to the "liberation of all oppressed peoples and the total destruction of the present system." *Autonomous* is the name given to an identity-based movement that surpasses the circuitous limitations of identity politics—lesbian politics would not end at lesbianism. They want a "strong lesbian movement" that targets "hetero-sexism and sexism, the institutions of patriarchy," and "domestic colonialism, the roots of racism, and imperialism—all the systems that oppress lesbians." Gibbs and Bennett argue that sterilization, racialized incarceration, and struggles against capitalism, apartheid, and colonialism in the United States, Puerto Rico, South Africa, and Chile are issues that imperil the lives of les-bians (and all people) everywhere to different degrees and with different outcomes. As a working-class, black lesbian, Gibbs wants a lesbian politics that can make sense of her life: the lynching and murder of her cousin, a black woman; her sister's drug addiction and incarceration on Rikers Island; the diffuse processes she calls "conditions" that lead to the death of "Black and Third World communities"; and struggles by Native people and multiple communities of color for liberation and land.[4]

Incarceration and capitalism are central to the essays in *Top Ranking*. In their introduction Gibbs and Bennett describe an emerging form of rac-ism in lesbian communities: "One way that racism in particular has mani-fested itself in both the lesbian and feminist community/movements is in some of the strategies devised for addressing violence against women, a legitimate concern of all women. Some of us have called for more police protection, lesbian police officers and/or participated in discussions with the police, completely disregarding the murder or shooting down of Third World women, men and children by the police and that the sole purpose of the police is to protect private property and maintain 'order.'"[5] Like the Street Transvestite Action Revolutionaries before them, Gibbs and Bennett worry about how white supremacy is changing the contours and directions of lesbian and queer desire in the era of the neoliberal-carceral state. The goal of the collection is to redirect the force of queerness. They see the capture of desire when lesbians and feminists want the racial state to pro-tect *some* lesbians against *some* forms of homophobic and sexist violence. Gibbs and Bennett see lesbians running toward the police, calling out for their regulation and violence to provide the contingent safety of death and dispossession. Lesbianism is going on patrol when Gibbs, Bennett, and so many others want it to make patrolling impossible. *Top Ranking* catalogues how desire leads from the individual to the biopolitical, the intimate to the colonial, from a group of lesbians afraid for their lives to the racial terror of the police. The editors instead want desire to lead to the continuation of a five-century-long struggle against the possession of the everyday by anti-blackness, white supremacy, and settler colonialism.

To that end the contributors to *Top Ranking* see a relationality among systems of power often conceived of as discrete under statist, Marxist, feminist, nationalist, lesbian, and radial epistemologies (racism and classism, as the title suggests) and between individuals and communities often considered oppositional or beyond the capacity of connection. In an essay titled "Prison Work and the Lesbian Issue: A Personal Statement," a white lesbian antiprison activist named Charoula responds to lesbians who believe that "doing prison work is antithetical to the 'lesbian movement.'" Grounded in an analysis of gendered poverty, the racialized regulation of welfare, criminalized survival strategies, and patriarchal violence, Charoula argues that incarcerated women "know who the enemy is, and the enemy is the same for both lesbians and straight women. I only wish we could acquire the same clear insight in our struggles out here." She imagines a lesbian politics that will attack "the state itself" by attacking prisons. By attacking the racial state, lesbians could launch an autonomous but coalitional movement grounded in the "differences amongst us." In the short term such a movement could support the resistance and survival of those most vulnerable to racialized and heteropatriarchal state violence. "In the long range, fighting for women in prison is fighting for our own interests as well—our own survival."[6] One cannot easily separate outside from inside, free from unfree, because the inside possesses the outside and the outside makes the inside possible.

Charoula's and other contributors' conception of coalition is echoed in Bernice Johnson Reagon's 1981 essay "Coalition Politics: Turning the Century," included in Barbara Smith's *Home Girls: A Black Feminist Anthology*. Reagon imagines an unruly and insurgent relationality when she argues against separatism and isolationism: "there's no chance that you can survive by staying inside the barred room" that communities create in the name of safety and security. She points out that you don't build a coalition to feel the warm, comforting embrace of home or because "you *like* it." You enter a coalition because it's the only way to survive.[7] Elsewhere Fred Moten similarly writes, "The coalition emerges out of your recognition that it's fucked up for you, in the same way that we've recognized it's fucked up for us. I don't need your help. I just need you to realize that this shit is killing you, too, however much more softly, you stupid motherfucker, you know?" By emphasizing relationality grounded in the fabricated differences that govern life and death, many of the collection's contributors work to have (neo)liberal subjectivity "unlawfully overcome by others" because a new way of being would not possess "a kind of agency that can hold the regulatory forces of subject hood."[8]

The collection imagines new ways of being that abolish (neo)liberal subjectivity in favor of a differential collective becoming grounded in being "fluent in each other's histories."[9] This conception of coalition as a different way of being in the world is evident in the flowers in June Jordan's "Letter to the Local Police."

Recall that the world of the flowers ontologically threatens the world of the neoliberal subject and so needs to be policed, named, and eradicated. Yet the world of the flowers is already in the world of the police. Their racialized queer fugitivity precedes the police. The police emerged and expanded to make their fugitivity impossible—to expel them to the realm of the forgotten. The existence of the flowers has to be forgotten, because their existence, even the memory of their existence, is a threat to the future. It cannot be known that they are known. The life of the flowers puts in ontological peril the law and order of the state. Their existence also threatens the security, normativity, and safety of the neoliberal subject who polices them so their promise of another way of being disappears and becomes unknowable. But the flowers are always there, living with each other, living amid the ways of life they threaten with other ways of being.

The underground was also in, but beyond, the world it worked to make unknowable. It was a vast world created inside the devastation and terror of the world as it existed. And critically, the underground required aboveground coalitional networks to provide housing, money, health care, information, friendship, feedback, and so much more. In other words, the fugitive is not a solitary figure. The threat of her escape lay in the collectivity of the underground, because there were thousands like her "abiding in a perpetual near riot / of wild behavior" beyond control or identity. While isolation was one of her tactics, other people made her escape possible. This means that building other modes of life was not an isolationist effort, nor is it unique to the underground. It is important to remember that this world beyond the world exists in so many places in so many times: in a Black Panther health clinic, when collective struggles over language and knowledge make possible new ways to inhabit a body, in the erotic connections forged in the hold of the ship, in the love and care between imprisoned people, in ways of living that do not know the logic of the market, in the whispers of the maroon outpost, on the dance floor after the drag show when everything disappears, in the lifeways that precede and supersede the settler state, when workers walk away from the factory and toward new ways of organizing life, and on and on and on. The underground is not an exceptional space, but it is one way to see a collective making of a different world in, but beyond, the impossibility of living in the current one.

"Somewhere" by Rita Brown, a George Jackson Brigade member and captured fugitive, is also included in *Top Ranking*. Gibbs and Bennett note that one of the many shortcomings of the collection is that Brown is the only imprisoned contributor. They also note that they did not know where Brown was—she was simply "somewhere," as the title of her essay suggests—because she was transferred due to her friendship with the recently escaped Assata Shakur.[10] Writing from a prison cell, Brown describes how an emergent neoliberal subjectivity was changing leftist, feminist, antiracist, and lesbian politics in the early 1980s. It is worth quoting her at length because her writing anticipates the colonization of the collective by the individual within contemporary neoliberalism:

> Somewhere along the roads to getting our consciousness raised we got angry at the discovery of our personal oppression. That anger sometimes distorts our view of the world. It makes us narrower instead of broader cuz it is so big and ugly. It clouds our brains and fogs our vision so that all we can see is "what they are doing to me." Even when we find theory that teaches us the importance/necessity of thinking in the broadest terms, we still react in narrow defensive ways. This is all [a] product of cultural brainwashing. We are all products of our "me first" environment. . . . We often let our righteous anger produce the behavior of spoiled brats. We forget that everything we feel, even our anger, is suspect. Not that it is bad to feel anger, but do we deal with it? i mean, look whose institutions taught it all to us, right?
>
> Somewhere along the roads to getting our consciousness raised we learned a new language with all sorts of "isms" & clever intellectual phraseology. Now we get even more arrogant cuz we know the lingo & know we have really learned something. We believe we are the only korrect ones & damn anyone else who don't agree with us. Some of us go so far as to order the korrect clothes to wear, the korrect people to sleep with, the korrect children to raise etc etc etc ad infinite nasium. . . . We create even more OTHERS to scorn & hate instead of dealing with "the man." Which is not to say we shouldn't get our own house in order. But we should realize that our misdirected energy is extremely dangerous, especially to us.[11]

One of the devastating effects of neoliberalism has been the eradication of collective movements for liberation in favor of single-issue policy organizations that focus on individual rights and transformation. Within this broader shift to the nonprofit-industrial complex, neoliberalism has shaped how we imagine what we want, what we need, and what tomorrow should look like.[12] Impossible demands—"Bring the war home!"; "Free our sisters, free ourselves!"; "Free all political prisoners!"; "Gay liberation now!"; "We cannot live without our lives"—have been supplanted by a bureaucracy of the practical: marriage, insurance, retirement, inclusion in the military and police, criminal justice reform, hate crimes laws, and so on. In this context, Brown observes that one's feelings and affects are produced by regimes of power far beyond the control of the individual. Feelings like anger, depression, anxiety, and fear are political, but not only in the sense that they are resistant. She argues that because feelings are political they are not innocent: "even our anger is suspect." Anger can lead to capture because neoliberalism and the prison shape the contours of our emotional lives. Our feelings and affects are possessed by what we imagine we refuse. Lorde gave this same warning in her poem about police violence, "Power," and her essay "The Uses of the Erotic." Lorde's erotics contain the potential of flight or of circling back to heteropatriarchy. Her anger about the murder of Clifford Glover could lead to a new order of things or to destruction without a new beginning. Thus emotions are incredibly powerful for Lorde, but they need to be nurtured with knowledge. Lorde has to "learn" how not to let her affective power "lie limp and useless" or "corrupt as poisonous mold." Brown implies that one's feelings are not the sole property of the sovereign (neo)liberal individual. They are instead produced and captured by other people, institutions, and regimes of power. Brown warns the readers of *Top Ranking* not to get lost in the disorienting cloud of terror created by state violence, to not allow rage and fury to lead to "narrow and defensive ways."

Brown's "me first environment" is another way of describing a leftist, neoliberal desire for inclusion and incorporation, as opposed to abolition and liberation.[13] This politics is founded on a desire for visibility and recognition so one is correctly seen by power—so what one opposes gives one a proper name. This neoliberal resistance says to the racial state and other institutional formations, "See me, name me, embrace me." It says, "Let me inside, give me a home, but keep the outside intact." By asking to be seen as a proper neoliberal individual this "me first" politics upholds the subjection and subordination of those not conceptualized as a necessary part of the self. "Me" requires a "you" not worthy of what "I" deserve. Alexander warns against this individual conception of the political and an antagonistic competition it creates. She writes that we must resist "and unlearn an impulse to claim first oppression, most-devastating oppression, one-of-a-kind oppression, defying comparison oppression. We would have to unlearn an impulse that allows mythologies about each other to replace knowing about one another. . . . We cannot afford to cease yearning for each other's company."[14] Desiring each other's company and "knowing about one another" are different political, affective, and epistemological projects from what Brown calls "me first." Yet she does not say that an individualizing politics should be abandoned in total. We still need to keep our house in order, after all. But she does hold on to the question of scale. She notes the destructive effects of infighting about how best to inhabit the subjectivity of a proper resistant neoliberal subject who is always one step in front of power's grasp. Doing the "korrect" thing is a way to feign resistant innocence in the face of so much complicity. It is a way to construct and solidify the neoliberal self in contradistinction to the failures of a lesser, backward, unenlightened, racialized, complicit Other. One's resistant freedom, which she calls being "korrect," requires an imaginary subject who is unfree, tethered to power, and worthy of derision and blame. Brown wants readers to "forgot the useless strive for perfection."[15] She wants lesbian anger and affect to be directed at an assemblage of forces coalesced under "the man." Yet doing so requires a profound radical humility open to embracing our collective complicities, mistakes, and shortcomings.

Early in the essay Brown writes, "We can only learn by doing. We have to stop being afraid that we might do something wrong."[16] She warns us not to mistake individual rights and expression for freedom or self-righteous fury for resistance. Indeed she reminds us that resistance is never solely resistant. As *American Woman* and *Top Ranking* make clear, resistance can also animate the shape of subjection. Resistance can open new pathways for power's operation. To perhaps point out the obvious, this is *Top Ranking's* argument about lesbianism. Lesbian politics took the shape of subjection when it left classism and racism unthought. White supremacy could possess a resistant lesbian politics and thus expand its systems of capture and control. Lesbian politics may contest heteropatriarchy, but that resistance can still bolster other methods of unevenly distributing value and disposability.

Brown thus argues that setting up a disciplinary politics that enforces a correct way to be, think, and act will distract from the regimes of power that are leading to the misery, subjection, terror, deaths, and slow deaths of everyone in different ways at different speeds by different means. Brown ends her essay by reminding readers, "Perfection is not a human characteristic. Only robots have predictable behavior. So let's get a strong hold on our patience, mix it thoroughly with determination, forget the useless strive for perfection, & let's continue our work building ourselves and our alliances. It sure won't be easy to build better ways & days . . . but we can do it!!"[17] Brown wants an emerging neoliberal subjectivity to be overcome by a politics of differential collective becoming. From prison she sees neoliberal individuality and its politics as a new form of capture that has to be contested. Individuality is not the sign of freedom but the mark that one has been caught. The challenge, as Foucault argues one year later, is "not to discover what we are, but to refuse what we are," to become something different, and to do so together. *Top Ranking* and its contemporaneous edited collections outline this politics of fugitivity and the fact that "there is no relationship of power without the means of escape or possible flight."[18] The way out is there—a world is here, beyond the world as it is. We need an affective politics and epistemology capable of seeing the exit.

In his correspondence with Barbara Smith, the editor of *Home Girls*, David Gilbert, a Weather Underground member and white antiracist and anti-imperialist political prisoner, describes the imperative to escape in his transcription of a poem written by the Turkish political prisoner Nazim Hikmet, "It's This Way":

I stand in the advancing light,
my hands hungry, the world beautiful.

My eyes can't get enough of the trees—they're so hopeful, so green.

A sunny road runs through the mulberries,
I'm at the window of the prison infirmary.

I can't smell the medicines—carnations must be blooming nearby.

It's this way:
being captured is beside the point,
the point is not to surrender.[19]

Even though Gilbert's body is immobilized, and will be until he dies, he remains committed to producing modes of thought that take flight. The challenge is not to find the innocence of the outside—escape is not so simple and being captured is beside the point. The prison's end must exceed the institution. This is the lesson of the fugitive, a lesson we must grasp if the affects, desires, discourses, and ideas that make the prison possible are to end along with its cages, corridors, and guard towers. The fugitive can lead the way. She shows that something else lives between escape and capture. Even if escape is impossible, we still have to run.

INTRODUCTION. "ESCAPE-BOUND CAPTIVES"

1. The George Jackson Brigade, "Capitalism Is Organized Crime," in Burton-Rose, *Creating a Movement with Teeth*, 107.

2. The George Jackson Brigade, "International Women's Day," in Burton-Rose, *Creating a Movement with Teeth*, 90.

3. John Brockhaus and Roxanne Park, "Ed Mead Speaks from Prison," in Burton-Rose, *Creating a Movement with Teeth*, 197.

4. The George Jackson Brigade, "The Power of the People Is the Force of Life: Political Statement of the George Jackson Brigade," in Burton-Rose, *Creating a Movement with Teeth*, 148.

5. Hewitt, *Political Violence and Terrorism in Modern America*, 105.

6. The George Jackson Brigade, "Olympia Bombing," in Burton-Rose, *Creating a Movement with Teeth*, 78–79.

7. John Dooly, "Rita Bo Brown: The Gentleman Bank Robber," *Portland (OR) Mercury*, June 12, 2003. http://www.portlandmercury.com/portland/Content?oid=29228&category=23483.

8. Brown, "A Short Autobiography," 15.

9. Brown, "Sentencing Statement," 19, 16, 17–19, 17.

10. The George Jackson Brigade, "Capitalism Is Organized Crime," 108.

11. This theorization of the prison as a warehouse is also remarkable because it is exactly how some contemporary scholars of the prison describe the function of incarceration in the post-1970s United States. For example, Gilmore, *Golden Gulags*, argues that imprisoned people are deindustrialized cities' working or workless poor. Similarly Herivel and Wright's *Prison Nation* documents the creation of the prison-industrial complex as a technology used to contain surplus populations under contemporary capitalism. Wacquant, *Punishing the Poor* and "The Penalization of Poverty and the Rise of Neoliberalism," argues that as social welfare policies were downsized in the 1970s and 1980s, the deregulated labor market became intimately connected to incarceration. According to Wacquant, the penal system functions as an apparatus to manage social insecurity and the social disorders created by deindustrialization, deregulation, and

privatization. In the late 1970s and early 1980s criminalization became the strategy of choice in dealing with the globalization of capital and the resistance it engendered. See also Parenti, *Lockdown America*; Sudbury, "Celling Black Bodies."

12. Davis, *Are Prisons Obsolete?*, 16.

13. Alex Fryer, "The Evolution of a Revolutionary—John Sherman, Radical-Turned-Robber, Now Follows a Spiritual Guru," *Seattle Times*, June 24, 1999, http://community .seattletimes.nwsource.com/archive/?date=19990624&slug=2968311.

14. Brockhaus and Park, "Ed Mead Speaks from Prison," 194.

15. Fryer, "The Evolution of a Revolutionary."

16. Camp, *Incarcerating the Crisis*.

17. Davis and Aptheker, *If They Come in the Morning*, xiii.

18. Aptheker, "The Social Function of Prisons," 57.

19. Baldwin, "An Open Letter to My Sister, Angela Y. Davis."

20. Foucault, "The Masked Assassination," 140, 156.

21. Baldwin, "An Open Letter to My Sister, Angela Y. Davis," 23.

22. Wacquant, *Punishing the Poor*, 61.

23. Sylvia River Law Project, *It's a War in Here*, 9.

24. Wacquant, *Punishing the Poor*, 69.

25. See in general Sylvia River Law Project, *It's a War in Here*; Mogul et al., *Queer (In)Justice*; Stanley and Smith, *Captive Genders*.

26. Gilmore, *Golden Gulags*, 28.

27. Davis and Aptheker, *If They Come in the Morning*, xiii.

28. Davis and Aptheker, *If They Come in the Morning*, vxiii, xv–xvii.

29. Davis and Aptheker, *If They Come in the Morning*, 43.

30. Edward Mead, "Ed Mead Replies," in Burton-Rose, *Creating a Movement with Teeth*, 228.

31. Shakur, "America Is the Prison."

32. Burton-Rose, "A Collective Interview with the George Jackson Brigade," in *Creating a Movement with Teeth*, 13, 257–58.

33. For one of the most detailed accounts of the rise of neoliberal economics see Jones, *Masters of the Universe*.

34. Jones, *Masters of the Universe*, 3.

35. Harvey, *Neoliberalism*, 11.

36. Wacquant, *Punishing the Poor*, 306.

37. Giroux, *The Terror of Neoliberalism*, xiii.

38. Hong, *Death beyond Disavowal*; Reddy, *Freedom with Violence*.

39. Goldberg, *The Threat of Race*, 341.

40. Gilmore, "Fatal Couplings of Power and Difference," 17.

41. Gilmore, *Golden Gulags*, 28.

42. Mohanty, *Feminism without Borders*, 234.

43. Jean Genet, introduction to Jackson, *Soledad Brother*, 332.

44. Rodríguez, *Forced Passages*; Hames-García, *Fugitive Thought*; James, introduction to *Warfare in the American Homeland*.

45. Rodríguez, *Forced Passages*, 202.

46. For a comprehensive overview of these movements see Burrough, *Days of Rage*.

47. Ferguson, *Aberrations in Black*, ix.

48. Burton-Rose, *Creating a Movement with Teeth*, 200.

49. Springer, *Living for the Revolution*.

50. Burton-Rose, *Creating a Movement with Teeth*, 200–201.

51. Keeling, "I = Another," 53.

52. Brockhaus and Park, "Ed Mead Speaks from Prison," 149.

53. Cohen, "Punks, Bulldaggers, and Welfare Queens," 447, 438, 440.

54. Haley, "'Like I Was a Man,'" 73.

55. Haley, *No Mercy Here*, 57.

56. Haley, *No Mercy Here*, 21.

57. Sharpe, *In the Wake*, 75–77.

58. Haley, *No Mercy Here*, 9.

59. Haley, "'Like I Was a Man,'" 73.

60. Spillers, "Mama's Baby, Papa's Maybe," 72.

61. Abdur-Rahman, "'The Strangest Freaks of Despotism,'" 230.

62. Spillers, "Mama's Baby, Papa's Maybe," 67.

63. Abdur-Rahman, "'The Strangest Freaks of Despotism,'" 234.

64. Tinsley, "Black Atlantic, Queer Atlantic," 209.

65. The George Jackson Brigade, *The Power of the People Is the Force of Life*, 5.

66. Stagecoach Mary Collective, "A Response to the George Jackson Brigade," in Burton-Rose, *Creating a Movement with Teeth*, 114–15.

67. Hong and Ferguson, introduction to *Strange Affinities*, 13.

68. Berlant, *Cruel Optimism*, 95–121.

69. Hanhardt, "Left Queer."

70. Hong and Ferguson, introduction to *Strange Affinities*, 13.

71. Richie, *Arrested Justice*, 103.

72. Butler, *War Frames*, 167–69.

73. Sandoval, *Methodology of the Oppressed*, 43, 77.

74. Hong, "Existentially Surplus"; Ferguson, *Aberrations in Black*, 110–37.

75. The George Jackson Brigade, "International Women's Day," 90–92.

76. The George Jackson Brigade, "International Women's Day," 93.

77. Keeling, "I = Another," 73; George Jackson Brigade, "International Women's Day," 92–93.

78. Mohanty, *Feminism without Borders*, 46.

79. The George Jackson Brigade, "International Women's Day," 94.

80. The George Jackson Brigade, "International Women's Day," 263, 262.

81. The George Jackson Brigade, "International Women's Day," 162.

82. Eng et al., "What's Queer about Queer Studies Now?," 3.

83. Davis, "Lessons from Soledad," in Davis and Aptheker, *If They Come in the Morning*, 44.

84. "Prohibited Items."

85. For more on solitary confinement see Kurshan, *Out of Control*; Rhodes, *Total Confinement*; Reiter, *23/7*; Guenther, *Solitary Confinement*.

86. Rita D. Brown, "Things Here," in Gibbs and Bennett, *Top Ranking*, 41.

87. Davis, "Lessons from Soledad," 44.

88. Moten and Harney, *The Undercommons*, 28.

89. Deleuze, *The Logic of Sense*, 80.

90. Lowe, *Immigrant Acts*, 57.

91. Butler, *Bodies That Matter*, 241.

92. Berger, "Marilyn Buck's Playlist," 115.

93. Gossett, "Making a Way Out of No Way."

1. "WE'RE NOT HIDING BUT WE'RE INVISIBLE"

1. Nixon, "What Has Happened to America?"

2. Nixon, "What Has Happened to America?"

3. Bernstein, *America Is the Prison*, 25–27.

4. Bourdieu, "The Essence of Neoliberalism."

5. Bourdieu, "The Essence of Neoliberalism."

6. Harvey, *Neoliberalism*, 19.

7. Scott, *Seeing like a State*, 82.

8. For example, see Flamm, *Law and Order*; Alexander, *The New Jim Crow*; Garland, *The Culture of Control*; Simon, *Governing through Crime*; Bernstein, *America Is the Prison*.

9. Goldwater, "1964 Acceptance Speech."

10. Goldwater, "1964 Acceptance Speech."

11. Elbaum, *Revolution in the Air*, 1.

12. Rodríguez, *Forced Passages*, 20–21.

13. Brown, *Regulating Aversion*, 149–76.

14. Hall, "The Neoliberal Revolution," 706.

15. Quoted in Hall, "The Neoliberal Revolution," 707.

16. Brown, "American Nightmare," 694.

17. Brown, "American Nightmare," 705.

18. Gordon, *Ghostly Matters*, 1.

19. Foucault, *The History of Sexuality*, 44.

20. Twenty years later Thatcher would similarly invoke the specter of white victimization in a metaphor of slavery: "Let me give you my vision: a man's right to work as he will, to spend what he earns, to own property, to have the State as servant not as master: these are the British inheritance. They are the essence of a free country and on that freedom all our other freedoms depend" (quoted in Hall, "The Neoliberal Revolution," 706).

21. Brown, *Regulating Aversion*, 166.

22. It's significant that as he is arguing for a "free" economy, Goldwater also argues that the government must maintain a "stable monetary and fiscal climate." Thus a free market requires an active and powerful state in the economic and penal sphere ("1964 Acceptance Speech").

23. Nixon, "Acceptance Speech, Delivered before the Republican National Convention."

24. Quoted in Flamm, *Law and Order*, 42.

25. Melamed, *Represent and Destroy*, xxi.

26. Hanhardt, "Left Queer."

27. Flamm, *Law and Order*, 11, emphasis added.

28. Quoted in Flamm, *Law and Order*, 98.

29. Nixon, "The First Civil Right."

30. In his acceptance speech Nixon acknowledged that many viewed law and order as fundamentally a racist project: "And to those who say that law and order is the code word for racism, here is a reply: Our goal is justice—justice for every American. If we are to have respect for law in America, we must have laws that deserve respect. Just as we cannot have progress without order, we cannot have order without progress."

31. On the development of official antiracism in the mid-twentieth century, see Melamed, *Represent and Destroy*, 2013.

32. Wilderson, *Red, White, and Black*, 222.

33. Edelman, *No Future*, 4; Nixon, "A Child's Face."

34. For Nixon and the governing imagination of the era, it was not the queer, as Edelman would have it, who opposed life and futurity; it was the threat of blackness that was the sign of the end of the future. As Keeling writes, "From within the logics of reproductive futurity and colonial reality, a black future looks like no future at all" (*Looking for M—*, 578).

35. Bourdieu, "The Essence of Neoliberalism."

36. For more on COINTELPRO see Blackstock, *Cointelpro*; Churchill and Vander Wall, *The COINTELPRO Papers*; Churchill and Vander Wall, *Agents of Repression*.

37. Burton-Rose, *Guerrilla USA*; Burton-Rose, *Creating a Movement with Teeth*.

38. See broadly, Burrough, *Days of Rage*.

39. Churchill, preface to Burton-Rose, *Creating a Movement with Teeth*, 14.

40. Ayers, *Fugitive Days*, 228.

41. Ayers, *Fugitive Days*, 216.

42. Burton-Rose, *Guerrilla USA*, 177–78.

43. Mark Rudd, a Weather Underground member, writes that the 1970s counterculture helped many fugitives stay hidden: "I'd eventually have to tell some vague story about dropping out of school in the East. Amazingly few people asked questions, probably because my story was not all that different from those of the people I was hanging out with—ex-students, ex–flight attendants, ex-secretaries, ex–everybody who had found acid or some other truth that led them to drop out of straight society" (*Underground*, 220).

44. Gilbert, *Love and Struggle*, 157, 158, 220.

45. Scott, *Seeing like a State*, 183–91, 183.

46. Foucault, *Security, Territory, Population*, 44.

47. Foucault, *Discipline and Punish*, 151, 152.

48. Ayers, *Fugitive Days*, 226.

49. Davis, *An Autobiography*, 5.

50. Dohrn et al., *Sing a Battle Song*, 151.

51. Gilbert, *Love and Struggle*, 162.

52. For a broader overview of the Weather Underground see Berger, *Outlaws of America*; Jacobs, *The Way the Wind Blew*.

53. Wilkerson, *Flying Close to the Sun*.

54. Dohrn et al., *Sing a Battle Song*, 150.

55. Dohrn et al., *Sing a Battle Song*, 152.

56. Dohrn et al., *Sing a Battle Song*, 169.

57. Dohrn et al., *Sing a Battle Song*, 225.

58. Dohrn et al., *Sing a Battle Song*, 160.

59. Dohrn et al., *Sing a Battle Song*, 176.

60. Dohrn et al., *Sing a Battle Song*, 198.

61. Dohrn et al., *Sing a Battle Song*, 108–9.

62. Singh, *Black Is a Country*, 204.

63. Churrah, "The State."

64. Singh, *Black Is a Country*, 204.

65. See Gilbert, *Love and Struggle*, 153–225.

66. Dohrn et al., *Sing a Battle Song*, 204.

67. Dohrn et al., *Sing a Battle Song*, 199–200.

68. In a fascinating and sometimes bizarre process, a number of FBI agents went underground and pretended to be fugitives in order to learn how the underground worked. The process largely failed. See Grathwohl, *Bringing Down America*; Eckstein, *Bad Moon Rising*.

69. The George Jackson Brigade took a similar risk when they publicly declared, "We're not all straight and we're not all men," because the police would be able to narrow down their search. Despite this information, the FBI continued to investigate the college-educated, white, aboveground left (Burton-Rose, *Guerrilla USA*, 178–81).

70. Dohrn et al., *Sing a Battle Song*, 200, 206, 201.

71. Dohrn et al., *Sing a Battle Song*, 218, 202, 74, 198, 209.

72. Dohrn et al., *Sing a Battle Song*, 214–15.

73. Dohrn et al., *Sing a Battle Song*, 215, 217.

74. Soss et al., *Disciplining the Poor*, 1.

75. Stoler, *Carnal Knowledge and Imperial Power*, 150.

76. Berlant, *Cruel Optimism*, 95.

77. Berlant, *Cruel Optimism*, 100.

78. Dohrn et al., *Sing a Battle Song*, 214–15.

79. Povinelli, *Economies of Abandonment*, 144, 145, 218.

80. I'm grateful to Regina Kunzel for making this point clear to me.

81. Ferreira da Silva, *Toward Global Idea of Race*, 28.

82. Dohrn et al., *Sing a Battle Song*, 216.

83. Muñoz, *Cruising Utopia*, 185.

84. Martin, *An Empire of Indifference*, 67.

85. Dohrn et al., *Sing a Battle Song*, 176.

86. Singh, *Black Is a Country*, 2–5.

87. Singh, *Black Is a Country*, 217.

1. Berrigan, *America Is Hard to Find*, 74–75, 51, 73, 35.

2. Berlant, *Cruel Optimism*, 2.

3. Messadra, "The Right to Escape," 267.

4. Koerner, "Line of Escape," 169.

5. Friedman, *Capitalism and Freedom*, 15.

6. Friedman, *Capitalism and Freedom*, 15, 13, 14, 13.

7. Jones, *Masters of the Universe*, 6, 31, 36, 69, 68, 92.

8. Friedman, *Capitalism and Freedom*, 109, 9.

9. Friedman, *Capitalism and Freedom*, 109, 110, 111.

10. In Friedman's theory, rage over a white supremacist economic system becomes a sign that one is not responsible enough for freedom. Responsibility means one takes individual action. To "bypass" the market's individuality and to target the system of "economic freedom" is to become an enemy. Rebellious populations disrupting the marketplace with uprisings and protest require the containment of law and order.

11. Friedman, *Capitalism and Freedom*, 112–13.

12. The state's use of force is of course not considered.

13. Friedman, *Capitalism and Freedom*, 113.

14. Jones, *Masters of the Universe*, 73–84.

15. Quoted in Harvey, *Neoliberalism*, 20, emphasis added.

16. Sharpe, *Monstrous Intimacies*, 22.

17. Lowe, *The Intimacies of Four Continents*, 39.

18. Wilderson, *Red, White and Black*, 20–21; Hartman, *Scenes of Subjection*, 115.

19. Lowe, *The Intimacies of Four Continents*, 39.

20. Friedman, *Capitalism and Freedom*, 14, 27, 2.

21. Rose, *Powers of Freedom*, 65.

22. Brown, *States of Injury*, 17.

23. Friedman, *Capitalism and Freedom*, 33.

24. Gilmore, *Golden Gulags*, 7.

25. Similar to Gilmore, Loïc Wacquant writes, "Thus the 'invisible hand' of the unskilled labor market . . . finds its ideological extension and institutional complement in the 'iron fist' of the penal state, which grows and redeploys in order to stem the disorder generated by social insecurity" (*Punishing the Poor*, 6).

26. Hartman, *Scenes of Subjection*, 125–26.

27. Posner, "An Economic Theory of Criminal Activity."

28. Harcourt, *The Illusion of the Free Market*, 131.

29. Harcourt, *The Illusion of the Free Market*, 134.

30. Posner writes, "Put differently, the prohibition against rape is to the marriage and sex 'market' as the prohibition against theft is to the explicit markets in goods and services" ("An Economic Theory of Criminal Activity," 1199).

31. Harcourt, *The Illusion of the Free Market*, 136.

32. Harcourt, *The Illusion of the Free Market*, 137, 241.

33. Rose, *Powers of Freedom*, 64.

34. Deleuze and Guattari, *Anti-Oedipus*, 81.

35. Chen, *Animacies*, 23.

36. Deleuze and Guattari, *Anti-Oedipus*, 76.

37. Rose, *Powers of Freedom*, 65.

38. Quoted in Rose, *Powers of Freedom*, 67.

39. Rose, *Powers of Freedom*, 95.

40. Kelley, *Freedom Dreams*.

41. Wilderson, *Red, White and Black*, 22.

42. Brown, *States of Injury*, 18.

43. Deleuze and Guattari, *A Thousand Plateaus*, 110.

44. Koerner, "Line of Escape," 165.

45. Chu, "The Trials of the Ethnic Novel," 533.

46. Choy, *Wendy . . . Uh . . . What's Her Name.*

47. Choi, *American Woman*, 323, 354–55.

48. Choi, *American Woman*, 323.

49. Eun, "American vs. Woman," 100.

50. Block, *Arm the Spirit*, 6.

51. Block, *Arm the Spirit*, 6.

52. Block, *Arm the Spirit*, 7, 252.

53. Deleuze, *Foucault*, 48.

54. Laaman, "Statement in Court," 112.

55. Spiotta, *Eat the Document*; Banks, *The Darling*.

56. Koerner, "Line of Escape," 164.

57. Trouillot, *Silencing the Past*, 52.

58. Gordon, *Ghostly Matters*, 11.

59. Trouillot, *Silencing the Past*, 5.

60. Trouillot, *Silencing the Past*, 53.

61. Trouillot describes the line between history and fiction: "The need for a different kind of credibility sets the historical narrative apart from fiction. This need is both contingent and necessary. It is contingent inasmuch as some narratives go back and forth over the line between fiction and history, while others occupy an undefined position that seems to deny the very existence of a line. It is necessary inasmuch as, at some point, historically specific groups of humans must decide if a particular narrative belongs to history or to fiction. In other words, the epistemological break between history and fiction is always expressed concretely through the historically situated evaluation of specific narratives" (*Silencing the Past*, 9).

62. Trouillot, *Silencing the Past*, 52.

63. Block, *Arm the Spirit*, 14, 20–21, 19.

64. Block, *Arm the Spirit*, 201, 204.

65. Davis, *An Autobiography*, 1, 4, 6.

66. Davis, *An Autobiography*, 4.

67. Davis, *An Autobiography*, 4–5.

68. Choi, *American Woman*, 281.

69. Choi, *American Woman*, 64–65.

70. Block, *Arm the Spirit*, 177, 186.
71. Puar, *Terrorist Assemblages*, 211–15.
72. Vlagopoulos, "The Beginning of History and Politics," 130.
73. Choi, *American Woman*, 53.
74. Choi, *American Woman*, 4, 542.
75. Choi, *American Woman*, 323, 319.
76. Trouillot, *Silencing the Past*, 82.
77. Trouillot, *Silencing the Past*, 547.
78. See Gilmore, "Fatal Couplings of Power and Difference"; Hardt and Negri, *Multitude*, 3–95.
79. Choi, *American Woman*, 221.
80. Choi, *American Woman*, 168.
81. Choi, *American Woman*, 168–69.
82. Choi, *American Woman*, 170.
83. Vlagopoulos, "The Beginning of History and Politics," 136.
84. Choi, *American Woman*, 140, 189, 141.
85. Vlagopoulos, "The Beginning of History and Politics," 136.
86. Choi, *American Woman*, 64.
87. Deleuze and Guattari, *A Thousand Plateaus*, 215.
88. Foucault, "The Subject of Power," 336; Foucault, preface to Deleuze and Guattari, *Anti-Oedipus*, xiii.
89. Sandoval, *Methodology of the Oppressed*, 164.
90. Koerner, "Line of Escape," 170.
91. Foucault, *The History of Sexuality*, 143.
92. Crosby et al., "Queer Studies, Materialism, and Crisis," 130.
93. Povinelli, *Economies of Abandonment*, 109.
94. Cahill and Thompson, "The Insurgency of Objects," 51.
95. Moten, *In the Break*, 1.
96. Huffer, *Mad for Foucault*, 271.
97. Negri, "Foucault between Past and Future," 80. Deleuze put it slightly differently: "Life becomes resistance to power when power takes life as its object" (*Foucault*, 92).
98. Koerner, "Line of Escape," 171.

3. POSSESSED BY DEATH

1. Shakur, "Women in Prison," 85.
2. Butler and Athanasiou, *Dispossession*, 19.
3. Ferguson, *Aberrations in Black*, 4.
4. Shakur, "Women in Prison," 79.
5. Parenti, "Assata Shakur Speaks from Exile."
6. Davis, "From the Prison of Slavery to the Slavery of Prison."
7. On the prison and slavery see Davis, "From the Prison of Slavery to the Slavery of Prison"; Oshinsky, *Worse than Slavery*; Lichtenstein, *Twice the Work of Free Labor*; Haley, *No Mercy Here*; Wacquant, "Deadly Symbiosis"; Rodríguez, *Forced Passages*;

Childs, *Slaves of the State*. On the prison and neoliberalism, see Gilmore, *Golden Gulags*; Wacquant, "The Penalization of Poverty and the Rise of Neoliberalism"; Wacquant, *Punishing the Poor*; Parenti, *Lockdown America*.

8. Hartman, *Lose Your Mother*, 6. Hartman writes, "This is the afterlife of slavery—skewed life chances, limited access to health and education, premature death, incarceration, and impoverishment."

9. Childs, "'You Ain't Seen Nothin' Yet,'" 273–75.

10. Sharpe, *In the Wake*, 2, 12.

11. Brand, *A Map to the Door of No Return*, 24–25.

12. Sharpe, *The Ghosts of Slavery*, 2.

13. Hartman, *Lose Your Mother*, 6.

14. Gordon, *Ghostly Matters*, 8, 139.

15. Definition at *Merriam-Webster* online.

16. Boggs, "The Black Revolution in America," 278, 276.

17. Childs, *Slaves of the State*, 11.

18. Gilmore, *Golden Gulags*, 28.

19. Jackson, *Soledad Brother*, 233–34.

20. Jackson, *Blood in My Eye*, 10.

21. Jackson, *Blood in My Eye*, 7.

22. Sharpe, *Monstrous Intimacies*, 3. For broader theorizations of the afterlife of slavery, also see Browne, *Dark Matters*; Brown, *The Repeating Body*.

23. Tinsley, "Black Atlantic, Queer Atlantic," 191.

24. Spillers, "Mama's Baby, Papa's Maybe," 68.

25. Hartman, *Scenes of Subjection*, 121.

26. Wilderson, *Red, White and Black*, 11, 14.

27. Baucom, *Specters of the Atlantic*, 29.

28. Morrison, *Beloved*, 210.

29. Shakur, "Women in Prison," 86.

30. Agathangelou et al., "Intimate Investments," 137.

31. Hong and Ferguson, introduction to *Strange Affinities*, 13.

32. Gordon, *Ghostly Matters*, 18; Hong, *The Ruptures of American Capital*, xxx.

33. Trouillot, *Silencing the Past*, 82.

34. Johnson, "The Pedestal and the Veil," 300.

35. Because slavery did not use wage labor, many Marxists have argued that it was wasteful and inflexible and thus does not meet a strict definition of capitalism. Marx himself did not consider slavery capitalist because, for him, the wage-labor exchange against capital was the essence of capitalism. In this theory, the forms of domination and subjugation used on the plantation are precapitalist and "extra-economic." In the teleology of some forms of Marxism, industrial capitalism would supersede the precapitalist mercantilism of the plantation. Plantations were understood as an aberration from the rational, efficient, commercial calculations of capitalism. Yet, as Robin Blackburn points out, the rational calculations used to measure "tight-packing" on slave ships, reproduction, health and life spans, insurance, finance and profit, and so on demonstrate the absolute modernity of the slave trade. Blackburn argues that

the slave trade anticipates and inaugurates many of the practices central to modern capitalism (*The Making of New World Slavery*, 309–400). For a useful discussion of this debate also see Baptist, *The Half Has Never Been Told*; Beckert and Rockman, *Slavery's Capitalism*; Johnson, *River of Dark Dreams*.

36. Harvey, *Neoliberalism*, 33. See also Braedley and Luxton, *Neoliberalism and Everyday Life*; Brown, "American Nightmare."

37. Harvey, *Neoliberalism*, 166.

38. Ong, *Neoliberalism as Exception*, 4.

39. Foucault, *The Birth of Biopolitics*, 268. Also see Harvey, *Neoliberalism*, 3.

40. Foucault, *The Birth of Biopolitics*, 242.

41. Brown, *Undoing the Demos*, 67.

42. Duggan, *The Twilight of Equality?*; Brown, "Neo-Liberalism and the End of Liberal Democracy."

43. Venn, "Neoliberal Political Economy, Biopolitics and Colonialism."

44. Hartman, "The Belly of the World," 166.

45. Spillers, "Mama's Baby, Papa's Maybe," 58.

46. Ong, *Neoliberalism as Exception*, 4.

47. Hong, *The Ruptures of American Capital*, xxx–xxxiv.

48. Williams, *Dessa Rose*, iii.

49. Lowe, *Immigrant Acts*, 22.

50. Tinsley, "Black Atlantic, Queer Atlantic," 193.

51. Lowe, *Immigrant Acts*, 29. Also see Gordon, *Ghostly Matters*.

52. McKittrick, *Demonic Grounds*, 33.

53. Hartman, *Lose Your Mother*, 15–16.

54. Hartman, "The Belly of the World," 171. Hartman is paraphrasing Hortense Spillers, "Interstices: A Small Drama of Words," in *Pleasure and Danger: Exploring Female Sexuality*, edited by Carol A. Vance (London: Pandora, 1992), 74.

55. Davis, "Reflections on the Black Woman's Role in the Community of Slaves," 126.

56. Davis, "Reflections on the Black Woman's Role in the Community of Slaves," 125.

57. Spillers, "Mama's Baby, Papa's Maybe," 68.

58. Spillers, "Mama's Baby, Papa's Maybe," 65.

59. Hill Collins, *Black Feminist Thought*.

60. Davis, "Reflections on the Black Woman's Role in the Community of Slaves," 116–17.

61. It is noteworthy that the prison could not exhaust Davis's intellectual and emotional capacity. Like the histories she recovers, there is a fugitivity in her thinking and writing in addition to the strength, compassion, and knowledge she passes on from prison.

62. Hartman, "The Belly of the World," 171.

63. Davis, "Reflections on the Black Woman's Role in the Community of Slaves," 111.

64. Sharpe, *The Ghosts of Slavery*, xxvi.

65. Williams, *Dessa Rose*, iii.

66. Vint, "'Only by Experience,'" 241.

67. Brendt, *Incidents in the Life of a Slave Girl*, 2.

68. Cited in Hartman, *Scenes of Subjection*, 107.

69. Cited in Vint, "'Only by Experience,'" 241.

70. Sharpe, *The Ghosts of Slavery*, xi.

71. Best and Hartman, "Fugitive Justice," 2–3.

72. Williams, *Dessa Rose*, 9.

73. Williams, *Dessa Rose*, 24.

74. Williams, *Dessa Rose*, 24, 176.

75. Williams, *Dessa Rose*, 17.

76. Sharpe, *The Ghosts of Slavery*, xii.

77. Williams, *Dessa Rose*, 87.

78. Baucom, *Specters of the Atlantic*, 11.

79. Baucom, *Specters of the Atlantic*, 12.

80. Brown, *The Reaper's Garden*, 48.

81. Baucom, *Specters of the Atlantic*, 333.

82. Davis, "Reflections on the Black Woman's Role in the Community of Slaves," 121, emphasis added.

83. Hartman, "The Belly of the World," 168–69. White supremacy wedded the market to flesh and bone, a process that is central to Achille Mbembe's concept of necropolitics. He writes, "Any historical account of the rise of modern terror needs to address slavery, which could be considered one of the first instances of biopolitical experimentation. . . . This power over the life of another takes the form of commerce: a person's humanity is dissolved to the point where it becomes possible to say that the slave's life is possessed by the master. Because the slave's life is like a 'thing,' possessed by another person, the slave's existence appears as a perfect figure of a shadow" ("Necropolitics," 21).

84. Hartman and Wilderson, "The Position of the Unthought," 184.

85. Davis, "Reflections on the Black Woman's Role in the Community of Slaves," 113.

86. Hartman, "The Belly of the World," 169.

87. Smallwood, *Saltwater Slavery*, 35–36.

88. Baucom, *Specters of the Atlantic*, 61.

89. Johnson, *Soul by Soul*, 58.

90. Baucom's *Specters of the Atlantic* demonstrates that even corpses remained valuable because of insurance policies. The dead were still money.

91. Baucom, *Specters of the Atlantic*, 63.

92. Williams, *Dessa Rose*, 99, emphasis added.

93. Williams, *Dessa Rose*, 100.

94. Williams, *Dessa Rose*, 138.

95. See Clough, "The Affective Turn," 220–21; Hardt and Negri, *Common Wealth*, 229–30; Harvey, *The Condition of Postmodernity*, 125–97.

96. Williams, *Dessa Rose*, 140.

97. Smallwood, *Saltwater Slavery*, 53.

98. Wilderson, *Red, White and Black*, 111.

99. Smallwood, *Saltwater Slavery*, 56.

100. Hartman, *Scenes of Subjection*, 116.

101. Rediker, *The Slave Ship*, 9. See also Johnson, "The Pedestal and the Veil"; Robinson, "Capitalism, Slavery and Bourgeois Historiography"; Rockman, "The Unfree Origins of American Capitalism."

102. Sexton, "People of Color Blindness," 44.

103. Hartman, *Lose Your Mother*, 6.

104. Mbembe, "Necropolitics," 21.

105. Agamben, *Homo Sacer*, 175.

106. Baucom, *Specters of the Atlantic*, 24.

107. On prison and death see Smith, *The Prison and the American Imagination*; Rodríguez, *Forced Passages*; Dayan, *The Story of Cruel and Unusual*.

108. Sudbury, "Celling Black Bodies."

109. Shakur, "Women in Prison," 81.

110. Shakur, "Women in Prison," 80

111. Hartman, "The Time of Slavery," 722. Regina Kunzel alerted me to the ways the social sciences and the state naturalize crime and poverty and thus obfuscate the terror with which they are intertwined.

112. Shakur, "Assata: An Autobiography," 60.

113. Bukhari, *The War Before*, 1, 2.

114. Bukhari, *The War Before*, 2, 10, 11.

115. Ferguson, *Aberrations in Black*, 4.

116. Shakur, "Assata: An Autobiography," 54.

117. See broadly, Gilmore, *Golden Gulags*.

118. Sudbury, "Celling Black Bodies"; Gilmore, "Globalisation and U.S. Prison Growth."

119. Shakur, "Women in Prison," 85.

120. Duggan, *The Twilight of Equality?*, 1–21. Also see Reddy, *Freedom with Violence*.

121. Shakur, "Assata: An Autobiography," 63–64.

122. Davis, "Reflections on the Black Woman's Role in the Community of Slaves," 127; Shakur, "Women in Prison," 86.

123. Shakur, "Women in Prison," 86.

124. Gilmore, "Globalisation and U.S. Prison Growth," 186.

125. Shakur, "Women in Prison," 86–87.

4. "ONLY THE SUN WILL BLEACH HIS BONES QUICKER"

1. Street Transvestites for Gay Power, "NYU Occupation."

2. For a broader overview of this process see Hanhardt, *Safe Space*.

3. Guattari, *Chaosophy*, 154.

4. Sandoval, *Methodology of the Oppressed*, 5.

5. For the most thorough discussion of Foucault's antiprison activism, see Zurn and Dilts, *Active Intolerance*.

6. Berlant, *Desire/Love*, 45.

7. Jordan, *Directed by Desire*, 267–69.

8. I'm grateful to an anonymous reader for this articulation and observation.

9. Moten and Harney, *The Undercommons*, 125.

10. Brown, *Undoing the Demos*, 47.

11. Deleuze, *Desert Islands and Other Texts*, 263.

12. Foucault, preface to Deleuze and Guattari, *Anti-Oedipus*, xiii.

13. Varon, *Bringing the War Home*, 6.

14. Foucault, preface to Deleuze and Guattari, *Anti-Oedipus*, xiv, xii, xiii.

15. Deleuze, *Desert Islands and Other Texts*, 263.

16. Deleuze, "Desire and Pleasure."

17. Deleuze and Guattari, *Anti-Oedipus*, 29.

18. Deleuze, *Desert Islands and Other Texts*, 228.

19. Grace, "Faux Amis," 62.

20. Deleuze and Guattari, *Anti-Oedipus*, 104.

21. Deleuze, "Desire and Pleasure."

22. Deleuze, "Desire and Pleasure."

23. Dean, "The Biopolitics of Pleasure," 479–80.

24. Dean writes, "It is not so much that the same concept goes by different names—*desire* in Deleuze, *pleasure* in Foucault—but rather that both philosophers were seeking a vocabulary to describe those forces that militate against the lures of identity, lures today that we can recognize as specifically biopolitical" ("The Biopolitics of Pleasure," 486).

25. Guattari, *Chaosophy*, 245.

26. Guattari, *Soft Subversions*, 142.

27. Deleuze and Guattari, *Anti-Oedipus*, 105, 116.

28. Deleuze and Guattari, *Anti-Oedipus*, 29.

29. Guattari, *Chaosophy*, 163, 171.

30. Holland, *The Erotic Life of Racism*, 43.

31. Guattari, *Chaosophy*, 236, 169, 237, 207.

32. Berlant, *Desire/Love*, 44.

33. Lordon, *Willing Slaves of Capital*, 80, 49, 61, 108.

34. Duggan, *The Twilight of Equality?*, 50.

35. Eng et al., "What's Queer about Queer Studies Now?," 1.

36. For a broader overview, see Agathangelou et al., "Intimate Investments"; Puar, *Terrorist Assemblages*; Reddy, *Freedom with Violence*; Lamble, "Queer Necropolitics and the Expanding Carceral State"; Vitulli, "A Defining Moment in Civil Rights History?"; Spade, *Normal Life*.

37. Lordon, *Willing Slaves of Capital*, 101.

38. Singh, "The Whiteness of Police," 1092, 1095.

39. I am grateful to an anonymous reader who made this aspect of the poem clear to me.

40. Butler, *The Psychic Life of Power*, 107.

41. See, for example, Alexander, *The New Jim Crow*; Rodríguez, *Forced Passages*; Gilmore, *Golden Gulags*; Irwin, *The Warehouse Prison*; Reiman and Leighton, *The Rich Get Richer and the Poor Get Prison*; Camp, *Incarcerating the Crisis*.

42. Murakawa, *The First Civil Right*, 14.

43. Butler, *The Psychic Life of Power*, 2, 5, 107, 108.

44. Bloom and Martin, *Black against Empire*; Newton, *War against the Panthers*.

45. Clough and Willse, "Beyond Biopolitics," 2.

46. Singh, "The Whiteness of Police," 1093.

47. Baldwin, "An Open Letter to My Sister, Angela Y. Davis," 19, 22.

48. Mitchell, "Rethinking Economy."

49. As queer and trans activists and scholars have observed over the past three decades, through the aforementioned processes queer politics has embraced and promoted inclusion, rights, reform, and racialized state power as the path to a more tolerable world. For example, same-sex marriage upholds the uneven distribution of resources, and thus life chances, based on legally recognized relationships. The legal inclusion of LGBTQ people in the military expands the ability of the military to recruit poor people of color and to colonize and kill people of color around the world. Hate crimes laws expand the ability of the racial state and prison-industrial complex to punish and cage human beings, thus strengthening a system that causes unimaginable harm to millions of people, including queer and trans people. These processes reinforce and expand regimes of racialized neoliberal capital and systems of caging and capture. These reforms operate, in part, by soliciting desire. See Puar, *Terrorist Assemblages*; Brandzel, *Against Citizenship*; Conrad, *Against Equality*; Spade, *Normal Life*; Audre Lorde Project, "Statement"; Farrow, "Is Gay Marriage Anti-Black?"; Queers for Economic Justice, "Beyond Same-Sex Marriage"; Schulman, *Gentrification of the Mind*; Hanhardt, *Safe Space*; Reddy, *Freedom with Violence*; Manalansan, "Race, Violence and Neoliberal Spatial Politics in the Global City."

50. Singh, "The Whiteness of Police," 1096.

51. "Biography: Audre Lorde."

52. Lorde, *The Collected Poems*, 215–16.

53. Cacho, *Social Death*, 31.

54. Lorde, *The Collected Poems*, 215.

55. Hong, *Death beyond Disavowal*, 144–45.

56. Lorde, *The Collected Poems*, 215–16.

57. Lorde, *Sister Outsider*, 53, 55, 56.

58. Deleuze and Guattari, *Anti-Oedipus*, 116.

59. Ferguson, "Of Sensual Matters," 289.

60. Lorde, *Sister Outsider*, 55.

61. Ferguson, "Of Sensual Matters," 300.

62. Deleuze and Guattari, *Anti-Oedipus*, 116.

63. Lorde, *Sister Outsider*, 59.

64. Lorde, *Sister Outsider*, 37, 36, 38.

CONCLUSION: "BEING CAPTURED IS BESIDE THE POINT"

1. I am grateful to A. J. Lewis for alerting me to this collection and discussing its significance on a number of occasions.

2. Alexander, *Pedagogies of Crossing*, 265

3. Alexander, *Pedagogies of Crossing*, 263.

4. Gibbs and Bennett, "Racism and Classism in the Lesbian Community," 1, 2–3.

5. Gibbs and Bennett, "Racism and Classism in the Lesbian Community," 29.

6. Charoula, "Prison Work and the Lesbian Issue: A Personal Statement," in Gibbs and Bennett, *Top Ranking*, 44, 46, 47, 48. In her addition to the collection, the classic "Open Letter to Mary Daly," Audre Lorde similarly argues that white and black lesbians share a differential connection but that relationality must be grounded in abolishing white supremacy and a politics that can account for the fact that heteropatriarchy knows no boundaries, "but that does not mean it is identical within those boundaries" ("An Open Letter to Mary Daly," in Gibbs and Bennett, *Top Ranking*, 92).

7. Reagon, "Coalition Politics," 358, 356–57.

8. Moten and Harney, *The Undercommons*, 140, 28.

9. Alexander, *Pedagogies of Crossing*, 269.

10. Gibbs and Bennett, *Top Ranking*, 41n. Brown is also mentioned in Shakur, *Assata: An Autobiography*, 254.

11. Rita D. Brown, "Somewhere," in Gibbs and Bennett, *Top Ranking*, 36–37.

12. Incite! Women of Color against Violence, *The Revolution Will Not Be Funded*; Spade and Mananzala, "The Nonprofit Industrial Complex and Trans Resistance."

13. Spade, *Normal Life*, 59.

14. Alexander, *Pedagogies of Crossing*, 269.

15. Brown, "Somewhere," 39.

16. Brown, "Somewhere," 36.

17. Brown, "Somewhere," 39.

18. Foucault, "The Subject of Power," 336, 346.

19. Gilbert, *No Surrender*, inscription.

Abdur-Rahman, Aliyyah. "'The Strangest Freaks of Despotism': Queer Sexuality in Antebellum African American Slave Narratives." *African American Review* 40, no. 2 (2006): 223–37.

Agamben, Giorgio. *Homo Sacer: Sovereign Power and Bare Life.* Stanford, CA: Stanford University Press, 1998.

Agathangelou, Anna M., M. Daniel Bassichis, and Tamara L. Spira. "Intimate Investments: Homonormativity, Global Lockdown, and the Seductions of Empire." *Radical History Review* 100 (winter 2008): 120–43.

Alexander, Jacqui. *Pedagogies of Crossing: Meditations on Feminism, Sexual Politics, Memory, and the Sacred.* Durham, NC: Duke University Press, 2006.

Alexander, Michelle. *The New Jim Crow: Mass Incarceration in the Age of Colorblindness.* New York: New Press, 2010.

Aptheker, Bettina. "The Social Function of Prisons." In *If They Come in the Morning: Voices of Resistance,* edited by Angela Davis and Bettina Aptheker, 51–59. New York: Third Press, 1971.

The Audre Lorde Project. "Statement: ALP Position Statement on Marriage." Accessed September, 20 2017. https://alp.org/alp-position-statement-marriage.

Ayers, Bill. *Fugitive Days: Memoirs of an Anti-War Activist.* Boston: Beacon Press, 2001.

Baldwin, James. "An Open Letter to My Sister, Angela Y. Davis." In *If They Come in the Morning: Voices of Resistance,* edited by Angela Davis and Bettina Aptheker, 19–23. New York: Third Press, 1971.

Banks, Russell. *The Darling: A Novel.* New York: HarperCollins, 2004.

Baptist, Edward. *The Half Has Never Been Told: Slavery and the Making of American Capitalism.* New York: Basic Books, 2014.

Baucom, Ian. *Specters of the Atlantic: Finance Capital, Slavery, and the Philosophy of History.* Durham, NC: Duke University Press, 2005.

Becker, Gary. "Crime and Punishment: An Economic Approach." *Journal of Political Economy* 76 (1968): 169–217.

Beckert, Sven, and Seth Rockman, eds. *Slavery's Capitalism: A New History of American Economic Development.* Philadelphia: University of Pennsylvania Press, 2016.

Berger, Dan. "Marilyn Buck's Playlist." *PolyGraph* 23–24 (2013): 111–25.

———. *Outlaws of America: The Weather Underground and the Politics of Solidarity.* Oakland, CA: AK Press, 2005.

Berlant, Lauren. *Cruel Optimism.* Durham, NC: Duke University Press, 2011.

———. *Desire/Love.* Brooklyn, NY: Punctum Books, 2012.

Bernstein, Lee. *America Is the Prison: Arts and Politics in Prison in the 1970s.* Chapel Hill: University of North Carolina Press, 2010.

Berrigan, Daniel. *America Is Hard to Find: Notes from the Underground and Letters from Danbury Prison.* New York: Doubleday, 1972.

Best, Stephen, and Saidiya Hartman. "Fugitive Justice: The Appeal of the Slave." *Representations* 92 (fall 2006): 1–15.

"Biography: Audre Lorde." *Poetry Foundation.* Accessed April 16, 2016. http://www .poetryfoundation.org/bio/audre-lorde.

Blackburn, Robin. *The American Crucible: Slavery, Emancipation, and Human Rights.* London: Verso Books, 2011.

———. *The Making of New World Slavery: From the Baroque to the Modern 1492–1800.* London: Verso, 1997.

Blackstock, Nelson. *Cointelpro: The FBI's Secret War on Political Freedom.* Atlanta: Pathfinder Press, 1975.

Block, Diana. *Arm the Spirit: A Woman's Journey Underground and Back.* Oakland, CA: AK Press, 2009.

Bloom, Joshua, and Waldo E. Martin. *Black against Empire: The History and Politics of the Black Panther Party.* Berkeley: University of California Press, 2013.

Boggs, Grace Lee. "The Black Revolution in America." In *The Black Woman: An Anthology,* edited by Toni Cade Bambara, 269–85. New York: Washington Square Press, 1970.

Bourdieu, Pierre. "The Essence of Neoliberalism." *Le Monde diplomatique,* December 1998. http://mondediplo.com/1998/12/08bourdieu/.

Braedley, Susan, and Meg Luxton, eds. *Neoliberalism and Everyday Life.* Montreal: McGill-Queen's University Press, 2010.

Brand, Dionne. *A Map to the Door of No Return: Notes to Belonging.* Toronto: Vintage Canada, 2002.

Brandzel, Amy L. *Against Citizenship: The Violence of the Normative.* Urbana: University of Illinois Press, 2016.

Brendt, Linda. *Incidents in the Life of a Slave Girl.* Mineola, NY: Dover, 2001.

Brown, Kimberly Juanita. *The Repeating Body: Slavery's Visual Resonance in the Contemporary.* Durham, NC: Duke University Press, 2015.

Brown, Rita Bo. "Sentencing Statement." In *Queer Fire: The George Jackson Brigade, Men against Sexism, and Gay Struggle against Prison,* 16–19. Bloomington, IN: Untorelli Press, 2014.

———. "A Short Autobiography." In *Queer Fire: The George Jackson Brigade, Men against Sexism, and Gay Struggle against Prison,* 14–17. Bloomington, IN: Untorelli Press, 2014.

———. *While Copping a Plea in Kangaroo Kourt 2/11/78.* Accessed April, 16, 2008. http://www.the Brigadeip.org/documents/bo_kangaroo_kort.htm.

Brown, Vincent. *The Reaper's Garden: Death and Power in the World of Atlantic Slavery.* Cambridge, MA: Harvard University Press, 2008.

Brown, Wendy. "American Nightmare: Neoliberalism, Neoconservatism, and De-Democratization." *Political Theory* 34, no. 6 (2006): 690–714.

———. "Neo-Liberalism and the End of Liberal Democracy." *Theory and Event* 7, no. 1 (2003). http://muse.jhu.edu/journals/theory_&_event/.

———. *Regulating Aversion: Tolerance in the Age of Identity and Empire.* Princeton, NJ: Princeton University Press, 2006.

———. *States of Injury: Power and Freedom in Late Modernity.* Princeton, NJ: Princeton University Press, 1995.

———. *Undoing the Demos: Neoliberalism's Stealth Revolution.* New York: Zone Books, 2015.

Browne, Simone. *Dark Matters: On the Surveillance of Blackness.* Durham, NC: Duke University Press, 2015.

Bukhari, Safiya. *The War Before: The True Life Story of Becoming a Black Panther, Keeping the Faith in Prison and Fighting for Those Left Behind.* New York: Feminist Press, 2010.

Burrough, Bryan. *Days of Rage: America's Radical Underground, the FBI, and the Forgotten Age of Revolutionary Violence.* New York: Penguin, 2015.

Burton-Rose, Daniel, ed. *Creating a Movement with Teeth: A Documentary History of the George Jackson Brigade.* Oakland, CA: PM Press, 2010.

———. *Guerrilla USA: The George Jackson Brigade and the Anticapitalist Underground of the 1970s.* Berkeley: University of California Press, 2010.

Butler, Judith. *Bodies That Matter: On the Discursive Limits of "Sex."* New York: Routledge, 1993.

———. *Precarious Life: The Powers of Mourning and Violence.* New York: Verso Press, 2004.

———. *The Psychic Life of Power: Theories in Subjection.* Stanford, CA: Stanford University Press, 1997.

———. *War Frames: When Is Life Grievable?* London: Verso, 2009.

Butler, Judith, and Athena Athanasiou. *Dispossession: The Performative in the Political.* Malden, MA: Polity Press, 2013.

Cacho, Lisa Marie. *Social Death: Racialized Rightlessness and the Criminalization of the Unprotected.* New York: New York University Press, 2012.

Cahill, James Leo, and Rachel Leah Thompson. "The Insurgency of Objects: A Conversation with Fred Moten." *Interview* 1 (fall 2005): 45–66.

Camp, Jordan T. *Incarcerating the Crisis: Freedom Struggles and the Rise of the Neoliberal State.* Berkeley: University of California Press, 2016.

Chen, Mel. *Animacies: Biopolitics, Racial Mattering, and Queer Affect.* Durham, NC: Duke University Press, 2012.

Childs, Dennis. *Slaves of the State: Black Incarceration from the Chain Gang to the Penitentiary.* Minneapolis: University of Minnesota Press, 2016.

———. "'You Ain't Seen Nothin' Yet': *Beloved*, the American Chain Gang, and the Middle Passage Remix." *American Quarterly* 61, no. 2 (June 2009): 271–97.

Choi, Susan. *American Woman.* New York: HarperCollins, 2003.

Choy, Curtis, dir. *Wendy . . . Uh . . . What's Her Name.* DVD. Chonk Moonhunter Productions, 1976.

Chu, Patricia E. "The Trials of the Ethnic Novel: Susan Choi's *American Woman* and the Post–Affirmative Action Era." *American Literary History* 23, no. 3 (2011): 529–54.

Churchill, Ward. Preface to *Creating a Movement with Teeth: A Documentary History of the George Jackson Brigade*, edited by Daniel Burton-Rose, 11–17. Oakland, CA: PM Press, 2010.

Churchill, Ward, and Jim Vander Wall. *Agents of Repression: The FBI's Secret Wars against the Black Panther Party and the American Indian Movement.* Cambridge, MA: South End Press, 1988.

———. *The COINTELPRO Papers: Documents from the FBI's Secret Wars against Dissent in the United States.* Cambridge, MA: South End Press, 1990.

Churrah, Paisley. "The State." *TSQ* 1, nos. 1–2 (2014): 197–200.

Clough, Patricia. "The Affective Turn: Political Economy, Biomedia, and Bodies." In *The Affect Theory Reader*, edited by Melissa Gregg and Gregory Seigworth, 206–28. Durham, NC: Duke University Press, 2011.

Clough, Patricia Ticineto, and Craig Willse. "Beyond Biopolitics: The Governance of Life and Death." In *Beyond Biopolitics: Essays on the Governance of Life and Death*, edited by Patricia Ticineto Clough and Craig Willse, 1–18. Durham, NC: Duke University Press, 2011.

Cohen, Cathy. "Punks, Bulldaggers, and Welfare Queens: The Radical Potential of Queer Politics?" *GLQ* 3, no. 4 (1997): 437–65.

Conrad, Ryan, ed. *Against Equality: Queer Resistance, Not Mere Inclusion.* Oakland, CA: AK Press, 2014.

Crosby, Christina, et al. "Queer Studies, Materialism, and Crisis: A Roundtable Discussion." *GLQ* 18, no. 1 (2011): 127–47.

Davis, Angela. *Angela Davis: An Autobiography.* New York: International Publishers, 1989.

———. *Are Prisons Obsolete?* New York: Seven Stories Press, 2003.

———. "From the Prison of Slavery to the Slavery of Prison: Frederick Douglass and the Convict Lease System." In *The Angela Y. Davis Reader*, edited by Joy James, 74–96. Malden, MA: Blackwell, 1998.

———. "Reflections on the Black Woman's Role in the Community of Slaves." In *The Angela Davis Reader*, edited by Joy James, 11–129. Malden, MA: Blackwell, 1998.

———. *Women, Race, and Class.* New York: Random House, 1983.

Davis, Angela, and Bettina Aptheker, eds. *If They Come in the Morning: Voices of Resistance.* New York: Third Press, 1971.

Dayan, Colin. *The Story of Cruel and Unusual.* Cambridge, MA: MIT Press, 2007.

Dean, Timothy. "The Biopolitics of Pleasure." *South Atlantic Quarterly* 11, no. 3 (summer 2012): 477–96.

Deleuze, Gilles. *Desert Islands and Other Texts 1953–1974.* Translated by Michael Taormina. Los Angeles: Semiotext(e), 2004.

———. "Desire and Pleasure." Translated by Melissa McMahon. Monash University. Accessed April 20, 2016. http://www.artdes.monash.edu.au/globe/delfou.html.

———. *Foucault.* Translated by Sean Hand. Minneapolis: University of Minnesota Press, 1988.

———. *The Logic of Sense.* Translated by Mark Lester with Charles Stivale. New York: Colombia University Press, 1990.

Deleuze, Gilles, and Félix Guattari. *Anti-Oedipus: Capitalism and Schizophrenia.* Translated by Robert Hurley, Mark Seem, and Helen R. Lane. Minneapolis: University of Minnesota Press, 1983.

———. *A Thousand Plateaus: Capitalism and Schizophrenia.* Translated by Brian Massumi. Minneapolis: University of Minnesota Press, 1987.

Deleuze, Gilles, and Claire Parnet. *Dialogues II.* Translated by Hugh Tomlinson and Barbara Habberjam. New York: Colombia University Press, 1987.

Dohrn, Bernardine, Bill Ayers, and Jeff Jones. *Sing a Battle Song: The Revolutionary Poetry, Statements, and Communiqués of the Weather Underground 1970–1974.* New York: Seven Stories Press, 2006.

Duggan, Lisa. *The Twilight of Equality? Neoliberalism, Cultural Politics, and the Attack on Democracy.* Boston: Beacon Press, 2003.

Eckstein, Arthur M. *Bad Moon Rising: How the Weather Underground Beat the FBI and Lost the Revolution.* New Haven, CT: Yale University Press, 2016.

Edelman, Lee. *No Future: Queer Theory and the Death Drive.* Durham, NC: Duke University Press, 2004.

Elbaum, Max. *Revolution in the Air: Sixties Radicals Turn to Lenin, Mao, and Che.* London: Verso, 2002.

Eng, David L., Judith Halberstam, and José Esteban Muñoz. "What's Queer about Queer Studies Now? Introduction." *Social Text* 84–85 (fall–winter 2005): 1–17.

Eun, Jae. "American vs. Woman: Asian American Identity and Queer Intimacy in *American Woman.*" *Feminist Studies in English Literature* 19, no. 3 (2011): 95–125.

Farrow, Kenyon. "Is Gay Marriage Anti-Black?" *Chicken Bones: A Journal.* Accessed November 26, 2016. http://www.nathanielturner.com/isgaymarriageantiblack.htm.

Ferguson, Roderick. *Aberrations in Black: Toward a Queer of Color Critique.* Minneapolis: University of Minnesota Press, 2004.

———. "Of Sensual Matters: On Audre Lorde's 'Poetry Is Not a Luxury' and 'Uses of the Erotic.'" *WSQ: Women's Studies Quarterly* 40, nos. 3–4 (fall–winter 2012): 295–300.

Ferreira da Silva, Denise. *Toward a Global Idea of Race.* Minneapolis: University of Minnesota, 2007.

Flamm, Michael M. *Law and Order: Street Crime, Civil Unrest, and the Crisis of Liberalism in the 1960s.* New York: Columbia University Press, 2005.

Floyd, Kevin. *The Reification of Desire: Toward a Queer Marxism.* Minneapolis: University of Minnesota Press, 2009.

Foucault, Michel. *The Birth of Biopolitics: Lectures at the Collège de France, 1978–1979.* New York: Palgrave Macmillan, 2010.

———. *Discipline and Punish: The Birth of the Prison.* New York: Vintage Books, 1977.

———. *The History of Sexuality,* Volume 1: *An Introduction.* New York: Vintage Books, 1978.

———. "The Masked Assassination." In *Warfare in the American Homeland: Policing and Prison in a Penal Democracy*, edited by Joy James, 140–58. Durham, NC: Duke University Press, 2007.

———. Preface to *Anti-Oedipus: Capitalism and Schizophrenia*, by Gilles Deleuze and Félix Guattari, xi–xiv. Minneapolis: University of Minnesota Press, 1983.

———. *Security, Territory, Population*. New York: Picador, 2007.

———. *Society Must Be Defended: Lectures at the Collège de France, 1975–1976*. New York: Picador, 1997.

———. "The Subject of Power." In *Michel Foucault: Power*, edited by Paul Rabinow, 326–48. New York: New Press, 1994.

Friedman, Milton. *Capitalism and Freedom*. Chicago: University of Chicago Press, 2002.

Garland, David. *The Culture of Control: Crime and Social Order in Contemporary Society*. Chicago: University of Chicago Press, 2001.

George Jackson Brigade. *The Power of the People Is the Force of Life: Political Statement of the George Jackson Brigade*. Montreal: Abraham Guillen Press, 2002.

Gibbs, Joan, and Sara Bennett. "Racism and Classism in the Lesbian Community: Towards the Building of a Radical Autonomous Lesbian Movement." In *Top Ranking: A Collection of Articles on Racism and Classism in the Lesbian Community*, edited by Joan Gibbs and Sara Bennett, 1–30. New York: Come! Unity Press, 1980.

———, eds. *Top Ranking: A Collection of Articles on Racism and Classism in the Lesbian Community*. New York: Come! Unity Press, 1980.

Gilbert, David. *Love and Struggle: My Life in SDS, the Weather Underground, and Beyond*. Oakland, CA: PM Press, 2012.

———. *No Surrender: Writings from an Anti-Imperialist Political Prisoner*. Montreal: Abraham Guillen Press, 2004.

Gilmore, Ruth Wilson. "Fatal Couplings of Power and Difference: Notes on Racism and Geography." *Professional Geographer* 54, no. 1 (2002): 15–24.

———. "Globalisation and U.S. Prison Growth: From Military Keynesianism to Post-Keynesian Militarism." *Race and Class* 40, nos. 2–3 (1998–99): 171–88.

———. *Golden Gulags: Prisons, Surplus, Crisis, and Opposition in Globalizing California*. Berkeley: University of California Press, 2007.

Giroux, Henry. *The Terror of Neoliberalism: Authoritarianism and the Eclipse of Democracy*. New York: Paradigm, 2004.

Goldberg, David Theo. *The Threat of Race: Reflections on Racial Neoliberalism*. Oxford: Wiley-Blackwell, 2009.

Goldwater, Barry. "1964 Acceptance Speech." *Washington Post Archives*. Accessed March 9, 2012. http://www.washingtonpost.com/wp-srv/politics/daily/may98/goldwaterspeech.htm.

Gordon, Avery. *Ghostly Matters: Haunting and the Sociological Imagination*. Minneapolis: University of Minnesota Press, 1997.

Gossett, Reina. "Making a Way Out of No Way." *Vimeo*, February 27, 2016. https://vimeo.com/157653800.

Grace, Wendy. "Faux Amis: Foucault and Deleuze on Sexuality and Desire." *Critical Inquiry* 36, no. 1 (autumn 2009): 52–75.

Grathwohl, Larry. *Bringing Down America: An FBI Informer with the Weathermen.* New Rochelle, NY: Arlington House, 1976.

Guattari, Félix. *Chaosophy: Texts and Interviews 1972–1977.* Translated by David L. Sweet, Jarred Becker, and Taylor Adkins. Los Angeles: Semiotext(e), 2009.

———. *Soft Subversions: Texts and Interviews 1977–1985.* Los Angeles: Semiotext(e), 2009.

Guenther, Lisa. *Solitary Confinement: Social Death and Its Afterlives.* Minneapolis: University of Minnesota Press, 2013.

———. "Subjects without a World? An Husserlian Analysis of Solitary Confinement." *Human Studies* 34 (2011): 257–76.

Haley, Sarah. "'Like I Was a Man': Chain Gangs, Gender, and the Domestic Carceral Sphere in Jim Crow Georgia." *Signs: Journal of Women and Culture in Society* 39, no. 1 (2013): 53–77.

———. *No Mercy Here: Gender, Punishment, and the Making of Jim Crow Modernity.* Chapel Hill: University of North Carolina Press, 2016.

Hall, Stuart. "The Neoliberal Revolution." *Cultural Studies* 25, no. 6 (November 2011): 705–28.

Hames-García, Michael. *Fugitive Thought: Prison Movements, Race, and the Meaning of Justice.* Minneapolis: University of Minnesota Press, 2004.

Hanhardt, Christina. "Left Queer." *Scholar and Feminist Online* 11, nos. 1–2 (2012–13). http://sfonline.barnard.edu/gender-justice-and-neoliberal-transformations/left-queer/.

———. *Safe Space: Gay Neighborhood History and the Politics of Violence.* Durham, NC: Duke University Press, 2013.

Harcourt, Bernard. *The Illusion of the Free Market: Punishment and the Myth of the Natural Order.* Cambridge, MA: Harvard University Press, 2011.

Hardt, Michael, and Antonio Negri. *Common Wealth.* Cambridge, MA: Harvard University Press, 2009.

———. *Multitude: War and Democracy in the Age of Empire.* New York: Penguin, 2005.

Hartman, Saidiya. "The Belly of the World: A Note on Black Women's Labors." *Souls* 18, no. 1 (2016): 166–73.

———. *Lose Your Mother: A Journey along the Atlantic Slave Route.* New York: Farrar, Straus and Giroux, 2007.

———. *Scenes of Subjection: Terror, Slavery, and Self-Making in Nineteenth-Century America.* Oxford: Oxford University Press, 1997.

———. "The Time of Slavery." *South Atlantic Quarterly* 101, no. 4 (2002): 757–77.

Hartman, Saidiya, and Frank B. Wilderson. "The Position of the Unthought." *Qui Parle* 13, no. 2 (spring/summer 2003): 183–201.

Harvey, David. *The Condition of Postmodernity.* Malden, MA: Blackwell, 1990.

———. *Neoliberalism: A Brief History.* Oxford: Oxford University Press, 2007.

Herivel, Tara, and Paul Wright, eds. *Prison Nation: The Warehousing of America's Poor.* New York: Routledge, 2003.

Hewitt, Christopher. *Political Violence and Terrorism in Modern America: A Chronology.* Westport, CT: Praeger Security International, 2005.

Hill Collins, Patricia. *Black Feminist Thought: Knowledge, Consciousness, and the Politics of Empowerment.* New York: Routledge, 2010.

Holland, Sharon Patricia. *The Erotic Life of Racism*. Durham, NC: Duke University Press, 2012.

Hong, Grace Kyungwon. *Death beyond Disavowal: The Impossible Politics of Difference*. Minneapolis: University of Minnesota Press, 2015.

———. "Existentially Surplus: Women of Color Feminism and the New Crises of Capitalism." GLQ 18, no. 1 (2012): 87–106.

———. *The Ruptures of American Capital: Women of Color Feminism and the Culture of Immigrant Labor*. Minneapolis: University of Minnesota, 2006.

Hong, Grace, and Roderick Ferguson. Introduction to *Strange Affinities: The Gender and Sexual Politics of Comparative Racialization*, edited by Grace Hong and Roderick Ferguson, 1–23. Durham, NC: Duke University Press, 2011.

Huffer, Lynne. *Mad for Foucault: Rethinking the Foundations of Queer Theory*. New York: Columbia University Press, 2009.

Incite! Women of Color against Violence, eds. *The Revolution Will Not Be Funded: Beyond the Non-Profit Industrial Complex*. New York: South End Press, 2009.

Irwin, John. *The Warehouse Prison: Disposal of the New Dangerous Class*. Oxford: Oxford University Press, 2004.

Jackson, George. *Blood in My Eye*. Baltimore: Black Classic Press, 1972.

———. *Soledad Brother: The Letters of George Jackson*. Chicago: Lawrence Hill Books, 1994.

Jacobs, Ron. *The Way the Wind Blew: A History of the Weather Underground*. London: Verso, 1997.

James, Joy. Introduction to *Warfare in the American Homeland: Policing and Prisons in a Penal Democracy*, edited by Joy James, 3–23. Durham, NC: Duke University Press, 2007.

Johnson, Walter. "The Pedestal and the Veil: Rethinking the Capitalism/Slavery Question." *Journal of the Early Republic* 24 (summer 2004): 299–308.

———. *River of Dark Dreams: Slavery and Empire in the Cotton Kingdom*. Cambridge, MA: Harvard University Press, 2013.

———. *Soul by Soul: Life inside the Antebellum Slave Market*. Cambridge, MA: Harvard University Press, 2001.

Jones, Daniel Stedman. *Masters of the Universe: Hayek, Friedman, and the Birth of Neoliberal Politics*. Princeton, NJ: Princeton University Press, 2012.

Jordan, June. *Directed by Desire: The Collected Poems of June Jordan*. Port Townsend, WA: Copper Canyon Press, 2005.

Keeling, Kara. "I=Another: Digital Identity Politics." In *Strange Affinities: The Gender and Sexual Politics of Comparative Racialization*, edited by Grace Kyungwon Hong and Roderick Ferguson, 53–75. Durham, NC: Duke University Press, 2011.

———. "Looking for M—: Queer Temporality, Black Political Possibility, and Poetry from the Future." GLQ 15, no. 4 (2009): 565–82.

———. *The Witch's Flight: The Cinematic, the Black Femme, and the Language of Common Sense*. Durham, NC: Duke University Press, 2007.

Kelley, Robin D. G. *Freedom Dreams: The Black Radical Imagination*. Boston: Beacon Press, 2002.

Koerner, Michelle. "Line of Escape: Gilles Deleuze's Encounter with George Jackson." *Genre* 44, no. 2 (2011): 157–80.

Kurshan, Nancy. *Out of Control: A Fifteen-Year Battle against Control Unit Prisons.* San Francisco: Freedom Archives, 2013.

Laaman, Jaan. "Statement in Court." In *Hauling Up the Morning: Writings and Art by Political Prisoners and Prisoners of War in the United States,* edited by Tim Blunk and Ray Luc Levasseur, 112. Trenton, NJ: Red Sea Press, 1990.

Lamble, Sarah. "Queer Necropolitics and the Expanding Carceral State: Interrogating Sexual Investments in Punishment." *Law and Critique* 24, no. 3 (2013): 229–53.

Lichtenstein, Alex. *Twice the Work of Free Labor: The Political Economy of Convict Labor in the New South.* London: Verso, 1996.

Lorde, Audre. *The Collected Poems of Audre Lorde.* New York: W. W. Norton, 1997.

———. *Sister Outsider: Essays and Speeches.* Berkeley: Crossings Press, 1984.

Lordon, Frédéric. *Willing Slaves of Capital: Spinoza and Marx on Desire.* London: Verso, 2014.

Lowe, Lisa. *Immigrant Acts: On Asian American Cultural Politics.* Durham, NC: Duke University Press, 1996.

———. "The Intimacies of Four Continents." In *Haunted by Empire: Geographies of Intimacy in North American History,* edited by Ann Laura Stoler, 191–213. Durham, NC: Duke University Press, 2006.

———. *The Intimacies of Four Continents.* Durham, NC: Duke University Press, 2015.

Manalansan, Martin. "Race, Violence and Neoliberal Spatial Politics in the Global City." *Social Text* 84–85 (2005): 141–56.

Martin, Randy. *An Empire of Indifference: American War and the Financial Logic of Risk Management.* Durham, NC: Duke University Press, 2007.

Massumi, Brian. *Parables for the Virtual: Movement, Affect, Sensation.* Durham, NC: Duke University Press, 2002.

Mbembe, Achille. "Necropolitics." *Public Culture* 15, no. 1 (2003): 11–40.

McKittrick, Katherine. *Demonic Grounds: Black Women and the Cartographies of Struggle.* Minneapolis: University of Minnesota Press, 2006.

Melamed, Jodi. *Represent and Destroy: Rationalizing Violence in the New Racial Capitalism.* Minneapolis: University of Minnesota Press, 2012.

Messadra, Sandro. "The Right to Escape." *Ephemera: Theory of the Multitude* 4, no. 3 (2004): 267–75.

Mitchell, Timothy. "Rethinking Economy." *Geoforum* 39, no. 3 (May 2008): 1116–21.

Mogul, Joey, Andre Ritchie, and Kay Whitlock. *Queer (In)Justice: The Criminalization of LGBT People in the United States.* Boston: Beacon Press, 2011.

Mohanty, Chandra. *Feminism without Borders: Decolonizing Theory, Practicing Solidarity.* Durham, NC: Duke University Press, 2003.

Morrison, Toni. *Beloved.* New York: Penguin, 1987.

Moten, Fred. *In the Break: The Aesthetics of the Black Radical Tradition.* Minneapolis: University of Minnesota Press, 2003.

Moten, Fred, and Stefano Harney. *The Undercommons: Fugitive Planning and Black Study.* New York: Autonomedia, 2013.

Muñoz, José Esteban. *Cruising Utopia: The Then and There of Queer Futurity.* New York: New York University Press, 2009.

Murakawa, Naomi. *The First Civil Right: How Liberals Built Prison America*. Oxford: Oxford University Press, 2014.

National Prison Project of the ACLU Foundation. "Report on the High Security Unit for Women, Federal Correctional Institutional, Lexington, Kentucky." *Social Justice* 15, no. 1 (spring 1988): 1–7.

Negri, Antonio. "Foucault between Past and Future." *Ephemera: Theory of the Multitude* 6, no. 1 (2006): 75–82.

Newton, Huey P. *War against the Panthers: A Study of Repression in America*. New York: Harlem River Press, 1996.

Nixon, Richard. "Acceptance Speech, Delivered before the Republican National Convention, August 8, 1968." *The American Presidency Project*. http://www.presidency .ucsb.edu/ws/?pid=25968.

———. "A Child's Face." Advertisement. *Museum of the Living Image*. Accessed on March 12, 2012. http://www.livingroomcandidate.org/commercials/1968/childs-face.

———. "The First Civil Right." Advertisement. *Museum of the Living Image*. Accessed April 17, 2016. http://www.livingroomcandidate.org/commercials/1968.

———."What Has Happened to America?" 1967. *Cengage*. http://www.wadsworth.com /history_d/templates/student_resources/0030724791_ayers/sources/ch29/29.4.nixon .html.

Ong, Aihwa. *Neoliberalism as Exception: Mutations in Citizenship and Sovereignty*. Durham, NC: Duke University Press, 2006.

Oshinsky, David. *Worse than Slavery: Parchman Farm and the Ordeal of Jim Crow Justice*. New York: Free Press, 1996.

Parenti, Christian. "Assata Shakur Speaks from Exile: Post-Modern Maroon in the Ultimate Palenque." October 24, 2000. http://www.scritub.com/limba/engleza/music /quotAssata-Shakur-Speaks-from-1941962116.php.

———. *Lockdown America: Prisons and Policing in an Age of Crises*. London: Verso, 1999.

Patterson, Orlando. *Slavery and Social Death: A Comparative Study*. Cambridge, MA: Harvard University Press, 1982.

Posner, Richard A. "An Economic Theory of Criminal Activity." *Columbia Law Review* 85, no. 6 (October 1984): 1193–231.

Povinelli, Elizabeth. *Economies of Abandonment: Social Belonging and Endurance in Late Liberalism*. Durham, NC: Duke University Press, 2011.

"Prohibited Items." *Corrections, Prisons, and Parole*. Accessed November 24, 2016. http:// www.corrections.vic.gov.au/home/prison/visiting+a+prisoner/prohibited+items/.

Puar, Jabir. "Prognosis Time: Toward a Geopolitics of Affect, Debility and Capacity." *Women and Performance: A Journal of Feminist Theory* 19, no. 2 (2009): 161–72.

———. *Terrorist Assemblages: Homonationalism in Queer Times*. Durham, NC: Duke University Press, 2009.

Queer Fire: The George Jackson Brigade, Men against Sexism, and Gay Struggle against Prison. Bloomington, IN: Untorelli Press, 2014.

Queers for Economic Justice. "Beyond Same-Sex Marriage: A New Strategic Vision for All Our Families and Relationships." *Monthly Review Online*, August 8, 2006. http:// mrzine.monthlyreview.org/2006/beyondmarriage080806.html.

Reagon, Bernice Johnson. "Coalition Politics: Turning the Century." In *Home Girls: A Black Feminist Anthology*, edited by Barbara Smith, 356–68. New York: Kitchen Table/Women of Color Press, 1983.

Reddy, Chandan. *Freedom with Violence: Race, Sexuality, and the U.S. State*. Durham, NC: Duke University Press, 2011.

Rediker, Marcus. *The Slave Ship: A Human History*. New York: Viking, 2008.

Reiman, Jeffrey, and Paul Leighton. *The Rich Get Richer and the Poor Get Prison: Ideology, Class, and Criminal Justice*. New York: Routledge, 2013.

Reiter, Keramet. *23/7: Pelican Bay Prison and the Rise of Long-Term Solitary Confinement*. New Haven, CT: Yale University Press, 2016.

Rhodes, Lorna. *Total Confinement: Madness and Reason in the Maximum Security Prison*. Berkeley: University of California Press, 2004.

Richie, Beth. *Arrested Justice: Black Women, Violence, and America's Prison Nation*. New York: New York University Press, 2012.

Roberts, Dorothy. *Killing the Black Body: Race, Reproduction, and the Meaning of Liberty*. New York: Vintage Books, 1997.

Robinson, Cedric. "Capitalism, Slavery and Bourgeois Historiography." *History Workshop Journal* 23, no. 1 (1987): 122–40.

Rockman, Seth. "The Unfree Origins of American Capitalism." In *The Economy of Early America: Historical Perspectives and New Directions*, edited by Cathy Matson, 335–63. University Park: Pennsylvania State University Press, 2006.

Rodríguez, Dylan. *Forced Passages: Imprisoned Radical Intellectuals and the U.S. Prison Regime*. Minneapolis: University of Minnesota Press, 2006.

Rose, Nikolas. *Powers of Freedom: Reframing Political Thought*. Cambridge: Cambridge University Press, 1999.

Rudd, Mark. *Underground: My Life with SDS and the Weathermen*. New York: HarperCollins, 2009.

Sandoval, Chela. *Methodology of the Oppressed*. Minneapolis: University of Minnesota Press, 2000.

Schulman, Sarah. *Gentrification of the Mind: Witness to a Lost Imagination*. Berkeley: University of California Press, 2013.

Scott, James C. *Seeing like a State: How Certain Schemes to Improve the Human Condition Have Failed*. New Haven, CT: Yale University Press, 1998.

Sexton, Jared. "People of Color Blindness: Notes on the Afterlife of Slavery." *Social Text* 103 (2010): 31–56.

Shakur, Assata. *Assata: An Autobiography*. Chicago: Lawrence Hill Books, 1987.

———. "Women in Prison: How We Are." In *The New Abolitionists: (Neo)Slave Narratives and the Contemporary Prison Writing*, edited by Joy James, 79–90. Albany: SUNY Press, 2005.

Shakur, Zayd. "America Is the Prison." In *Off the Pigs! The History and Literature of the Black Panther Party*, edited by G. Louis Heath, 247–80. Metuchen, NJ: Scarecrow, 1976.

Sharpe, Christina. *In the Wake: On Blackness and Being*. Durham, NC: Duke University Press, 2016.

————. *Monstrous Intimacies: Making Post-Slavery Subjects.* Durham, NC: Duke University Press, 2010.

Sharpe, Jenny. *The Ghosts of Slavery: A Literary Archeology of Black Women's Lives.* Minneapolis: University of Minnesota Press, 2003.

Simon, Jonathon. *Governing through Crime: How the War on Crime Transformed American Democracy and Created a Culture of Fear.* New York: Oxford University Press, 2007.

Singh, Nikhil Pal. *Black Is a Country: Race and the Unfinished Struggle for Democracy.* Cambridge, MA: Harvard University Press, 2004.

————. "The Whiteness of Police." *American Quarterly* 66, no. 4 (December 2014): 1091–99.

Smallwood, Stephanie. *Saltwater Slavery: A Middle Passage from Africa to American Diaspora.* Cambridge, MA: Harvard University Press, 2008.

Smith, Caleb. *The Prison and the American Imagination.* New Haven, CT: Yale University Press, 2009.

Soss, Joe, Richard C. Fording, and Sanford F. Schram. *Disciplining the Poor: Neoliberal Paternalism and the Persistent Power of Race.* Chicago: University of Chicago Press, 2011.

Spade, Dean. *Normal Life: Administrative Violence, Critical Trans Politics, and the Limits of the Law.* Brooklyn, NY: South End Press, 2011.

Spade, Dean, and Rickke Mananzala. "The Nonprofit Industrial Complex and Trans Resistance." *Sexuality Research and Social Policy* 5, no. 1 (March 2008): 53–71.

Spillers, Hortense. "Mama's Baby, Papa's Maybe: An American Grammar Book." *Diacritics* 17, no. 2 (summer 1987): 65–81.

Spiotta, Dana. *Eat the Document: A Novel.* New York: Scribner, 2006.

Springer, Kimberly. *Living for the Revolution: Black Feminist Organizations, 1968–1980.* Durham, NC: Duke University Press, 2005.

Stanley, Eric, and Nat Smith, eds. *Captive Genders: Trans Embodiment and the Prison Industrial Complex.* Oakland, CA: AK Press, 2011.

Stoler, Ann Laura. *Carnal Knowledge and Imperial Power: Race and the Intimate in Colonial Rule.* Berkeley: University of California Press, 2002.

Street Transvestites for Gay Power. "NYU Occupation: Street Transvestites for Gay Power State." *The Spirit Was,* February 22, 2013. http://thespiritwas.tumblr.com/post/43780113854/nyu-occupation-street-transvestites-for-gay-power.

Sudbury, Julia. "Celling Black Bodies: Black Women in the Global Prison Industrial Complex." *Feminist Review* 80 (2005): 162–79.

Sylvia River Law Project. *It's a War in Here: A Report on the Treatment of Transgender and Intersex People in New York State Men's Prisons.* New York: Sylvia Rivera Law Project, 2007.

Tinsley, Omise'eke Natasha. "Black Atlantic, Queer Atlantic: Queer Imaginings of the Middle Passage." *GLQ* 14, nos. 2–3 (2008): 191–215.

Trouillot, Michel-Rolph. *Silencing the Past: Power and the Production of History.* Boston: Beacon Press, 1995.

Varon, Jeremy. *Bringing the War Home: The Weather Underground, the Red Army Faction, and Revolutionary Violence in the Sixties and Seventies.* Berkeley: University of California Press, 2004.

Venn, Couze. "Neoliberal Political Economy, Biopolitics and Colonialism: A Transcolonial Genealogy of Inequality." *Culture and Society* 26, no. 6 (2009): 206–33.

Vint, Sherryl. "'Only by Experience': Embodiment and the Limitations of Realism in Neo-Slave Narratives." *Science Fiction Studies* 34, no. 2 (2007): 241–61.

Vitulli, Elias. "A Defining Moment in Civil Rights History? The Employment Non-Discrimination Act, Trans-Inclusion, and Homonormativity." *Sexuality Research and Social Policy* 7, no. 3 (2010): 155–67.

Vlagopoulos, Penny. "The Beginning of History and Politics: Susan Choi's *American Woman* and the Shadow of U.S. Imperialism." *Studies in American Fiction* 37, no. 1 (2010): 127–51.

Wacquant, Loïc. "Deadly Symbiosis: When Ghetto and Prison Meet and Mesh." *Punishment and Society* 31, no. 1 (2001): 95–134.

———. "The Penalization of Poverty and the Rise of Neoliberalism." *European Journal on Criminal Policy and Research* 9, no. 1 (2001): 401–12.

———. *Punishing the Poor: The Neoliberal Government of Social Insecurity.* Durham, NC: Duke University Press, 2009.

Wilderson, Frank. "Gramsci's Black Marx: Whither the Slave in Civil Society." *We Write* 2, no. 1 (2005): 1–17.

———. *Red, White and Black: Cinema and the Structure of U.S. Antagonisms.* Durham, NC: Duke University Press, 2010.

Wilderson, Frank, and Saidiya Hartman. "The Position of the Unthought." *Qui Parle* 13, no. 2 (spring/summer 2003): 183–201.

Wilkerson, Cathy. *Flying Close to the Sun: My Life and Times as a Weatherman.* New York: Seven Stories Press, 2007.

Williams, Sherley Anne. *Dessa Rose.* New York: William Morrow, 1986.

Zurn, Perry, and Andrew Dilts, eds. *Active Intolerance: Michel Foucault, the Prisons Information Group, and the Future of Abolition.* New York: Palgrave-Macmillan, 2016.

Davis, Angela Y., 4, 5–9, 13, 18, 21–22, 24–25, 42, 73–75, 86–87, 91, 94, 98–102, 105–8, 110, 116–18, 135, 143–44, 146, 165n61

Dean, Timothy, 127

deindustrialization. See neoliberal economics

Deleuze, Gilles, 54, 66–69, 81, 121–22, 125–28, 136, 140–41, 163n97, 168n24

desire, 25–26, 126–42; "captured" by state, 25, 121, 126, 127, 134, 136, 147; fugitive, 25–26, 81, 120, 122, 126, 134, 139–42, 154; for police and prisons, 25, 121, 122, 124–25, 127–28, 130–36; white supremacy and, 110, 128, 130–31, 135–36

Duggan, Lisa, 129

Edelman, Lee, 37

escape, 5, 18, 22, 26, 65, 70, 114, 124, 145, 153–54; desire and, 26, 81, 120–21, 136, 140; "escape–bound captives" (escape as ontologically prior to capture), 21, 54; erasure as, 71–74; from prison, 20–21, 85, 150; from slavery, 102–3, 111; underground as escape from neoliberal logics, 24, 46–47, 55–57, 67–69, 78, 80–83, 120, 149, 153–54

fascism, 6, 8, 79, 81, 121, 125–28; "psychofascist control," 2

feminism: activism, feminist, 1–5, 10, 13, 20, 23, 39, 47–49; black feminism, 24–25, 36, 78, 84–92, 93–94, 97–107, 110, 113–18, 136–40, 141–42, 144–48; coalitional, 13–14, 18, 20, 47–51, 148–53; nonnormative feminisms, 23–25, 26, 29, 49–51, 85, 87, 94, 98–99, 120–21; white feminism, 36, 47, 93–94, 113, 147; women of color feminism, 10, 13, 18, 94, 97, 122

Ferguson, Roderick, 12–13, 17–18

Ferreira da Silva, Denise, 50

Flamm, Michael, 35

Foucault, Michel, 6, 41, 65, 81–82, 95–96, 121–22, 125–28, 133, 141, 153, 168n24

freedom, 61–63, 67, 152–53; fugitive, 5, 14, 23–24, 53, 54–57, 67–73, 75–76, 78, 81–83, 144; neoliberal, 8–11, 22–24, 28–38, 56–67, 92–93, 97, 116–17, 158n20, 158n22, 161n10; prison and free world, coextension of, 9–10, 94–95, 111, 114, 148; racialized (un)freedom, 57, 60–64, 90, 92–93, 96, 111–12, 114;

unfreedom vs., 53, 61–66, 152; of whiteness, 59–63, 92, 135–36, 158n20

free market. See neoliberal economics

Friedman, Milton, 10, 11, 23–24, 56–67, 80, 161n10

fugitivity: desire and, 120–22, 128, 141–42, 154; freedom and, 5, 14, 23–24, 53, 54–57, 67–73, 75–76, 78, 81–83, 144; neoliberal-carceral state and, 23, 26, 29, 31, 40–41, 56, 65, 75, 106, 122, 124–25, 141, 144; queer/nonnormative possibilities of, 5, 7, 12–13, 18–20, 22–24, 25–26, 29, 31, 40, 42–43, 46–48, 50–53, 54–57, 67–71, 81–83, 98, 120–22, 124–25, 141–42, 144–54; slavery and, 24, 85–87, 98–106, 111

future: desire and, 129, 135–36, 141–42; fugitivity and, 19–21, 74, 83, 145–46, 149; in law-and-order discourse, 22–23, 28–38, 52, 134–35, 159n34; possessed (by past), 29, 45, 50–53, 83, 90, 92–95, 107, 111–12, 120, 135; queerness and, 18, 20, 29, 119–20; of whiteness, 34, 37. See also temporality

Genet, Jean, 12

George Jackson Brigade, 1–4, 7–10, 13–14, 16, 19–20, 22, 39, 44, 76, 146, 150, 160n69

Gibbs, Joan, 146–47, 150

Gilbert, David, 40, 42, 153

Gilmore, Ruth Wilson, 7, 11, 64, 90, 155n11, 161n25

Glover, Clifford, 43, 45, 136–39, 151

Goldwater, Barry, 3, 19, 22–23, 31–35, 51, 136

Gordon, Avery, 72, 89

Guattari, Félix, 66–69, 81, 119, 121–22, 125–28, 136, 140–41

Haley, Sarah, 14–15

Hall, Stuart, 32

Hames-Garcia, Michael, 12

Hartman, Saidiya, 62, 86, 88, 96, 98, 107–8, 164n8, 166n83

Harvey, David, 30, 95

haunting, 11, 23, 25, 28–29, 40, 58, 62, 77, 86, 89, 90, 93, 111, 113, 118, 135, 138. See also possession

Hayek, Friedrich, 10, 58, 61, 65, 67

Health, Education, and Welfare, Department of (HEW), 48–52

Hearst, Patty, 24, 69–70